THE ANCIENT
EARTHWORKS AND
TEMPLES OF THE
AMERICAN
INDIANS

ALTAR-PIECE, TEMPLE OF THE CROSS, PALENQUE.

THE ANCIENT EARTHWORKS AND TEMPLES OF THE AMERICAN INDIANS

LINDESEY BRINE

ORACLE

Ancient Earthworks and Temples of the American Indians

First published by Farmer and Sons, London

This edition published in 1996 by Oracle Publishing Ltd.,
2A Kingsway, Royston, Hertfordshire,
SE8 5EG, England.

ISBN 1 86196 000 X

Printed and bound in Guernsey by
The Guernsey Press Co. Ltd

PREFACE.

THE attention of archæologists and students of the ancient Mexican hieroglyphs has latterly been directed to the mysterious subject of the origin of the astronomical and architectural knowledge that existed in Mexico, Guatemala, and Yucatan before the discovery of America. In the United States researches have also been made for the purpose of establishing, upon a scientific basis, conclusions respecting the tribes who made the extraordinary ramparts and geometrically planned inclosures in Ohio.

It is a remarkable fact that although, since the period when Mexico was conquered by Cortes, an almost uninterrupted series of investigations have taken place into the peculiar conditions of civilization of the Mexican and Central American Indians, nothing satisfactory has yet been ascertained which explains the manner in which that civilization could have arisen amongst those exceptionally instructed races.

Las Casas who, in the sixteenth century, lived for many years amongst the Indians in his diocese of Chiapas and Yucatan and saw several of the temples in that region, declared that the land contained a secret. That secret may possibly be discovered if the hieroglyphs and symbolic characters of the Toltecs and Aztecs can be interpreted. But until trustworthy methods of decipherment are determined, all conclusions, in default of other evidence, must necessarily be conjectural.

It was with the vague expectation that I should observe, either amongst the earthworks in the North or in the constructions at Palenque and Uxmal, analogies with the works of other races in Asia or Polynesia, that the travels described in this volume were undertaken. After my arrival in England a brief paper upon the subject of those travels, so far as they related to Guatemala and Mexico, was read before the British Association in Edinburgh and was afterwards published in 1872 under the title of "The Ruined Cities of Central America."

More than twenty years then elapsed before the approaching termination of my naval career gave me sufficient leisure to examine my journals with that exclusive attention which the complicated and perplexing nature of the subject required. This interval of time has enabled me to obtain a more vivid perception of the relative proportions of the problem, and to bring together in a more defined focus the impressions and observations which had been written during the journey. The theories then adopted have been modified or strengthened by the knowledge that has been subsequently acquired in other quarters of the world.

It will be observed, upon an examination of the illustrations of the ruins of Uxmal, that the Indians in Yucatan must have possessed great architectural capacities. Pyramids, Temples, Monasteries and other religious structures were built under most difficult circumstances, in a manner which commands admiration.

But it is not only the later civilization of the Mexican Indians that has to be taken into consideration in any attempts that may be made to solve the difficult and complex problem of this Indian advance towards higher conditions of life. Underlying the whole question are the native proclivities based upon the strange and significant practices of earlier forms of Pagan superstitions and sacrifices. Some of the profoundly interesting characteristics of these developments of the aboriginal Indian belief in supernatural influences have formed the subject of that chapter which relates to the ancient religious observances of the North American Indians.

ATHENÆUM CLUB, *May* 15, 1894.

CONTENTS.

CHAPTER I.

CHAPTER II.

CHAPTER III.

CHAPTER IV.

CHAPTER VIII.

CHAPTER IX.

CHAPTER X.

CHAPTER XI.

CHAPTER XII.

CHAPTER XIII.

CHAPTER XIV.

CHAPTER XVIII.

CHAPTER XIX.

CHAPTER XX.

ILLUSTRATIONS.

PLATES.

MAPS AND PLANS.

ILLUSTRATIONS IN THE TEXT.

NOTE.—The illustration of the Serpent Emblem in the Casa de las Monjas is reproduced from a large photograph taken at Uxmal by William D. James, Esq. It will be observed that the details of the sculpture of the rattlesnake are very clearly defined.

The illustrations marked † are from a series of valuable

photographs, also taken at Uxmal, by Captain Herbert Dowding, Royal Navy, who placed at my disposal such of them as I considered to be required for the purposes of this work.

I wish to call particular attention to the representation of that part of the Casa de las Monjas where the adjacent Temple of the Dwarf is seen. In comparing the structures with the pyramid, it has to be remembered that the Casa de las Monjas is placed upon a raised platform not less than seventeen feet in height. The Pyramid of the Dwarf is completely detached.

Upon an examination of the frontispiece it will be noticed that the centre stone which, when I saw it lying on the ground at Palenque, was uninjured, is there shown in two portions which are kept in position by iron clamps.

It was accidentally broken when being removed from Palenque to the museum in the City of Mexico.

The left slab, upon which is graven the smaller figure, is from a photograph of a moulding made by M. Desiré Charnay. The right slab is from a photograph of the original stone now placed in the museum at Washington, and which was represented in the Memoir upon the Palenque Tablet written by Professor Rau, and published by the Smithsonian Institution. The photographs of the right and left slabs have been reduced to the size of that of the centre, and thus an exact reproduction of the whole of the Tablet of the Cross has been obtained. The representation in the frontispiece is, approximately, upon the scale of one inch to the foot and is therefore a twelfth of the size of the original tablet when it was in its position within the temple.

The illustrations of Indians are from photographs collected by me during my travels and were selected as being typical of the respective tribes. My small sketch of the entrance to the Casa de las Monjas at Uxmal is drawn to scale, and the character of the Indian horizontal arch is delineated in its architectural proportions.

TRAVELS AMONGST AMERICAN INDIANS:

THEIR

ANCIENT EARTHWORKS AND TEMPLES.

CHAPTER I.

New York.—Mr. Grinnell.—Search for Sir John Franklin.—
Southern States.—The Negroes and their prospects.—Naval
Academy at Annapolis.—Military Academy at West Point.—
Shakers.—Boston.—Professor Agassiz.—Prairies and Glacial
Action.—Coral Reefs in Florida.—Mr. Ticknor.—Shell Mounds
in Florida.—Schools.—Dr. Howe's Institution for the Blind.—
Laura Bridgman.

UPON my return to England, after having completed
several years of foreign service, I obtained permission
from the Admiralty to proceed upon a journey into
North and Central America.

There were certain subjects that I particularly
wished to examine, especially those that were connected with the mounds or earthworks in the valley
of the Ohio, and the ruined temples of the southern
regions of Mexico and Guatemala. In the lands inhabited, at the time of the Spanish Conquest, by
Indian tribes who had reached a singular form of

civilisation, the origin of which has not yet been
traced, it is probable that some discovery will be
made which will throw light upon the manner in
which their knowledge was obtained.

The problems which have yet to be solved with
respect to the ruins at Palenque, and in Yucatan,
have a fascination for those who are interested in the
endeavour to seek an explanation of the strange
events that must have happened amongst the Indians
who inhabited that part of the world.   It is possible
that evidences may be found which will lead to the
conclusion that at some period, not very remote, there
has been an introduction amongst the aboriginal races
of influences derived from Europe or Asia, and it is
not unreasonable to expect that when the hieroglyphs
within the altars of Palenque are interpreted, much
that is now unintelligible will be made clear.   The
investigations of Mr. Stephens, in 1840, together with
the earlier reports of Del Rio and Dupaix, directed
attention to the extraordinary character of the pyramids and stone structures that were found deserted
and ruined within the tropical lands and forests.

In the North the field of research has been carefully examined by competent explorers, but, even in
that region, there is much that is open to theory or
conjecture with regard to the purposes for which the
great earthworks in the interior of the Continent
were raised.   There is also an almost complete
absence of definite knowledge respecting the race
and subsequent migrations of the tribes that dwelt
within those embankments.   The extensive shell
heaps or kitchen middens found near the sea coasts,
have been partly excavated, and, judging from the

implements of bone and the weapons which they contain, it has been made evident that the Indians must have had customs singularly corresponding with those of the tribes who formed the shell mounds in Europe.

I had no theories to establish, but I expected to find that the tribes in the West and North-West resembled the Manchu race I had seen in the North of China, and that the Indians in Central America would show traces of kindred with the Malays. I also thought that, in the ruined temples, there would be seen architectural affinities with the Buddhist monasteries in Upper Burmah and Cambodia. These were however only surmises, and I was prepared to recognise that it would be necessary to adopt other conclusions.

It was difficult to arrange for any decided plan of travel, but I intended, in the first instance, to visit the Navy Yards and observe what progress was being made with respect to ships and their armaments; and then to proceed to those parts of America where the principal works of the aboriginal tribes still remain. Finally, I hoped to be able to cross the Continent and go down the Mexican and Guatemalan coasts, and from one of the ports on the Western seaboard, cross Central America from the Pacific to the Atlantic towards Yucatan. Such was the outline of the direction that I proposed to follow, but which would be varied or changed as circumstances might require.

We left Liverpool in the Samaria on the 15th of March, 1869, and reached New York late in the evening of the 28th, after having experienced a continuation of head winds and stormy weather, which made our passage across the Atlantic long and tedious. My first care, upon arrival, was to call upon Mr. Henry Grinnell,* whose exertions and services in prosecuting, at his own expense, the search for Sir John Franklin and the ships beset in the Arctic ice, are so well known.

In the year 1850 Lady Franklin sent her appeal to the President of the United States, in which she urged the Americans, as a kindred people, to help in the enterprise of rescuing our sailors from perishing from cold and starvation in those Northern latitudes. The appeal was not unanswered, but in consequence of the unavoidable delays incidental to obtaining the sanction of Congress for the necessary expenditure, there was much risk of the season becoming too advanced for reaching the channels in time, and that, consequently, a whole year's work would be lost. It was then that Mr. Grinnell, a leading merchant and shipowner, prepared and fitted out for Arctic service two of his own vessels. These ships, respectively called the "Advance" and the "Rescue," were officered and manned by the Naval Department and reached the ice in time to do useful work. The fate, however, of Sir John Franklin and his crew was not ascertained, although traces of his winter quarters were discovered.

---

*Many of those who were interested in Arctic research and the then unknown fate of Sir John Franklin, will remember the meetings at Lady Franklin's house at Kensington Gore, and how greatly Mr. Grinnell's exertions and enterprise were appreciated.

At Washington, I found that Congress was sitting. Political affairs were in an unusually excited condition in consequence of the state of things resulting from the Civil War and the admission of negroes to the franchise. Soon after my arrival I attended the Levée of President Grant, and in the evening dined with our Minister, Mr. Thornton, at the Legation. Several members of the Diplomatic body were present, some of whom I had previously met in Europe.

The question of the capacity of the negroes with respect to their taking an equal share with the white citizens in the management of the government policy occupied the attention of politicians. It was thought impossible to foresee what would be the effect of the emancipation of over three millions of slaves. It seemed certain that the Americans would have eventually a complicated problem to deal with, presenting grave difficulties.

From Washington I went into the Southern States. In the districts where large numbers of slaves had been employed, the subject of their education was being seriously considered, and schools were established for the purpose of advancing the intelligence of the black children. The ignorant and hopeful parents were speculating upon the brilliant future that seemed to be opening before them. They had vague dreams that some new and prosperous destiny was going to be granted to their race. They thought that, as a result of freedom and education, their children would become active and useful citizens, equal, if they had fair opportunities, to those who had been their masters.

Such was the universal belief amongst the elders, and great will be the disappointment amongst the children upon growing up into manhood to discover, that, in obedience to an unexplained law, there seems to be a limit to their power of reaching the standard of proficiency to which they aspired.

I had seen the emancipated negroes in the islands of the West Indies, and the extraordinary condition of Hayti when under the rule of the black emperor Soulouque. It was therefore not possible to think that there was any probability of these school children rising to an equality with the white races around them. There was something almost painful in listening to the faith of the fathers in the prospects of their sons, and the earnest manner in which they spoke of their future career, if they worked hard and did their best to deserve success.

After passing through the low-lying lands near the coast, which had in previous years been cultivated by this race, I proceeded up the Chesapeake Bay, and stopped at Annapolis for the purpose of looking at the Naval Academy. The system of training officers for sea service is, in many respects, radically different from that which is followed in England. With regard to the comparative results it is difficult to form an opinion. It is presumable that the English system is the best for developing the naval capacity of English lads, and the regulations carried out at Annapolis may be more suitable for the Americans. Both schools succeed in producing efficient young officers.

The principle underlying the policy of the training system in England is youth. It is thought that in

order to make a good sailor, officer or man, the future
seaman must be entered when young, and thus begin
his sea life while he is still capable of being naturally
accustomed to the performance of his duties. In
America and also with the maritime powers on the
European continent different conclusions are held.
At Annapolis the age for entry is between fourteen
and sixteen, and as the entries usually take place at
the latest period, the age upon passing out into sea
service is about twenty. The preliminary training is
thoroughly carried out, and the Academy is exceptionally fortunate in being situated on the shores of
a large and well-sheltered bay where there is room
for practising the necessary gunnery exercises.

The Military Academy at West Point is placed
in a very beautiful situation. Nothing can be
finer than the scenery at that part of the Hudson
river. The site has been well selected with regard
to the various requirements for training officers for
general service, with reference to drills, cavalry
exercises, and topographical and engineering studies.
Professor Bartlett, to whom I had a letter of introduction from Professor Henry, of the Smithsonian
Institute, did everything that was in his power to
make my stay agreeable. I was also much indebted
to General Pitcher, the officer in command, who
made me acquainted with all the details of the system
in operation.

The Cadets are chosen in the same manner as at
Annapolis. Ten are appointed annually by the President, and the remainder are usually nominated by
members of Congress from their respective states.
Private allowances are discouraged, and the Govern-

ment make a grant of 500 dollars a year for each pupil, or the same allowance that is given to the midshipmen at Annapolis. General Pitcher told me that about one half of the candidates usually failed at the preliminary examination, and that, upon the average, one-third of the remainder were rejected at the succeeding examinations, a proportion of failures which corresponds with that at the Naval Academy. They rise at five, clean their rooms, place everything in order, attend early drills, and are constantly at work throughout the day. The series of drills and studies is very continuous, and there is only just sufficient time allowed for meals, and very little time for recreation. The average age of the lads is over twenty-one ; the term is for four years. Many distinguished officers have graduated here and habits of self-reliance are strictly enforced. The principle which governs the system which is maintained during the earlier part of the training is that of accustoming each cadet to be independent of help.

In proceeding from West Point, I visited the Shakers at their settlements, near the village of Lebanon. I was received by their chief Elder, a man named Evans, who, by his energy and firmness of will, had obtained much personal influence over the community. The Shakers had been successful in securing for themselves a considerable degree of financial prosperity which was the result of their economy and industry.

Evans was acquainted with the scheme of life contemplated by Mr. Harris, near Brocton. The community established there had been joined by Mr.

Laurence Oliphant,* and I was interested in hearing the opinions of the Shakers about them. Evans thought that they could not long keep together, because marriage was permitted amongst its members. Marriage, he said, meant personal property and where that existed a communistic society could not succeed.

A few days after arriving at Boston, I dined with Mr. Charles Francis Adams, who had for many years been the United States Minister in England. I had met him frequently at the house of Sir Charles Lyell in London. The conversation turned chiefly upon the conduct of the troops in the Civil War,§ all the details of which were eagerly discussed.

An officer present, who had commanded a brigade with distinction throughout the campaign, gave us

---

*Mr. Laurence Oliphant, whom I had known in other parts of the world, was then living with his community upon the Southern shores of Lake Erie.

The last time that I saw him was at a Levée, held in St. James's Palace, in the year 1880, under circumstances which were in extreme contrast with his daily life of labour at Brocton. I understood that he had come over to England to arrange some business matters connected with the affairs of his society.

America is the home of many groups of people endeavouring to carry out their various schemes of communistic life. I visited several of their settlements and found that their methods of management were very different. The prosperity and the harmony of the men and women, evidently depended upon their faith in their own strange forms of religion. It was also observable that, in all cases, the leaders were men of dogmatic character.

§The question respecting the proportion of foreigners in the armies of the North came under consideration.

It had been supposed that a large number of the troops consisted of men of foreign nationalities, but an investigation that

some information with regard to the behaviour of the
troops of the Northern army under fire, from the point
of view of their respective nationalities. Of the
negroes he spoke highly from personal knowledge,
for during a part of his service, a regiment of those
troops was placed under his command. He said that
they were not intelligent, but were easily disciplined
and controlled. They were found to be useful in
covering an assault as they did not appear to be
shaken in their courage or firmness by any great
slaughter in their ranks.

The Germans were expected to be cool and phleg-
matic, but it was found that they were excitable and
easily startled and unsettled. The Irish were always
ready to fight, but they were soon depressed by any
reverses. The Americans were excellent as cavalry,
as infantry they were steady and deliberate.

I mentioned that, at West Point, I had met General

---

had been made into the subject has proved that the alien strength
of the army had been the subject of much exaggeration.

Upon the examination of the numbers it will be seen, however,
that the composition of the forces deserves attention. Their
classification was as follows :—

British Americans (volunteers from British possessions in N. America)	53,500
English	45,000
Irish	144,000
German	176,800
Men of unknown nationality	74,900
Negroes (about)	140,000
National Americans	1,523,000

National Americans include all emigrants who in consequence
of having been five years in the States are entitled to become
citizens.

Vogdes, who had commanded a negro regiment, and that he considered his men to have proved that they were reliable and obedient, and capable upon occasions of showing that they were not wanting in daring. In the operations around Nashville, a great proportion of the losses in the army fell upon the coloured troops in consequence, as the general commanding reported, of the brilliant manner in which they charged the enemy's earthworks. This kind of dashing courage on the part of negroes, who had been bred in slavery, was surprising. I was deeply interested in hearing the details of the war, particularly such of them as related to the conduct of the black troops when under fire.

I had seen in the South, the emotional side of the character of the American born negroes, as shown in their political meetings and their religious services, but I had not been previously aware that these apparently lethargic people had by nature, the capacity for becoming brave and impulsive soldiers. It is obvious that they felt they were fighting for freedom, and for the emancipation of their wives and children, the most powerful incentives that could stimulate their actions. They were ready and willing to face the risk of death in order to obtain that freedom which, to those that have it not, must be the most coveted prize that this world can give.

One afternoon I went to Cambridge for the purpose of meeting Mr. Bartlett, a partner in the publishing firm of Messrs. Little and Brown. I was indebted to him for many kind acts in assisting me in visiting the museums, and we had arranged to go to the Harvard University together, in order to have an interview with Professor Agassiz, who had returned from Florida, where he had been engaged in the examination of the coral reefs.

After looking at the extensive collection of corals and shells which had been placed in the Museum, we walked across the college grounds to the Professor's house. I delivered my letter of introduction, and was received with great courtesy. Agassiz for some time talked about his varied experiences in many parts of the world and his recent researches, but upon hearing that I was going to visit the prairies in the North-west, he showed much interest in the details of the journey that I proposed to take.

He said that he had been in many parts of those prairies, and had made several careful investigations with the object of establishing certain facts with regard to their formation, and had come to the conclusion that they were caused by glacial action. He thought that the theory that they were once sea beaches was erroneous, for he was convinced that the sea had never been in those regions. He also spoke about the consequences of the habits of the numerous herds of buffaloes that had roamed, in remote times, over those lands and had made their wallows there. These shallow depressions collected large quantities of water, and influenced the manner in which many of the streams originated.

After having drawn my attention to the chief objects of geological interest that might possibly come within my notice in the region to the south of Lake Superior, Agassiz mentioned his work in Florida. He had given much consideration to the outlying banks fringing the southern coasts of that promontory. The facts he had established were not in accordance with the views of Darwin and Lyell. "If," he said, " the Pacific formations were as described by Darwin and others, those on the coast of Florida were entirely different. In no way could Darwin's theory explain the Florida formations." He had ascertained that the corals grew up from great depths, for he had dredged to a depth of eight hundred fathoms and had brought up live corallines; thus proving that they existed and worked in very deep waters. It was his opinion that Darwin's coral theories had not had a sufficient study of evidence given to them.

In the evening, at Mr. Ticknor's house, there were present at dinner Commodore Rogers, Superintendent of the Navy Yard; Mr. Francis Parkman, author of several historical works relating to the early European settlements in North America; Mr. Hillard, also an author of considerable reputation, and Mr. Frank Parker. Mr. Ticknor* told us anecdotes of his travels in Europe soon after the restoration of Louis XVIII. He had known many of the celebrities of that time, and spoke of Sir Walter Scott, Sir Humphrey Davy, Mrs. Siddons, Lord and Lady Byron, Talleyrand, Madame de Stael and Madame Récamier.

There was a long discussion upon the uncertain future of the republic. It seemed to be considered that as America became more populated, it was much

---

*Mr. Ticknor preceded Mr. Longfellow at Harvard University as Professor of Modern Languages. As an author he is well known by his History of Spanish Literature, and the biography of his friend Mr. Prescott, the historian.

to be feared that universal suffrage, freedom and equality of race, would lead to disorder.   Mr. Ticknor mentioned that Prince Metternich, when speaking to him about this subject, remarked that there was a great difference between old Austria and America. In Austria he had always to look out for mischief and prepare to meet it or contrive a remedy.   In America, he said, a mischief, if it exists, takes time and grows until it gradually forces itself upon the attention of the people.   Finally, if it becomes alarming, the mass deals with it and arrests its progress as it best can, and then things go on as before.

Professor Jeffries Wyman,* who had discovered several extensive shell banks on the eastern coasts of Florida, gave me, at his house at Cambridge, an interesting account of his investigations.   He thought that the mounds were entirely formed by the refuse of the food eaten by the tribes dwelling near the sea ; but, whether by a large settlement of tribes in a comparatively short time, or by a small tribe in a long time, it was difficult to determine. Some of the banks were from fourteen to twenty-five feet high.   They varied in length from one hundred to five hundred yards.   On the tops of several of them he had seen large trees, whose age he estimated to be not less than eight hundred years. It did not appear that the mounds followed the outlines of any particular plan of encampment, except in an instance where one of the longest of them had the shape of an amphitheatre.

----

*Then Professor of Anatomy in Harvard College, and Curator of the Peabody Museum of Archæology and Ethnology.

He also examined some fresh water shell heaps. These, he thought, were made in the same manner as the sea shell mounds, by the Indians eating the fish and piling up the shells. In all of them he had dis-covered fragments of pottery and other marks of human life. The Professor proposed that I should make an appointment with him in order to have a thorough examination of his collection, not only from the shell heaps, but also from the tumuli of the mound builders and other Indian tribes. A day for this purpose was accordingly fixed. In the mean-while my time was occupied in visiting the public schools : Mr. Frank Parker, who was interested in educational work, usually went with me.

From a national point of view it was considered of great importance that the children of the emigrants should receive a sound education so as to enable them to become useful and self-respecting citizens. The majority of the parents upon their arrival at New York or Boston, do not attempt to seek their fortunes away in the West, but settle in those quar-ters of these cities where they find that others of their race are already established. The elder members of the emigrating families are quite aware that their age or other circumstances practically debar them from all hope of success in any attempts to gain a livelihood by their own work. Thus their attention is directed to the training of their children, so that these may have a fair start in life. For this purpose, the free and thoroughly practical system of education carried out in the schools seems to be excellent.

It is needless to dwell upon the methods adopted in American cities for raising the standard of know-

ledge among the boys and girls of the poorer classes,
for they are well known.   Nothing can be more
pleasing than to observe the development of the
minds of these young wanderers from other lands,
where their fate was adverse and their lives were
without hope.   They appear to seize with eagerness
the chances that are given them to attain, by their
own intelligence, higher and more secure positions,
and thus break away from the discouraging conditions into which they were born.   The construction
and size of the school buildings were well adapted for
their purpose.   The health and attention of the
students are, therefore, not affected by close confinement or the insufficiency of pure air.

There was an institution in Boston, devoted to the
work of teaching the blind, which had an especial
interest of its own, and I was therefore glad to accept
Dr. Howe's invitation to dine with him and then see
Laura Bridgman,*the blind girl, whose education had
been so successfully managed, and whose history had,
for many years, attracted observation.

After dinner Laura came into the room.   I noticed
that she was of average height and looked thin, pale
and delicate.   She had a shy and peculiar manner.
Mrs. Howe placed herself in communication with her,
and Laura immediately became more assured.   When
I was introduced she expressed, by the movements
of her fingers, that she was much pleased to have
my companionship.   I asked if she wished to inquire

-----

*Laura Bridgman was born in 1829 so, at the time that I saw
her, she was forty years old.

about any English friends? She replied, "Yes. Do
you know Dickens, how is he?" Then suddenly, before I had made any answer, she felt Mrs. Howe's
sleeve and said, "You have a new dress," and named
the material—a sort of French silk. Mrs. Howe said
that the guess was correct. She then became more
animated and bright, but showed a singularly quick
impatience when wanting Mrs. Howe to listen to her.
When not occupied in maintaining a conversation
she became quiet and looked sad.

Mrs. Howe asked in what way she amused herself and what was her greatest pleasure. She replied,
"reading." "What reading do you like best?" To
this question Laura replied, "Bible, hymns and
psalms." Mrs. Howe turned round to me and said
this answer was very curious as Dr. Howe had
brought her up without any religious training, because he did not wish to give her mind any especial
bent in that matter; but owing, it was supposed, to
the influence and teaching of some friend, she had
been made acquainted with the Bible and had become
intensely attached to it.

It was said that Laura was able to articulate two
words—"Doctor" and "Grandmother"—and I asked
her to say them. "Doctor," was pronounced in a
distinct manner giving the sound "Dok-tá." The
word "Grandmother" was not so clearly spoken and
she gave the sound very rapidly. It was however
sufficiently expressed to be understood. I was told
that these words had in some manner been learnt
by feeling the throats of other people who pronounced
them, and finding that certain expansions of the mus-
cles occurred when the sounds were made. She con-

versed by holding out one hand and moving the fingers. Mrs. Howe held her wrist and communicated her remarks by touch upon it. In this manner an intelligent conversation was carried on. Laura evidently enjoyed the excitement caused by this interchange of ideas, for when thus engaged she looked very happy.

She was blind, deaf and dumb.

CHAPTER II.

UPON the day arranged for my visit to Cambridge, I found Professor Wyman prepared to employ several hours in examining the Indian collections. He proposed that we should begin by looking carefully over the contents of a case within which was placed everything that had been discovered in a burial mound in Illinois. The mound had contained the bones of nine adults, several fragments of rude stone implements, and some arrowheads. The skulls had been flattened and shaped by pressure.

We then examined the collections of human skulls that had been received from all parts of the continent. Amongst these, were several of an important character, obtained by Mr. Squier in Central America. They were long and flattened upon the top, and were supposed to have belonged to the race that built the stone temples in Yucatan. Other groups were then compared. It was observable that some tribes had the custom of pressing in the back of the head to such an extent as to make it nearly perpendicular.

Others pressed the skulls so as to give them great length. In a few instances, they were given a tall, oval form. The Californian Indians appear to have given their children a high, receding forehead. This method of shaping the head is still followed by the Flathead Indians in the West. It is done by the pressure of boards tied together in such a manner that the infant gets its skull shaped when it is in the cradle.

A question arose as to the effect of the artificial shapes of the head upon the character of the tribes ; and particularly, whether, in accordance with certain theories, there was any known difference in disposition between the tribes who flattened the forehead and those who flattened the skull at the back. The Professor said that the matter had been the subject of inquiry. It was considered, as far as could be ascertained, that the alterations in shape made no difference in the character, and that the Indians, whether with long, high, or flat heads, were similar in their savage nature.

Amongst the Mexican antiquities were a number of terra-cotta figures which were thought to be emblematic of the worship of serpents, lizards, and other reptiles. There were also idols carved out of hard, volcanic stone. After having seen these, and also quantities of rudely shaped stones, which were probably used by the Indians on the north-east coast for sinking their nets, the Professor began to examine the various things that had been taken from the American shell mounds.

First, in order, were the collections that had been brought from Maine and Massachusetts. There were oyster shells, the bones of wolves, deer and birds, fragments of coarse pottery, layers of charcoal, and bone awls. In the shell heaps at Concord there had been discovered various stone weapons and flint arrowheads. In the Florida mounds there were found the remains of crocodiles, implements made of stone, the bones of deer, and numbers of small sharp needles, made from bird bones, which had been used by hand.

It appears from the evidence obtained by the investigation of the shell banks, that tribes of similar habits dwelt on the cold coasts of New England and the almost tropical shores of Florida. It is also clear, that in many of their customs and methods of obtaining food they resembled the races that formed the kitchen middens in Denmark. Their stone and flint implements and their bone awls and needles were of the same shapes as those used by the pre-historic people who lived upon the shores of the Swiss lakes.

Many of the stone axes and arrowheads that have been found in the burial mounds, or in the neighbourhood of the ancient Indian encampments in North America are of the same type, and show the same system of workmanship as those that were made by the aboriginal tribes in Western Europe. The similarities in form, size and methods of adaptation for use are remarkable, for, although it may be expected that men, in an uncivilised condition would, in all parts of the world, have the same wants or necessities, yet it must be considered surprising that in the construction of the implements for war and for domestic purposes, the methods of design should be so singularly alike amongst the savages of the old and new continents.

Upon a subsequent occasion, when the doubtful question of the influence of the formation of the skull upon the mind was discussed, Mr. Ticknor mentioned the singular fact that the head of Daniel Webster* grew larger after he had passed middle age. His attention had been drawn to this circumstance by observing a change in the likeness of that statesman, and, as he knew Webster intimately, he asked him about the matter, and Webster said, "Yes, I find that I have constantly to increase the size of my hats."

Towards the latter part of my stay in Boston, I received a letter from Mr. Ralph Waldo Emerson, asking me to dine with him at Concord, and mentioning that he had also invited Mrs. Julia Ward Howe. Upon the day he had fixed for the purpose, we travelled down to the station, and were met by Miss Emerson, who drove us home in her quaint old-fashioned carriage. The pony, she told us, was a friend who had been in the family for twenty years. We were received by Mr. and Mrs. Emerson. A few other guests came from Cambridge, and then we went in to dinner. Mr. Emerson talked much of De Quincey, whom he had known

---

*In one of the many brilliant speeches made by this orator, the following graceful allusion to the mother-country may be mentioned here. "Great Britain," he said, "had dotted over the whole surface of the globe with her possessions and military posts, whose morning drum-beat, following the sun and keeping company with the hours, circles the earth daily with one continuous and unbroken strain of martial music."

at Lasswade, near Edinburgh, and then referring to
our English poets, mentioned with admiration, Ten-
nyson's poem, "Tithonus." One of his daughters
spoke with enthusiasm about Professor Agassiz's deep
sea dredgings, the lectures upon which she had been
attending.

Finally, the (always) absorbing topic of American
politics was dwelt upon, especially with respect to the
effect of democratic institutions upon the character of
the people. Mr. Emerson alluded with much sadness
to those evil influences of political corruption and office-
seeking which appeared to be inevitable blots upon all
systems of democracy, but he said that he thought
things would come right in the end. Upon the
various occasions that I met and conversed with
leading politicians (amongst whom was Chief Justice
Chase), I observed that they usually spoke of the
future of their country with the same anxiety.

There was much doubt and uncertainty as to what
was going to happen in the Southern States, which
had so recently been made desolate. Men's minds
were still agitated by the memory of the serious
events that had happened during the Civil War.
That great national convulsion had engaged the
thoughts and actions of all American citizens to the
fullest extent, and had necessarily diverted the conduct of affairs from the ordinary channels. There
was consequently a feeling of disquietude amongst
those who loved their country, their freedom and
their laws. But this temporary form of misgiving
was always accompanied by the firm conviction that
in some manner, not then quite clear, the nation
would ultimately triumph over all difficulties.

After dinner, Mr. Emerson took me into the library, and began to look over his books and point out his favourites. He said that what he most delighted in were the translations from Persian and other Eastern works. Finding that I was interested in his Oriental studies, he did not care to quit his books, and so we remained in the library until it was time to leave. In the meanwhile, he had taken down from the shelves many volumes. He also showed me photographs of his friends, and drew my attention to a likeness of Margaret Fuller, whom he had known for many years, and for whom he had felt great regard and esteem.

Margaret Fuller, who must have been a woman of extraordinary genius, was one of the leaders of the school of thought called Transcendentalism. Her end was as strange as her life. She crossed the Atlantic, travelled in Italy, married the Marchese d'Ossoli and was in Europe when the Revolution of 1848 broke out. Her sympathies being entirely with the cause of Italian freedom, she took a prominent part, under the direction of Mazzini, Garibaldi and other patriots, in the defence of Rome, doing much good service in the hospitals. After the adverse events of 1849, she embarked with her husband on board a sailing vessel bound for her own land, on the shores of which she was wrecked in a storm and all perished.

Before we went away, Mr. Emerson suggested that I should look at the exterior of the house, in which he seemed to take great interest. He told me that he had lived in it thirty-five years and had only made one change—the addition of the drawing room. It was an unpretending plank building of two stories, standing in its own small grounds, and was chiefly noticeable in consequence of having some fine chestnut trees in front between the door and the road.

Upon our return to the city, the President of the University asked me to be the guest of the Alumni of Harvard. His letter ran thus :—

"*June* 23.

" MY DEAR SIR,

" On behalf of the Alumni of Harvard College, I invite you to be present at the Commencement Dinner in Harvard Hall, Cambridge, on Tuesday, the 29th inst. The Alumni and their guests will assemble in Gore Hall, the Library, at 2 p.m. on that day. I hope to receive your acceptance, and to have the pleasure of meeting you on the occasion.

" Very respectfully yours,

" WM. GRAY,

" *Pres. of Alumni Assoc.*"

At one of the customary afternoon meetings of the members of the Saturday Club, I dined with them, as the guest of Dr. Howe. Among those present

-----

In the following year I accepted the invitation of Mr. Ticknor to stay a few days with him before leaving America, and I was fortunate in meeting at his house, Mr. Longfellow, who, at the time of my previous visit to Boston, was away from home, travelling in England, chiefly, as he afterwards told me, amongst the English lakes and in Devonshire. He proposed that I should go and see him at Cambridge, and this was arranged, and I went down there upon the first available day. I found him in his study, a small room looking out upon the lawn, and commanding a view of the country towards the bridge.

Before dinner, he showed me a bill of fare which had been given to him at a public banquet in London, which was framed and placed on the mantel piece of the dining-room. It was a coloured drawing of a scene described in his poem of "Hiawatha."

were Mr. Sumner, Professor Wyman, Mr. Lowell, Judge Hoar, Mr. Oliver Wendell Holmes, and Professor Gurney, the editor of the North American Review. Mr. Emerson was the chairman. The possibility of spontaneous generation, was the topic that happened to be chiefly discussed. Professor Wyman had been carrying out a series of experiments at Cambridge, and he told us what had been the results of his experience. He said that he had ascertained that the theory that boiling water killed life was, to a certain extent, erroneous. A first boiling killed some of the living creatures, a second boiling killed more, living organisms being reduced gradually in quantity. After a fourth severe boiling he failed to trace any life whatever. Finally after having carried out with great care, tests of all natures, he doubted the possibility of creating life where no life had previously existed.

Later in the day, I witnessed a most important triumph of mechanics, as applied to the removal of a

---

The sun was shining on the still waters of a lake, or inland sea, and a group of Indians were gazing at it. I think it was meant to represent the final departure of Hiawatha, westwards towards the sunset.

Mr. Longfellow said that he was much pleased with this mark of attention, not only on account of the merit of the picture, but because he appreciated the feeling that prompted the gift, as "Hiawatha" was the poem by which he most cared to be remembered.

He expressed strong sympathies with the poetical legends and traditions of the Iroquois and Dakota Indians. His conversation was, however, chiefly directed to the question of the future social and political condition of the negroes in the Southern States.

heavy building. The house that was being moved was large and strongly constructed of stone. It stood at the corner of a street which was about to be widened, and therefore it was necessary, either to pull it down or place it in another position, and it had been decided to execute the latter operation. The building had a frontage of seventy feet and a depth of one hundred feet. It was composed of a basement, five principal stories and a Mansard roof. The engineer in charge of the works told me that his calculations were based upon having to move a weight of fifty thousand tons. At the time I saw the house, it was full of residents, many of whom were looking out of the windows and watching the proceedings. The contractor permitted me to go underneath and observe the process of moving. The weight was taken by a vast number of screw jacks, and the building was lifted off the foundations. It was progressing towards its new site at the rate of fourteen inches in one hour.

On Commencement Day I went down to Cambridge early in the afternoon, and after being received by the President, fell into my place in the ranks of the procession formed in the college grounds. We then marched into dinner and I took my seat at the table. My immediate neighbours were Mr. Lowell, Mr. Oliver Wendell Holmes, Judge Hoar and Judge Grey. About six hundred were present in the hall and three hundred dined in another room. The gradations of age corresponded with the positions of the tables. The seats towards the left were occupied by comparatively young men, but on the right, were successive rows of heads, showing advancing years, until upon the extreme right were the white haired seniors.

At the conclusion of the dinner, in accordance with an ancient custom, all stood up and sang a Psalm to the tune known by the name of St. Martin. The President then gave his annual address and the usual speeches followed. Mr. Adams made a good speech and referred to his late absence as the United States Minister to Great Britain. The President then rose and told the Alumni that a "representative of Great Britain" was present and called upon me to respond. This I did as briefly as possible, and upon resuming my seat I was astonished at the enthusiastic manner with which the said representative was received. After much cheering, the band played "God save the Queen," which was again the occasion for a strong outburst of cordial good feeling towards England. As I looked down the hall I saw the slight, tall form of Mr. Emerson bending forward as he joined in our National Anthem. Mr. Holmes then recited a poem and Mr. Lowell gave a speech in which he alluded to the question of the Alabama which was causing such bitter feeling in America, and after speaking of the volcanic ground into which he had wandered, said

> " O matre pulchra filia pulchrior,
> Pout if you will, but sulk not into war.
> Had Adams stayed, this danger had not been,
> This less than kindness of two more than kin."

The singing of "Auld Lang Syne" was the fitting conclusion to an interesting day.

Professor Wyman told me that, before leaving the States, I ought to visit the shell mounds at Damariscotta in Maine and also those near Concord. The

latter were considered to be remarkable on account
of their being composed of fresh-water shells. Mr.
Emerson had offered to help me in my examination of
them, but not wishing to occupy his time in this unusual manner, I went down to Concord and tried to
find them by myself. In this attempt I failed, and,
finally, I decided to obtain his help. Fortunately,
he was at home and at once put the harness on his
pony and drove me down to the place. We crossed
some fields and found the shell heaps near a sharp
bend of the river. They were about a hundred and
fifty yards long, twenty yards wide and twelve feet
high, and were chiefly composed of mussel shells.
For more than an hour we worked zealously and
made slight excavations at different parts of the
banks, and found some fragments of bones which
had been shaped by hand, but we were not successful in
seeing any stone celts. We then went to an adjoining hillock upon which the Indians were accustomed
to encamp and there we picked up three rudely-made
arrow heads which had been formed out of hard por-
phyritic stone.

After finishing the inspection of the middens, we
went back to the house, and remained for an hour or
two in the library where we had tea. Mr. Emerson
told me that in order to pass through, with comparative comfort, the long winter, he and others had
formed a society of twenty-five members and arrangements were made for meeting at their respective
houses. Each member gave a reception in turn upon
Tuesdays. When the time was at hand for going to
the train he went to the stable, and again harnessed
the pony, and drove me to the station. When say-

ing "Good bye," he expressed many kind wishes
with regard to my projected journey.

Americans must naturally feel interested in whatever relates to the past history of the native races
who were the original inhabitants of their country,
and who possessed, in combination with their savage
nature and cruel practices, certain qualities of
honour and fortitude which seem to point to the
existence of latent conditions of mind placing them
upon a different footing from other ordinary savage
races. Theories which relate to the migrations of
the tribes who entered Mexico from the North have
also much attraction. As years roll onwards, and
the events, that then occurred, are more distant or
obscure, the causes of those movements and the origin
of the influences that created the subsequent advance
in civilisation amongst those Indians are becoming
almost incomprehensible.

On the way from Concord towards Canada I
stopped at Portsmouth for the purpose of seeing the
Navy Yard,* which was the last naval establishment
that I had to visit on the eastern coast, and then
proceeded to the remotely situated village of Damariscotta.

---

*The geographical conditions of the Atlantic sea-board are so
favourable for the development of naval power, that it is evident
that the United States have every possible natural advantage placed
at their disposal to enable them to become a great maritime
nation.

There is, however, a difficulty for them to surmount. Serviceable American-born men do not readily volunteer to join their
ships of war, and, consequently, the crews are largely composed
of foreigners, chiefly of English and German origin. The
reasons for this disinclination on the part of the Americans to

The shell mounds near the adjacent river far exceeded in magnitude what I had expected to find. They were placed about twelve miles from the sea within the limits of the ebb and the flow of the tides, and formed the banks of a small promontory round which the river made a sharp bend. Within these banks was a flat space of land which had been used by the Indians for their camping ground, and which is known to have been visited by small bands of them as late as the end of the last century. The heaps extend along the shores of the river and round the promontory for a length of about six hundred yards, and vary in height from fifteen to thirty-five feet. It was difficult to estimate their average width, but in many places it was not less than twenty-two yards.

The mound that I chiefly examined rose directly from the beach close to the line of the present high water mark. It was thirty-three feet high, sixty feet wide and one hundred and fifty feet long. Looking

---

accept sea service seem to be caused by the fact that the prospects for success in life in other directions are sufficiently good to prevent them from seeking an employment in which they would be subject to discipline and have to sacrifice their habits of independence. It will probably be found expedient, ultimately, to adopt a system of entry and training for seamen similar to that which has been found to succeed in England. The systems followed on the European continent, and which are based upon conscription, could find no place amongst a people with whom all service must be essentially voluntary.

If the difficulties with regard to men can be overcome, the naval strength of the United States may be as great as Congress may deem desirable, for, with respect to the capacities of harbours and dockyards and the means available for the construction and armaments of ships, there is practically no limit to the power of fitting out and maintaining large fleets.

from the river, it presented the appearance of a steep
cliff formed of compact layers of large oyster shells.
In consequence of the face of this cliff being exposed,
it was possible to trace all the horizontal strata.
Beginning from the top of the bank there was, in
the first place, a deposit of shells closely packed
about eighteen inches thick. Then there was a well
defined layer of earth or mould, averaging a thickness of half-an-inch throughout the whole length of
the bank without any break or change in its width.
The next layer was not so deep as that on the top,
and was one foot thick. Then came another deposit
of mould, half-an-inch in thickness, resting upon
another layer of shells. In this manner, the alter-
nating deposits of earth and shells succeeded each
other down to the base.

There were not any signs of kitchen midden refuse
amongst the shells, but in the intermediate layers
of earth I saw fragments of broken pottery, charred
wood, several rounded stones, small quantities of
bones of animals, and one bone awl which had evidently been much used. A portion of the cliff which
had been undermined by the action of the river had
slipped down upon the beach, consequently the interior of the mound was exposed. I made an excavation into this new face and found a stone knife, or
scraper, and a small stone chisel. In another part
of the bank I discovered a plank lying flat upon the
third layer of mould below the surface. It was
made of fir, and was four feet six inches long, six
inches wide and half-an-inch thick.

These shell heaps, the relics of the feasts and food
of the Indians, although interesting as evidences of

the habits of life of the savage races that once occupied this part of America, prove but little more than the fact that those races have existed and passed away. The successive layers of earth in the heaps would enable an estimate to be made of their age, if the length of the intervals of time that elapsed between the encampments could be known. The saw-cut plank, resting upon the third layer is an evidence that the two upper deposits of shells were made since the arrival of the English colonists. The Indians then dwelling on these lands were called the Abenakis. These oyster heaps may have been raised by them when they visited the coast of Maine after leaving their hunting grounds.*

----

*In the summer of 1870 I went to the village of Dighton to look at the inscribed stone in the river near that place.

Upon my arrival there it was high water and the rock was covered. The next day, when the tide was low, I hired a boat, pulled down the stream and stopped by its side, which was then fully exposed, and examined it with care. It was a boulder formed of hard close grained granite.

As the inscription was originally supposed by Danish and other antiquarians to have had some relation with the history of the arrival of the Northmen upon that coast, I traced the figures and rude characters with particular attention.

I have seen rolls of birch bark scratched in the same manner by Chippewas, for the purpose of giving information of the movements of their hunting parties, and I think that the figures on the Dighton stone were meant to represent similar events. As, however, the inscriptions are deeply cut, and as it must have taken some considerable time to execute them, it may be granted that the Indians wished to leave, near the mouth of the river, a permanent record which would be intelligible to others.

At many parts of this sea-board the New England tribes, as at Damariscotta visited the tidal waters to obtain food.

CHAPTER III.

FROM Damariscotta I went up the valley of the
St. Lawrence, and visited the reservation lands of the
Algonquins, Hurons, and other tribes that had
originally held possession of that part of the country.
The most important assemblage of Indians was placed
upon a large tract of land near the banks of the Grand
river in Upper Canada. There I saw, dwelling in
their separate villages, the descendants of the once
powerful confederacy of the Iroquois, who had been
our faithful allies in our wars.

Nearly three thousand Indians were gathered
together belonging to the tribes of the Senecas,
Onondagas, Mohawks, Cayugas, Oneidas and Tuscaroras. Some of them had been converted, but
many still maintained their ancient faiths and performed their customary Pagan ceremonies.

It was extraordinary to observe how unavailing
had been the influence of European civilisation in
advancing the intellectual capacities of the tribes.
The French missionaries at Lorette, Oka, and St.
Régis, many of whom were well acquainted with the

language of the converts put under their care, told me that all their efforts were useless, and that the labours of nearly three centuries were absolutely without any practical result.

After having passed a few weeks in the vicinity of the lakes, for the purpose of seeing the condition of various remnants of certain North American Indian

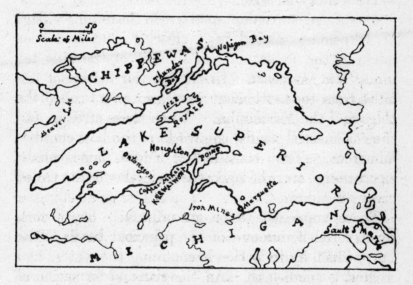

Plan of the Lake Superior Iron and Copper region.

tribes placed upon reservations, I reached the shores of the Georgian bay, and then proceeded to the port of Marquette in Michigan.

My chief object in landing upon the southern shores of Lake Superior, was to visit the places where ancient Indian mining operations had been discovered, in order that I might be, in some degree conversant

with matters relating to the origin of the copper
ornaments that had been found in some of the burial
mounds in Ohio. I also wished to make some excursions into the forests where, amongst the numerous
lakes and rivers, the beavers were still constructing
their dams and building their lodges. I desired to
see something of beaver life and work before the
advance of civilisation had removed these forests and
beavers away for ever.

I obtained convenient quarters in the mining village
of Ishpeming, placed in a clearing that had been
made in the forest, on the summit of the hills ten
miles from the coast. In the interior, within a few
miles from the settlement were two rivers called the
Carp and the Esconauba. Upon these streams and
their connected ponds, the works of the beavers were
numerous. They consisted of lodges, dams, canals,
excavations, and the open spaces in the forests called
beaver meadows.

There happened to be an unusually large work
constructed across one of the principal bends of the
Carp, which by its action in confining the waters had
created a small lake. As the size and formation of
that dam give a good knowledge of the capacity of
the beavers, and their powers of executing works of
considerable magnitude, it will be interesting to
describe it with some detail.

It was two hundred and sixty-two feet in length
and nearly six feet high in the centre, where the
water was deep. This height diminished gradually
towards the banks. The average width upon the top
was two feet. The slope outwards was in the
direction of the angle which happened to give the

Beaver Dam, Lodge and Pond, near Ishpeming, Michigan.

utmost resisting power. The base was about fourteen feet wide. The dam was not made in a direct line across the stream, but had curves which were convex towards the current, and were placed at the points of the greatest pressure. The slopes were formed in such a manner that the upper side acted as a barrier against the water, and the opposite side acted as a supporting buttress.

The entire construction was evidently made with a correct knowledge of the strength that was necessary to resist the outward pushing force that was exerted against it. When an engineering work of this nature, so great in proportion to the power and intelligence of its constructors, is examined, and its fitness for the object for which it has been made and for the duty it has to perform, has been ascertained, it occurs to the mind to consider whether such operations are the results of instinct or of some exceptional degree of reasoning faculties.

Within the pond was the lodge. It was placed near to the bank which by its curve gave the most shelter. It was shaped like a rounded bee-hive and measured nearly eight feet in diameter, and twenty-two feet over the outer circumference. The exterior was composed of small sticks cut in nearly equal lengths, and so intertwined, crossed and plastered with mud as to give great cohesion.

There were three entrances, two of them leading in the direction of the bank, and one towards the middle of the pond. The former are said to be used as the approaches to the inner room, and the latter for escape. All these entrances were below the surface of the water, and ran upwards into the dwelling room

which was a dry comfortable apartment, the floor
being well above the highest water level.

The beavers, when cutting the branches of the
trees into the requisite lengths, seem to have an
accurate perception of what is necessary for the special
works that are then in progress. Thus in their
lodges, which are chiefly made for shelter and warmth,
the sticks composing them are small, and when well
plastered together with mud make a good compact
residence. The dams which have a different purpose
are differently built, and in these the sticks are often
of considerable size, being sometimes fully six feet
long. Some of the cuttings, however, are small and
many of them are like short poles, having a diameter
about the size of a man's arm.

The methods of forming the foundations of their
dams are most practical, and the manner in which
earth, stones, mud, twigs, fibres and brushwood are
combined, not only show marvellous ingenuity, but
prove that beavers work perseveringly together with
incessant labour for long periods of time.

The superstructures are differently made. They
are composed of a framework of sticks placed at
various angles inclined upwards. This open form of
disposition appears to be intended to allow the surface
waters to escape to the extent that is necessary to
keep the level of the pond at the uniform height that
is desirable.

Although it is usually considered that the intelligence of the beaver communities is chiefly shown by
their ability in raising works of construction, I was
informed by men who were intimately acquainted
with the habits of these animals, that a greater

sagacity was displayed in the methods adopted by
them, under especial circumstances, for maintaining
communications between their dwelling places and
the woods from which they obtained their food and
building materials.

These rare and singular works of excavation are
called beaver canals. One of these, which was the
largest that was known to occur in this part of
Michigan, I examined with the utmost attention.
It was an open trench or channel, about half a mile
long, two to three feet wide, and from one to two
feet deep. The bottom was of the same width as
the surface, the sides being perpendicular. It connected a large pond with the adjacent forest. The
canal was sufficiently large to give room for a beaver
to swim in it and push in front of him the cutting of
birchwood that was to be conveyed to the lodge and
there stored for the winter supply of food. The
depth was enough for the purpose of concealment.

I also examined some other canals connecting the
ponds with trees, which were of a different character
and much smaller. The Indians were of opinion that
these must have been made exclusively for escape
when the beavers, whilst at work, were suddenly
alarmed.

But the most important results of the actions of
the beavers are the alterations made by them in the
aspect of the country, in consequence of their raising
the levels of the water and causing large spaces of
land to be subject to overflow. Thus, when the dams
are in order and efficiently maintained, much of the
adjoining land, when it lies low, becomes a swamp
and the trees decay and fall. Then if the works

are neglected and the waters follow their usual direction, the lands become dry and are changed into fertile grass meadows. Some of these meadows are of considerable extent. Around Ishpeming they supply the fodder required for the cattle employed at the mines. One of them, which occupies a large acreage, yields over fifty tons of hay annually.

An explorer who happened to pass through a region of this nature after it had been deserted by the beavers, would be surprised, when following the trail through the forest, to find himself entering into one of these open spaces, which have the appearance of small savannahs, and he would be unable to understand how such sharply defined inclosures could have been formed.

Near the borders of the meadows and ponds, several birches were undergoing the process of being felled. The operations were extremely curious, and it was evident that the beavers are both careful and ingenious in the execution of the work.

The trees selected for their purposes are generally about three or four feet in circumference at the part that is within reach. The trunk of each tree is, in the first place, gnawed evenly round, until only a portion of the centre, about two inches in diameter, is left to maintain it in an upright position. It is then carefully gnawed from the direction towards which the tree is intended to fall, which is often a matter of some importance. When it is lying upon the ground, the bark is stripped and stored for food, the branches are cut into the requisite lengths and used also partly for winter provision, but chiefly with regard to what may be wanted for the construction and repair of the dams and lodges.

Upon returning one afternoon from the River Carp,
I found that, by some inattention, I had left the
track and had wandered into the forest. Men who
are accustomed to explore this region had stated that
the safest course to adopt when such an event occurred
was to observe the position of the marks of the
weather upon the trunks of the trees. In Michigan,
it had been noticed that these evidences of exposure,
consisting of moss or lichen, were upon the Northern
sides, and it was considered that by watching these
indications, a line of direction could be followed.

It is possible that in places where the trees are
much exposed this system may be useful, but in this
case I did not find it so.

The indications of weather were often very faint
and difficult to trace. Where they did clearly exist,
they varied so greatly in their position, that it was
impossible to follow a straight line. I consequently
soon gave up the attempt to find the trail by this
method. Night was approaching, and the outlook
was becoming grave. In all directions but one, there
was nothing but many miles of dense forest, which it
would be hopeless to attempt to pass through.

The direction which was available had a broad
base, being the road from Ishpeming to Marquette.
This I knew must lie between south and south-
west. Consequently if I could follow a line between
these points, it was probable that the road would
soon be reached, as its distance was less than three
miles. I had my watch with me, and fortunately,
the sun could be seen occasionally, so it was possible
to make that my guide.

Upon a rough calculation of the true bearing of

the approaching sunset, I found that by keeping the
glimmer of the light on the right hand, and walking
steadily forward, the road ought to be reached before
dark. It was, however, anxious work and it was
getting late when I unexpectedly emerged into an
open clearing, where a squatter had temporarily
settled. It was with no slight pleasure that I heard
the sounds of life, the lowing of cattle, and the
welcome movements of a busy farmyard.*

After concluding my expeditions to the lands and
ponds of the beavers, I went to that part of Michigan
where the ancient mining pits and trenches have
been discovered. The earliest knowledge of them
was obtained by an American explorer who, in the
year 1847, when seeking for indications of metal ore,

---

*When afterwards passing through the forests near Palenque, in
Central America, I observed that whenever the Indians found it
necessary to quit the track, they immediately broke off small
branches from the trees, and placed them on the ground over
which they had trodden. As an additional precaution, they also
made marks on the trunks with their hatchets. It was thus easy
for them to get back to the place from which they had started.
It is however evident, that this plan is only useful in those cases
where the path is intentionally left. When the path is accidentally
missed, it is of the greatest importance not to lose touch with the
spot where you happen to be when your error is discovered.
This position will necessarily be within a short distance by a
straight line from the place from which you wandered. It has
been ascertained that it is the tendency of men who have lost
their way to unconsciously move in a circle, and thus much time
may be wasted in trusting to personal judgment. It is a good
plan to make a series of short tentative marches in different
directions, in straight lines from your starting point, which should
be considered as a central position to which you can always
return if necessary. Such straight lines of direction can be made

noticed several depressions in the ground, and saw lying in a heap, near what seemed to be an ancient excavation, a number of rude stone hammers that he thought had probably been used by hand.

In the following year another excavation was discovered, and after clearing this out to a depth of eighteen feet, there was found a detached mass of copper weighing over six tons which rested upon oak sleepers, and beneath it there was a vein of copper five feet thick.   There were also several stone hammers, grooved for the purpose of having handles attached to them, and a copper chisel with a socket for a wooden handle, a fragment of which although much decayed, was still in its place.   In an adjoining pit at a depth of ten feet, there was a wooden bowl and some charcoal.*   In some workings, subsequently discovered upon Isle Royale and near the end of

---

by marking trees, and keeping them as much as possible in line with each other.   In dense forests a watch is not serviceable, as the sun does not penetrate them, and its bearing cannot be seen. A compass is useful to a certain extent, but the constant deviations that have to be made to avoid obstacles, tend to make the line of progress a succession of broken curves, and it becomes unsafe to rely upon the accuracy of the direction.   Explorers have found it desirable to send men occasionally to the tops of the tallest trees to observe the nature of the country that is being traversed. When Cortes made his celebrated expedition from Mexico to Honduras, he maintained a straight march by the use of a ship's compass, but in that case there was no difficulty, for the direction was followed by cutting down the trees that were in the line of the advance.

*See " Report on the Geology and Topography of a portion of the Lake Superior Land District," by I. W. Foster and I. D. Whitney.   Washington, 1850.

the Kee-wai-wona promontory, a number of wooden
wedges were seen, together with traces of extensive
trenches.

In consequence of these discoveries further investigations were made, and a large number of
ancient pits were found in the forests, especially in
the districts where are now placed the towns of
Ontonagon and Houghton. It was within a few
miles from the latter town, that the explorers observed the heap of stone hammers, and their attention
was directed to the fact that they had been preceded
in the search for copper by men of some unknown
race, who possessed capacities for mining operations
greater than could be attributed to the Chippewas
who then occupied the land.

In order to examine this heap I engaged a man
—who knew the mining and forest region—to guide
me to the spot where the hammers still remained.
After crossing the Portage Lake and passing over
some low neighbouring hills, we came to a depression
in the ground which looked like an old ditch or
trench. At the side of this ditch, I saw several
hundreds of rounded water-worn stones of various
sizes. These had evidently been chosen on account
of the convenience of their shape, for the purpose
of being used for crushing the rocks that contained
metal.

A few of the stones appeared to have been
partly shaped by hand, but the majority of them
were in their natural form. Several were perforated
by small round holes, caused probably by the action
of water. Some men who happened to be employed
at one of the mines in the neighbourhood, told me

that in their opinion they had been made for thumb holes. They were, however, much too small for such a purpose.

Upon my return to Houghton I met Mr. I. H. Forster, who was the agent for mines and a Senator for the State. He proposed to accompany me to the sites of those ancient workings that he had personally inspected. After passing through a forest of birch and pine trees, we reached an open space where we saw the evidences of the nature of the operations that had been executed.

The direction of the trenches could be easily traced, although they were filled with earth and leaves. Several of the pits had been cleared out by the men employed at one of the new mines, and it was therefore possible to go down to the bottom of them and observe the methods of excavation. The first that I examined was twelve feet deep; from the base there ran two nearly horizontal galleries or adits, following the direction of the lode which ran N.W. and S.E. These adits were five feet wide and extended laterally about six feet. Upon the surface, near the edge of the pit, was the stump of a basswood tree, six feet in circumference, and at the opposite edge was the stump of a pine, four feet in circumference.

The second pit was twenty yards from the first, and had evidently been sunk in the direction required in order to reach the same lode. It was ten feet deep. From the base there was one adit following the direction of the deposit of copper. Close to the edge of this pit was the stump of a small birch tree. Beyond this were seven other pits, from twenty to fifty yards apart, and in connection with these, there were several short trenches from two to four feet wide.

The pits were discovered in 1865. Some animals were being driven along a track in the forest, when one of them straying from the path, plunged his feet deep into the ground ; this was noticed, and an explorer for copper examined the place and pushed his stick down it. This led to a further search, and the hole was found to be an ancient pit. Shafts were sunk, and the result has been, that, one of the most important mines in the district was established near the spot.

Upon another occasion I went with Mr. Forster to look at the trenches and pits that had been found in a more distant part of the forest. These pits were smaller than those that I had previously seen, but the trenches were frequently of considerable depth. I measured several that exceeded six feet deep. These trenches were usually in short lengths, but one of them was nearly two hundred feet long. Upon making inquiries amongst the leading men of the various copper mines that have been placed in the neighbourhood of the earlier workings, I was told that the practical miners were of opinion that these excavations were of considerable antiquity. It has, however, been proved by the condition of the things that were found in the pits that these conjectures are not well founded.

Near Ontonagon, to the south-west of Portage Lake, a line of trenches was observed in 1863, and a shaft was sunk in a depression which was considered to be an old pit. At a depth of nine feet, one of the workmen drew out upon the point of his pickaxe, a small untanned leather bag in a good state of preservation. It was noticed that the mouth of the bag was traversed by a leather string, which was in its place and could be used for drawing the opening together. The bag was seven inches wide and eleven inches deep.

Two years afterwards, some men exploring the same part of the forest, observed a small mound about six feet high. After digging through it down to the ground, they reached the surface of a pit, which was carefully excavated by them. At the top there was a deposit of sand; below that, were many closely pressed layers of decayed leaves. At the bottom of the pit they saw a birch bark basket, in all respects, similar to those that are made and used by the modern Chippewas. Near the basket they also found a bit of beaver or otter skin with the fur upon it, portions of the jaw of a bear, several pieces of charcoal, a beating block—fourteen inches square and three inches thick—made out of a lump of copper conglomerate, some lengths of knotted strips of buckskin, and a rough bit of wood about three feet long, which the miners call a digging stick. A collection of these things had been placed in an office at Houghton, where I saw them. I noticed that the digging stick was worn and frayed at the end where it had been used, and that the fur on the beaver skin was still in good condition.

In the same forest country as that where the pits were dug, several copper spear heads have been picked up. Those examined by me were unquestionably made by persons skilled in the work-

ing of metal.   Several of the members attached to the
mission at Sault Ste. Marie,* in the early part of the
eighteenth century, made crosses and ornaments
from copper that was brought to them by Indians,
who had found small lumps of the metal on the surface of the ground.   The spear heads may have been
made at the mission house.

After the cession of the Canadas to Great Britain
in 1763, an English Company was formed for the
purpose of searching for metal in this region.   The
operations were conducted by Mr. Alexander Henry,
and it has been ascertained that for several years he
worked near Ontonagon, and at other places upon
the Kee-wai-wona promontory.   Judging from the
method in which, at the ancient workings, the lodes
of copper have been traced through dense forests, it
is evident that fixed plans of operations must have
been pursued, and I came to the conclusion that the
surveyor who directed them, must have had a competent knowledge of the use of the compass.   It is

---

*The Jesuit Mission that was placed at Sault Ste. Marie, at the
entrance of Lake Superior was, during the seventeenth and
eighteenth centuries, one of the most important and influential
of the missionary establishments in North America.   Many of
the Fathers who were attached to it had received a good
mathematical education and were capable of making accurate
geographical surveys.   An excellent plan of Lake Superior and
its islands was made by them in 1670, and the coast lines and
bays were traced over a distance exceeding fifteen hundred
miles.   Amongst the distinguished men who worked at the mission were the Fathers Jogues, Allouez, Mesnard (who lost his
way and perished in the forest when travelling across the Kee-wai-
wona promontory), Dablon, and the well-known and devoted
missionary, Jacques Marquette.

therefore not unreasonable to assume, that all the pits and trenches were excavated under the superintendence of Europeans, at some period later than the sixteenth century.

Several miles to the south of these works I was shown the spot where the last and decisive battle was fought between the Chippewas and Iroquois. This battle field, which was on a point of land near Kee-wai-wona bay, was remarkable because it affords an instance of the great distances that were sometimes traversed by Indians when conducting their wars of extermination. The Iroquois whose territories and villages were upon the southern shores of Lakes Ontario and Erie, crossed into the Chippewa lands by the way of the channels leading to Sault Ste. Marie. Therefore, supposing that they followed the most direct line to the place where the battle was fought, they must have passed over a distance of not less than six hundred miles.

One of the burial mounds which had been opened, contained a large skull, a pipe made of dark slate and a stone hatchet. Upon the top of the mound was a pine tree which measured thirty inches in circumference. The scattered descendants of the Chippewa tribes dwell in the districts to the west of Lake Superior, but they occasionally wander into their original country. I met some of them near the shores of that great inland sea.

During the time that I was travelling in these iron and copper regions, I took the opportunity of accompanying the superintendent of one of the mines to look at the evidences of the action of the glacial drift upon the surfaces of the hills that had been cleared for the purpose of executing some preliminary mining operations. Some of these hills were composed of solid hematite iron and jasper, and yet these hard rocks were deeply grooved by the pressure that had been exerted against them.

Near Ishpeming there was a low range of hills or knobs, whose formation was a compact greenstone with wide veins of iron, which had been subjected to a severe grinding, and was furrowed with grooves two feet wide and five and a half inches deep. The general direction of this range was from E.N.E. to W.S.W. and the action of pressure was greatest where the sides of the hills faced towards the north. The grooves were about nine hundred feet above the level of Lake Superior. Large erratic boulders covered the surface of the land. I measured one of them which was lying exposed in a depression between two conical hills, eight hundred and fifty feet above the lake. It must have weighed over twenty tons. The boulders were usually masses of basalt, black or red granite, porphyry and jasper. Rounded boulders of pure copper are sometimes found. One of these, of exceptional size, was in the forest, in the direction of Ontonagon, and was estimated to weigh about eighteen tons.

Near Houghton, Mr. Forster showed me the surface of a hill, four hundred feet above the lake, which had been made perfectly smooth by the action of the drift passing over it. At another part where the rock was exposed we counted fifty-seven grooves over a space of sixty-seven feet of surface. Judging from the direction of the groovings on the Kee-wai-wona promontory and the iron hills of Michigan,

CHIPPEWA CHIEF.

(WEST OF LAKE SUPERIOR.)

the boulders appear to have been carried from Labrador.

The waters and floating icebergs must have swept over this country with much force for in many places the pressure exerted seems to have been enormous.

On my way south from this land, which contained so much that attracted attention, I visited the reservation of the Oneidas, at the spot where the council fire of that tribe was originally established, near Lake Ontario. I was received by the hereditary chief of that tribe, who was named Beech-tree. As he could not speak a word of English, our conversation was carried on with the assistance of his grandson, who acted as interpreter. Beech-tree was a large, broad shouldered man, with a remarkably massive head. If I had met him in the north of China, I should have taken him for a Manchu Tartar. His hair was very long and black, and tinged with grey.

He told his grandson to say that he was proud of his unmixed descent from the ancient chiefs of his nation, which had once been powerful, and that the land upon which we stood belonged by right to the Oneidas, and was the place where they held their great councils and decided upon questions of war or peace. After having made, with assumed dignity, this brief oration, Beech-tree retired into the interior of his hut, and I returned to my country cart, which had conveyed me to his territory, and finally reached the shores of Lake Erie. After traversing Lakes Huron and Michigan, I proceeded to the banks of the Ohio river, with the purpose of making expeditions to the works of the Mound Builders.

Before quitting the Oneida reservation, I made enquiries about a man named Williams, concerning whom I had heard, when at Boston, a strange and romantic story. It appears that Williams, whose parentage was uncertain or unknown, was sent early in the present century from the Indian village of St. Regis, to act as a missionary among the Oneidas. Some years later, rumours were spread to the effect that he was the true Dauphin, the son of Louis XVI. These rumours were stated to be based upon grounds which warranted a fair degree of belief.

The story as told to me at Oneida was that Williams was supposed to have been born at St. Regis (a picturesque village reservation on the South bank of the St. Lawrence, and which, at the time that I saw it, contained a population of fifteen hundred Iroquois, the majority of whom were half-breeds).

In early manhood he was sent to a college, trained for missionary work, and ultimately appointed to preach among the Oneidas. I was informed, by those who had previously known him, that he was an honest, zealous missionary, who was quite incapable of attempting any form of imposture.

It however happened (such is the story,) that the Prince de Joinville, when travelling in America, came to Oneida and saw Williams. It is also stated that he visited him on a second occasion. After this second meeting, it was thought by the residents in the neighbourhood, that Williams was possibly the Dauphin.

A picture of Simon, the gaoler who treated the young prisoner in the Temple with such incredible brutality, was shown to him, and he instantly started back with horror, as if recalling some painful memory. Williams had no recollection of anything about his youth before the age of fourteen.

In consequence of these apparent corroborations of the local surmises, it was conjectured that after the execution of Louis XVI., the young Dauphin was removed from the prison, sent to America and placed in an Indian family at St. Régis. Williams lived for many years with the Oneidas, and died at an advanced age. He was described as having been a man of portly physique, with large features and big hands and feet. His complexion was rather dark. I think it is probable that he was descended from half-breed Indian parents.

It will be observed, that, the whole value of the evidence supporting the theory of his being the Dauphin, depends upon the accuracy of the story that he received two visits from the Prince de Joinville. This statement, if correct, appears however to establish the presumption that the Royal Family of France, may have had some doubts with regard to the truth of the report of the death of Louis XVII. in the Temple. It is certain that a boy, said to have been that young prince, was buried by the orders of the Commune in an obscure churchyard in the Faubourg St. Antoine, in the year 1795; but the evidence is scarcely conclusive upon the subject.

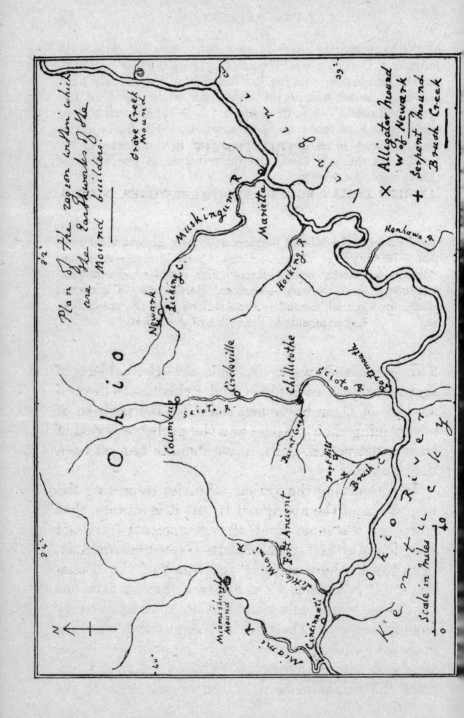

Plan of the region within which are the Earthworks of the Mound builders.

Ohio

Grave Creek Mound

Muskingum R.

Marietta

Newark

Licking C.

Hocking R.

Kentawa R.

Columbus

Sciota R.

Circleville

Chillicothe

Scioto R.

Paint Creek

Portsmouth

Fort Hill

Brush C.

Fort Ancient

Little Miami R.

Miami R.

Miamisburg Mound

Cincinnati

Ohio River Kentucky

Scale in miles

0   40

N

× Alligator Mound
   w. of Newark
+ Serpent Mound
   Brush Creek

CHAPTER IV.

ANCIENT INDIAN MOUNDS AND EARTHWORKS IN OHIO.

Earthworks of the Mound Builders and their geographical position.—Miamisburgh Mound.— Grave Creek Mound.—Ages and contents of burial mounds.—Rectangular, circular and octagonal Inclosures near Newark.—Marietta Earthworks.—Discoveries made in a burial mound.—Fortifications near Portsmouth.— Encampments in the valley of the Scioto.

THE great earthworks in Ohio are the subject of much antiquarian interest and conjecture. Several surveys of them have been made for the purpose of ascertaining their purpose and the probable period of their construction, but nothing definite has yet been determined.

In considering the various theories respecting the migrations of the aboriginal tribes, it is strange that traces of the same kind of encampments have not been found either in the North-West towards Asia, or in the southern parts of the valley of the Mississippi. It is difficult to understand how it happens that these works only occur within a comparatively confined region. Their actual geographical limits are contained within an area bounded approximately, towards the South, by the left bank of the river Ohio, from the neighbourhood of Cincinnati towards the

West, to Wheeling towards the East, and not extending northwards beyond a line drawn from East
to West through the centre of Ohio.

Consequently it will be seen, upon making a reference to the map, that the works of the people called
the Mound Builders, are situated within the southern division of the State including both banks of the
Ohio river. These were their extreme limits, but the
part of the country chiefly occupied by them has a
much lesser area.

It is evident from the positions of the earthworks,
that the tribes which raised them thought it necessary
to maintain their communications by water with the
valley of the Ohio, and on the banks of that river
they had several important fortifications or encampments. It is, however, upon the banks of the tributaries that fall into the Ohio from the North, that
their settlements were most numerous, especially
upon the Scioto, the Muskinghum and the streams
entering those rivers near Newark and Chillicothe.

The first earthwork that I visited was the great
mound of Miamisburgh, which is situated upon the
summit of high ground overlooking the valley of the
Little Miami river. It was opened and examined in
1869, a few months before I saw it. In appearance
and shape it resembled the largest of the Tumuli that
were raised upon the plains of Troy, but the dimensions of this American mound are much greater. It
is sixty-eight feet high, and has a circumference at
the base of about eight hundred and thirty feet.

A perpendicular shaft was sunk from the centre of
the summit to the centre of the base, and two horizontal shafts were made, one at eighteen feet, and

another at thirty-six feet respectively. At a depth
of four feet from the top, there was a layer of wood
ashes. At eight feet there was discovered a skeleton
and some decayed wood. At fifteen feet there was a
layer of charcoal and lime. At the depth of twenty-
four feet a singular construction was found. It consisted of an upright stone, standing upon two flat
stones, together with a number of rounded water worn
stones. With these there was some closely pressed
material, looking like a kind of cloth made from
wood fibre. Upon reaching the depth of thirty feet,
there was discovered a quantity of charcoal and
ashes. Six feet below this was a hollow space and,
from the character of the contents within, it was
supposed that there must have been a vault there,
which had been surrounded and covered with logs of
wood. At the base of the mound there was a large
quantity of charcoal.

Before the tumulus was opened, it had been conjectured that it was raised by the Indians for the
purposes of observation. It is situated at the extreme
western limit of the territories of the Mound Builders,
and at a considerable distance from any of their other
earthworks. The other great burial mound was placed
in a similar manner beyond the eastern boundary at
the confluence of a small stream called the Grave
Creek with the Ohio, near Wheeling. On my way
there by the river, I passed the mouths of the
Scioto and Muskinghum, and the towns of Portsmouth and Marietta,* where are the remains of

---

*At Marietta, there still exists an ancient Indian mound or
tumulus, about thirty feet high. It is situated near the south-

extensive encampments.

The Grave Creek Mound is similar to that at Miamisburgh, but it is, in all its measurements, rather larger and rises to a height of seventy feet. In the early part of the present century, some slight excavations were made upon the slopes, and it was then ascertained that numerous skeletons were buried there.

In the year 1838, a more thorough system of examination was adopted. A shaft was carried through horizontally from the surface of the ground at the base to the centre. Then a perpendicular shaft was sunk from the centre of the summit to the base, connecting these with the passage already opened. At three feet from the summit there was found a skeleton in a complete state of decay. Thirty-two feet lower down, there was a small vault or structure of logs of wood, within which was another skeleton also decayed. At the base there was a larger vault, containing two skeletons which were in a sufficiently well preserved condition to enable them, subsequently, to be exhibited. These skeletons were found to be partly enveloped in a fibrous material, and they were placed within a structure, formed by a number of upright logs of wood, covered by other similar logs placed horizontally. Upon the top of this roof there had been piled a small heap of stones.

The excavation of the horizontal shaft, near the surface, disclosed a very singular system of burial.

Dr. Clemens,* in his account of this operation,

---

cast limits of the inclosures. When I saw it, it was under the care of the local authorities.

* Morton's Crania Americana, pp. 221.

states that at a distance of twelve or fifteen feet were found masses of a substance composed of charcoal and burnt bones, and also that when enlarging the lower vault, in which were the two skeletons, ten more skeletons were discovered, all of them in a sitting posture, but in a state so fragile as to defy all attempts to preserve them. In this lower vault there were six hundred and fifty beads made of shell and perforated in the centre. In the smaller vault above, in which was the single skeleton, there were seventeen hundred shell beads, about one hundred and fifty small plates of mica perforated at their sides and corners, five hundred marine shells and five copper bands or bracelets which were placed on the bones of the arms.

There was a tree growing upon the top of the mound which interfered with the operations. Dr. Clemens stated that it was two-and-a-half feet in diameter, and had three hundred growths from centre to circumference. Some years earlier another oak which had become decayed was cut down by the proprietor, who said that he had counted upon it nearly five hundred annual rings. The number of rings in the trunk of a tree, growing upon any part of the mound, gives clear evidence upon the question of its least age, and therefore it may be assumed that the date of the completion of the burial mound cannot be later than the fourteenth century. It is, however, possible that there may have been several successive growths of trees on the slopes, and in that case it may have been raised at some earlier period. The Miamisburgh mound, at the time when I saw it, was covered with trees, none of which appeared to be of great age.

They must have been preceded by other growths.

The nature of the ornaments buried with the skeletons in the Grave Creek mound, seems to prove that there must have been communications between these Ohio races, and the tribes dwelling to the South of the Mississippi valley,* for the small sea shells were considered to be of the same kind as those seen on the beaches in Florida. The glittering flat slabs of mica, which hung over the breast, either as ornaments or marks of distinction, were similar to those discovered in burial mounds in the Iroquois country, near Lake Ontario. The copper bracelets were of rude workmanship, and were probably hammered into their shape from lumps of native copper. Similar bracelets have been found

---

*It is known that a communication between the south-western extremity of Lake Superior and the Mississippi Valley, existed from an early time. When I was at Toronto, Professor Daniel Wilson, to whom I was indebted for much information upon subjects relating to American archæology, told me that it had been ascertained that the copper found in these mounds, was of the same character as that in the Lake Superior Mines: so that the question of its origin was practically settled. It thus seems probable that some of the small lumps of pure copper found in the forests and on the shores of the lake, near the Kee-wai-wona promontory, were brought into Ohio.

A mound that was opened near Lake Ontario, and whose contents I examined, was stated to have been twelve feet high. Within it were about twenty skeletons, some coarse pottery, a number of arrow heads made of a hard flinty stone and several flat rectangular stones, pierced with one or two holes, which had been used as breast ornaments, possibly denoting a certain rank. There were also stone gouges, some stone axes and many fragments of charred wood. This was probably an Iroquois grave.

in some smaller burial mounds in other parts of Ohio. Those examined by me were made in the most rough and simple manner. The copper seems to have been beaten out into the required lengths, and then bent over to form the bracelets. The shapes resembled the bangles made in Hindostan and Persia.

There are circumstances with respect to the manner of burial by the Mound Builders which require to be noticed. It seems from the evidence of the various excavations that have been made, that it was frequently the custom to construct in the centre of the spot intended to be a burial place, a vault surrounded by upright logs of wood. In this was put the earliest burial, which was probably that of a chief. This vault was then covered with a roof of logs, and over it was piled a heap of stones. Other mounds were added in the course of time, and were placed on the surface of the ground in a circle surrounding the vault. This system of placing mounds was then continued in circles, one outside the other, until the space or area intended to be occupied was filled up. The later interments were probably made successively one above the other, until the tumulus was completed. The time that would elapse before a tribe had raised such a high mound as that at the Grave Creek, would necessarily be very long.

In the town of Newark, situated in a part of the country which appears to have been much occupied by the races that built the ancient earthworks, a very interesting collection of local antiquities had been brought together. Amongst the various relics discovered in the mounds were, stone axes and chisels, quantities of rude coarse pottery, many shell beads, and some copper bracelets.

Dr. Wilson, who was a resident in the neighbour-hood, and took much personal interest in antiquarian investigations, told me he had observed that the larger burial places seemed to have been raised grad-ually, and at intervals.   He had formed the opinion that the Indians usually traced upon the surface of the ground the outer base of the tumulus.   Within the inclosed space a number of skeletons were then laid and covered over with layers of earth or small mounds.   Over these, after a certain time had elapsed, more skeletons were placed and similarly covered.   This system of burial was continued until the mound was completed.   There were evidences of a great burning having taken place upon the top of every successive series of burials.   The nature of the contents of such of the smaller mounds as had been opened varied in many respects.   In some instances nothing was found except ashes and broken pottery. In others were skeletons together with stone pipes, chisels made of hard greenstone, flint arrow heads, bone awls and numerous beads.   There were also occasionally found a few rudely made copper rings. In a mound which was supposed to be a child's grave, a necklace of beads, strung upon a kind of fibre, was placed round the neck of the skeleton.

There was a large cairn, above forty feet in height, placed a few miles south of the town, which was de-stroyed about the middle of the present century in order to obtain materials for constructing a portion of the banks of a canal.   When the stones were re-moved, fifteen small mounds composed of earth were discovered ranged in a circle at some distance from the centre, and near the outer part of the base. There was also a central mound which contained a quantity of human bones. In one of the outer mounds the explorers saw a hollow wooden trough, in which was a skeleton and several rings made of copper. I examined some fragments of this trough that were preserved in the Museum. The wood was black and very hard. It was considered that the mounds beneath the cairn contained earth that must have been brought from a distance. This singular fact is in accordance with what has been observed in other Indian works, and probably has a special significance.

Judging from the character of the relics that have been discovered in the Ohio mounds,* it does not appear that there is any reason to justify the conclu-

---

*In the valley of the Mississippi, especially in the northern part which had been occupied by the Dakotas, I afterwards saw many burial mounds, which, with the exception of the unusually great mounds near Miamisburgh and Wheeling, resembled in all respects those in Ohio. The methods of burial with the Sioux were evidently similar to those of the Mound Builders, with respect to the custom of conveying skeletons from considerable distances for the purpose of placing them together in one burying heap.

In several of the ancient burial mounds in Ohio, thin flat plates or slabs of mica are placed with the skeletons. This shining and silvery looking mineral appears to have been greatly valued by Indians. When I was on the coast of California, I happened to be present when a shell bank was cut open and a section of it examined. There was found, piled within it, a confused heap of skulls and shells, together with a larger quantity of rough pieces of mica. It is remarkable that the use of mica as an ornament should have been prevalent over such a wide geographical area amongst tribes dwelling so far apart.

sion that the Mound Builders differed in their condition of civilisation from the other Indian tribes. The consideration of this subject has been made perplexing in consequence of the existence of the numerous burial places of the tribes who were settled in this region after the arrival of the Europeans. In several mounds were found gun barrels, silver crosses and other objects which are undoubtedly of foreign workmanship. The crosses were usually placed upon the breasts of the skeletons, and from this circumstance it is probable that they belonged to Indians who had been converted by the French missionaries.

After I had seen the principal burial places of the Mound Builders, I proceeded to look at the largest and most important group of that class of earthworks, which were considered by Messrs. Squier and Davis, who surveyed them in 1845, to have been raised for the purpose of religious ceremonial, and who accordingly called them sacred inclosures. It has also been conjectured that they may have been fortified camps.

They are situated a few miles from Newark, upon a slightly elevated plain, about forty feet above a river now called the Licking Creek. Upon two sides of them there are smaller streams, respectively named, South Fork and Racoon Creek : thus the camps are surrounded on three sides by water. The site chosen by the Indians was well adapted for the purpose of defence, when the habits or requirements of the tribes were such as to make it desirable for them to establish their dwelling places as near as possible to a river. The inclosures are designed with skill, and their construction must have involved arduous and long continued labour, which was probably executed in consequence of the apprehension of serious danger from the attacks of enemies. Upon an examination of their formation, it becomes evident that the men who traced the lines of the embankments, followed clear and well-defined rules.

As these earthworks are, with respect to their principles of construction, the most remarkable of their kind in North America, it is expedient to investigate their plans with careful attention. The inclosure, which is marked A on the annexed ground plan, consists of a large octagonal work connected with a smaller circular work. The octagon contains an area of about forty acres, surrounded by an embankment whose existing average height slightly exceeds five feet. There are eight entrances or gateways placed at equal distances from each other. They are guarded by mounds, made sufficiently wide to extend a little beyond the width of the openings and thus cover the approach. These mounds are of the same height as the ramparts, and are placed within them. They were made flat upon the top, and possibly the platform thus made was useful for defensive operations.

At one end of the inclosure the ramparts leave the octagon, and form two parallel banks leading into the circle B. This approach is nearly one hundred yards long and about fifteen yards wide. At its termination the banks turn to the right and left, and form a circular work containing an area of twenty acres. At the outer edge of the circle and opposite to the entrance, is placed a large flat-topped mound, attached to, but outside the general line of the banks. This mound, according to my measure-

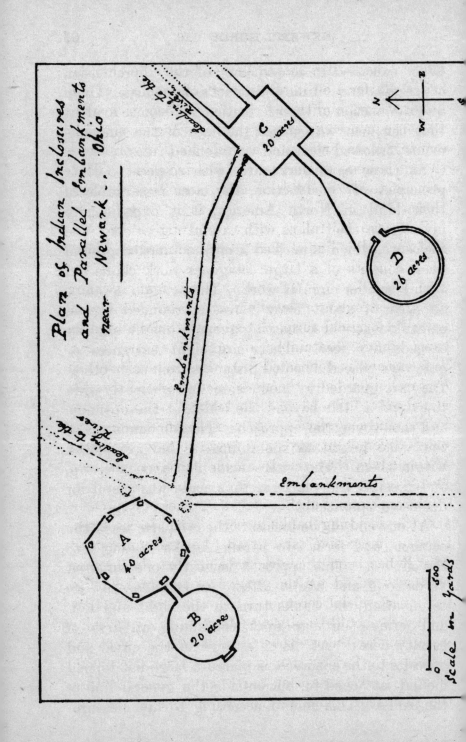

Plan of Indian Inclosures
and Parallel Embankments
near Newark — Ohio

N

C
20 acres

Feeding Ditches

D
26 acres

Embankments

Feeding to the
River

Embankments

A
40 acres

B
20 acres

scale in yards
0 — 500

ments, was twelve feet in perpendicular height, and
had a platform on its summit which was about one
hundred and eighty feet long by thirty feet wide.
In consequence of being several feet higher than the
embankments and outside their line, it commands
the approaches to that part of the inclosure. There
is no exterior or interior ditch to either of these
works.

From the central, or eastern opening of the octagon a long low line of parallel embankments connect
it with another group of earthworks which, in the
plan, is marked c. The inclosure has been, in many
parts, destroyed or levelled, but it is possible to
trace its original form. It appears to have been an
exact square, containing an area of twenty acres.
This square is connected with the circular work D
by parallel banks in the same manner as the octagon
is joined to the circle B, but they are of greater
length and magnitude. At the entrance, where the
banks diverge outwards and begin to form the curve
of the circle, they rise to a height exceeding fifteen
feet.

The appearance of these great avenues of approach,
and the inclosing banks, covered with forest trees,
is very impressive, and it can be well understood
why it has been thought probable that the circular
work was raised for the purpose of performing religious or sacrificial ceremonies. With respect to that
opinion it should be observed that, in this particular
instance, the theory that the lofty banks were intended as a fortification is to some extent doubtful,
because it happens that the ditch is placed within
the ramparts. This method of defence is unques-

tionably opposed to all the rules of European fortification. Possibly in the systems of Indian warfare
where stockades were generally used, and sometimes
placed on the sides of sloping banks, an inner ditch
may have been considered more capable of defence
than one placed externally.

The inclosure, like that at B, is in the shape of a
circle. It contains an area of about twenty-six
acres. The ramparts have an average height of
nearly twelve feet, and the depth of the ditch is over
nine feet. At that part of the work which is near
the entrance, the dimensions are, however, of still
greater importance, and the perpendicular height
measured from the bottom of the ditch exceeds
twenty-eight feet. The length of the inner slope
may be estimated as being about forty-two feet. In
the centre of the inclosure, there is a low heap of
earth and stones which, in consequence of its shape,
has received the name of the eagle mound. It is not
improbable that this was the spot where, after the
Indians returned from their wars, their prisoners
were tied to a stake, then tortured, and burnt in
accordance with the usual customs, and war dances
with other savage ceremonies, were performed in
the presence of the women and children assembled
around.

When taking into consideration the various circumstances which are apparent in the *Newark

---

*I have seen a re-survey of the Newark inclosures made
on behalf of the Smithsonian Institution, under the direction
of Professor Cyrus Thomas. The results of this survey are
very useful. The measurements have evidently been taken with

inclosures, particular attention should be given to the fact that their ground plans are geometrical figures. Thus the circle B is accurately traced. D has some small difference in the lengths of its diameters, but is very nearly a true circle. The square has its four sides equal, and all its angles are right angles. The octagon is carefully laid down, and its angles are almost mathematically correct.

The plans and measurements are evidences of the existence of mental capacities which were far in

---

much care. With respect to the Octagon, Professor Thomas observes that, " The angles at the crossings of the diagonals and diameters at the centre o, are so nearly right angles as to be worthy of notice in this connection. For instance, the angles at the crossings of the diagonals BF and DH, differ but 10′ from true right angles, while those at the crossing of the diameters AE and CG differ but 2′."

As regards the Square he states, that, " This inclosure varies but slightly from a true square, the course of the opposite sides in one case differing but 31′, and the other but 6′. The greatest variation at the corners from a true right angle is 57′."

The large Circle D is said to have a difference of diameters of twenty-six feet, these being respectively 1189 feet and 1163 feet.

The Observatory Circle, which is the inclosure connected with the Octagon, was found to have been made with remarkable correctness. " The widest divergence between the line of the survey and the circumference of the true circle is four feet. It is therefore evident that the inclosure approaches in form very nearly an absolute circle."

Professor Thomas also states with reference to the Observatory Circle, that the radius is almost an exact multiple of the surveyor's chain.

The geometrical accuracy of the lines of embankments and of the inclosed areas in earthworks of such great dimensions, covering such large spaces of ground, is not the least strange fact concerning these works.

advance of those of the present Indian races, who are remarkable for their extreme indifference to all ideas of regularity of form, and who have not, and never could have had, the slightest acquaintance with the rules of geometry.

The Licking river, after passing these inclosures, finally enters the Muskinghum, and the Muskinghum falls into the Ohio. The confluence takes place near the town of Marietta, where there are groups of earthworks which, in many respects, resemble those at Newark, and some of the areas were equal. The positions for the inclosures were evidently chosen upon similar principles. They were upon a comparatively elevated plateau, and had direct communication with the river.

In the early part of the present century some discoveries were made, which were considered to be of the utmost importance. It was thought that they had a direct bearing upon the question of the civilisation and antiquity of the Mound Builders, and a letter, written by Dr. Hildreth, has been acknowledged to be a very important contribution to the evidence upon these subjects.*

The letter ran as follows :—

" Marietta, July 19th, 1819.
" In removing the earth which composed an " ancient mound in one of the streets of Marietta, " on the margin of the plain, near the fortifications, " several curious articles were discovered the latter " part of June last. They appear to have been

---

*Archæologia Americana, Vol. I. The plan of the Marietta Inclosures is a reduction of a part of the survey made in 1837 by Mr. Charles Whittlesea, and published by the Smithsonian Institution in 1848.

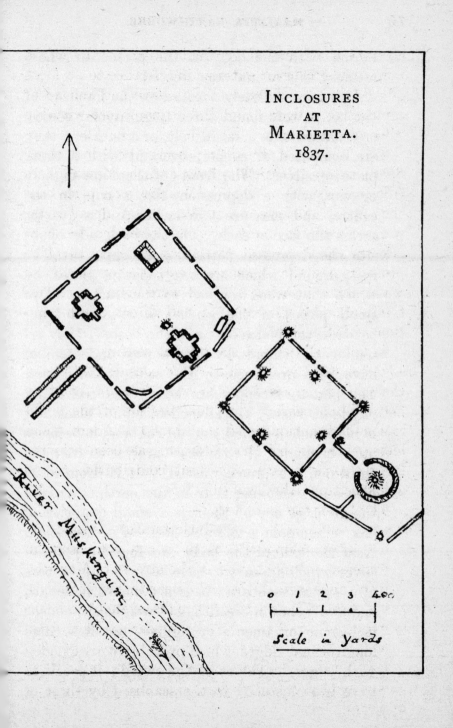

INCLOSURES
AT
MARIETTA.
1837.

River Muskingum

0 1 2 3 4 00

Scale in yards

"buried with the body of the person to whose
"memory this mound was erected.

"Lying immediately over, or on the forehead of
"the body, were found three large circular bosses,
"or ornaments for a sword belt, or a buckler; they
"are composed of copper, overlaid with a thick
"plate of silver. The fronts of them are slightly
"convex, with a depression, like a cup, in the
"centre, and measure two inches and a quarter
"across the face of each. On the back side, oppo-
"site the depressed portion, is a copper rivet or
"nail, around which are two separate plates, by
"which they were fastened to the leather. Two
"small pieces of the leather were found lying
"between the plates of one of the bosses; they re-
"semble the skin of an old mummy, and seem to
"have been preserved by the salts of the copper.
"The plates of copper are nearly reduced to an
"oxyde, or rust. The silver looks quite black, but
"is not much corroded, and on rubbing, it becomes
"quite brilliant. Two of these are yet entire; the
"third one is so much wasted, that it dropped in
"pieces on removing it from the earth. Around
"the rivet of one of them is a small quantity of
"flax or hemp, in a tolerable state of preservation.
"Near the side of the body was found a plate of
"silver which appears to have been the upper part
"of a sword scabbard; it is six inches in length
"and two inches in breadth, and weighs one ounce;
"it has no ornaments or figures, but has three
"longitudinal ridges, which probably corresponded
"with edges, or ridges of the sword; it seems to
"have been fastened to the scabbard by three or

"four rivets, the holes of which yet remain in the
"silver.

"Two or three broken pieces of a copper tube,
"were also found, filled with iron rust. These
"pieces, from their appearance, composed the lower
"end of the scabbard, near the point of the sword.
"No sign of the sword itself was discovered, except
"the appearance of rust above mentioned.

"Near the feet, was found a piece of copper,
"weighing three ounces. From its shape it appears
"to have been used as a plumb, or for an ornament,
"as near one of the ends is a circular crease, or
"groove, for tying a thread ; it is round, two inches
"and a half in length, one inch in diameter at the
"centre, and half an inch at each end. It is com-
"posed of small pieces of native copper, pounded
"together ; and in the cracks between the pieces,
"are stuck several pieces of silver ; one nearly the
"size of a four-penny piece, or half a dime. This
"copper ornament was covered with a coat of
"green rust, and is considerably corroded. A
"piece of red ochre, or paint, and a piece of iron
"ore, which has the appearance of having been
"partially vitrified, or melted, were also found.
"The ore is about the specific gravity of pure iron.

"The body of the person here buried, was laid
"on the surface of the earth, with his face upwards,
"and his feet pointing to the north-east, and head
"to the south-west. From the appearance of
"several pieces of charcoal, and bits of partially
"burnt fossil coal, and the black colour of the
"earth, it would appear that the funeral obsequies
"had been celebrated by fire ; and while the ashes

"were yet hot and smoking, a circle of flat stones
"had been laid around and over the body. The
"circular covering is about eight feet in diameter,
"and the stones yet look black, as if stained by
"fire and smoke. This circle of stones seems to
"have been the nucleus on which the mound was
"formed, as immediately over them is heaped the
"common earth of the adjacent plain, composed of
"a clayey sand and coarse gravel. This mound
"must originally have been about ten feet high,
"and thirty feet in diameter at its base. At the
"time of opening it, the height was six feet, and
"diameter between thirty and forty. It has every
"appearance of being as old as any in the neigh-
"bourhood, and was, at the first settlement of
"Marietta, covered with large trees, the remains
"of whose roots were yet apparent in digging away
"the earth. It also seems to have been made for
"this single personage, as the remains of one
"skeleton only were discovered. The bones were
"much decayed, and many of them crumbled to
"dust on exposure to the air. From the length of
"some of them, it is supposed the person was
"about six feet in height.

"Nothing unusual was discovered in their form,
"except that those of the skull were uncommonly
"thick. The situation of the mound on high
"ground, near the margin of the plain, and the
"porous quality of the earth, are admirably calcu-
"lated to preserve any perishable substance from
"the certain decay which would attend it in
"many other situations. To these circumstances,
"is attributed the tolerable state of preservation in

" which several of the articles above described were
" found, after lying in the earth for several cen-
" turies. We say *centuries*, from the fact that
" trees were found growing on those ancient works,
" whose ages were ascertained to amount to between
" four and five hundred years each, by counting the
" concentric circles in the stumps after the trees
" were cut down ; and on the ground, besides them,
" were other trees in a state of decay, that appeared
" to have fallen from old age."

It should be observed with reference to the statements made in the above letter, that the age of the
trees, said to have been estimated by the early
settlers at Marietta, has generally been accepted as
being correct, and based upon direct and accurate
evidence. Consequently it would be necessary to
admit that the earthworks were raised at some period
before the fifteenth century.

Passing from the question of this date, as calculated
by the annular rings counted upon the trees, to the
subject of the contents of the burial mound which
was excavated in the presence of Dr. Hildreth ; the
problem that has chiefly to be solved is the age of
the silver-plated ornaments. It is difficult to fix
the time when these were made, but judging from
the sketches of them, as published in the account of
these discoveries, the ornaments appear to have been
such as would have been placed upon the sword belt
and scabbard of a European officer of rank.

When the inclosures and their ramparts were for
the first time surveyed and described in the year
1805, it was observed that there were parallel pas-
sages or protected ways leading from the larger of

the forts down to the river.   These appear to correspond with the parallels that can still be traced at Newark, and which also lead to the river.   Those at Marietta were however more remarkable, because, in order to obtain the gradual approach which was required, it was necessary, apparently, to excavate the river bank in such a manner as to make a sunken road.   A conveniently sloped communication with the water was thus constructed.   It is probable that at the river side where the protecting embankments terminated, a fleet of canoes was kept ready for use or escape.

The next confluence of rivers below Marietta, occurs at the point where the Scioto falls into the Ohio.   Near the spot where the town of Portsmouth is now situated, are traces of an extensive series of low embankments which seem to have been made for temporary entrenchments.   On the opposite or south bank of the river, there was an inclosure constructed in the shape of a square, each of the sides being eight hundred feet long ; the area inclosed was nearly fifteen acres.   The embankments were over twelve feet high : and there was no ditch.

This fort was brought into especial notice in consequence of a strange discovery.   A large number of iron pickaxes, shovels and gunbarrels were found buried in the ramparts.   It has been conjectured that they were hidden there by the French soldiers when they retreated down the Ohio after the capture of Fort Du Quesne* by the British forces in the year

---

*Fort Du Quesne was built about the year 1752.   It was situated near the spot where is now the town of Pittsburgh.   In 1731

1758. The Indian fortifications on the banks of that river were placed upon the direct line of the communication with the other French forts in the valley of the Mississippi and Louisiana. In the ordinary course of events they would probably have been used by the French and their Indian allies, when they happened to be in their neighbourhood.

The valley of the river Scioto above Portsmouth, towards Chillicothe, was evidently much frequented by the Indians, who dwelt in inclosures resembling in their formation the square and circular works at Newark, although the embankments were of smaller dimensions. A brief description of one of them as it existed when first surveyed, is sufficient to give a knowledge of the usual plans of these encampments. It was situated on the left bank of a tributary of the Scioto, called Paint Creek.

There was a square inclosure, each of whose sides was one thousand and eighty feet in length. Attached to this square, which contained an area of twenty-seven acres, was a large circular inclosure having a diameter of about seventeen hundred feet. This circle had another smaller work connected with it which was also circular, and had a diameter of eight hundred feet. The embankments of all these inclosures were low, and did not anywhere

---

the Indians who then occupied the lands near Marietta formed an alliance with the French, and obtained their assistance in protecting them from the attacks of hostile tribes. These were probably the Iroquois, who at that period had made a treaty with the English, and were their allies during the wars against the French in Canada and this part of North America.

exceed five feet in height.   The position of the gateways and the mounds protecting them was the same
as in the octagonal work at Newark.   The large
circle had an opening into it leading out of the
square, and the small circle had also one opening
which connected it with the other.

This part of Ohio was, in the eighteenth century,
occupied by settlements of the Shawnee tribes.   In
several of the burial mounds, which are supposed to
have belonged to them, there have been found copper kettles, silver crosses and iron gun-barrels—all
of which must have been unquestionably made by
workmen of European descent.

CHAPTER V.

MOUNDS AND EARTHWORKS IN OHIO.

Ancient Fortified Inclosures at Circleville.—Discoveries in a
Burial Mound.—Alligator Totem near Newark.—Fort Ancient.
—Age of Trees growing upon the Ramparts at Fort Hill.—
Traditions.—Geometrical Ground Plans of Indian Inclosures.—
Conclusions.

BEFORE quitting the subject of those ancient earthworks, which were planned upon geometrical figures,
it is necessary to take into consideration certain
inclosures that were situated in the higher parts of
the Scioto Valley, in a position which is at the
present time, occupied by the town of Circleville.

The embankments or ramparts have been razed to
the ground, and no traces remain of what appears to
have been one of the most perfect examples of the
mathematical accuracy of that type of construction.
It is fortunate that during the demolition of the
works, there happened to be present an antiquarian
of such an acknowledged reputation as Mr. Atwater,
for he has written a full account of their form and
dimensions,* together with a report upon the strange

---

*Archæologia Americana, Vol. I.

discoveries made when excavating a burial mound, inside the circular inclosure near its centre. Mr. Atwater, who evidently took careful measurements,[*] wrote a statement which includes the following extracts :—

"There are two forts, one being an exact circle, "the other an exact square. The former is sur-"rounded by two walls, with a deep ditch between "them. The latter is encompassed by one wall, "without any ditch. The former was sixty-nine "rods in diameter, measuring from outside to out-"side of the circular outer wall ; the latter is "exactly fifty-five rods square measuring the same "way. The walls of the circular fort were at least "twenty feet in height, measuring from the bottom "of the ditch, before the town of Circleville was "built. The inner wall was of clay, taken up prob-"ably in the northern part of the fort, where was a "low place, and is still considerably lower than "any other part of the work. The outside wall "was taken from the ditch which is between these "walls, and is alluvial, consisting of pebbles worn "smooth in water, and sand, to a very considerable "depth, more than fifty feet at least. The outside "of the walls is about five or six feet in height "now ; on the inside, the ditch is, at present, "generally not more than fifteen feet. They are "disappearing before us daily, and will soon be "gone. The walls of the square fort are at this time, "where left standing, about ten feet in height.

*See Plan.

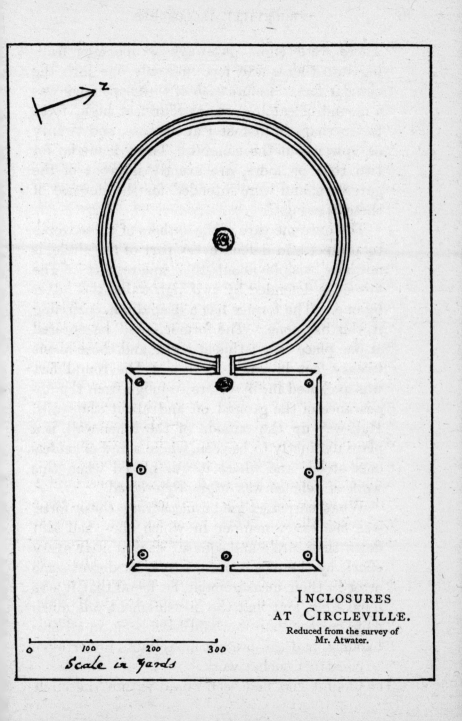

INCLOSURES
AT CIRCLEVILLE.

Reduced from the survey of
Mr. Atwater.

0   100   200   300
Scale in yards

" There were eight gateways or openings lead-
" ing into the square fort, and only one into the
" circular fort.   Before each of these openings was
" a mound of earth, perhaps four feet high, forty
" feet perhaps in diameter at the base, and twenty
" or upwards at the summit.   These mounds, for
" two rods or more, are exactly in front of the
" gateways, and were intended for the defence of
" these openings."   .   .   .   .   .

" The extreme care of the authors of these works
" to protect and defend every part of the circle, is
" nowhere visible about this square fort.   The
" former is defended by two high walls, the latter
" by one.   The former has a deep ditch encircling
" it, this has none.   The former could be entered
" at one place only ; this at eight, and those about
" twenty feet broad."   .   .   .   " The round fort
" was picketed in, if we are to judge from the ap-
" pearance of the ground on and about the walls.
" Half-way up the outside of the inner wall, is a
" place distinctly to be seen, where a row of *pickets*
" once stood, and where it was placed when this
" work of defence was originally erected."   .   .   .

" What surprised me on measuring these forts,
" was the exact manner in which they had laid
" down their circle and square ; so that after every
" effort, by the most careful survey, to detect some
" error in their measurement, we found that it was
" impossible, and that the measurement was much
" more correct than it would have been, in all pro-
" bability, had the present inhabitants undertaken
" to construct such a work."

The mound that had been raised within the circle

was ten feet high. Its summit had been levelled in order to obtain a platform which had a diameter of nearly thirty feet, and had probably been used as a site for the dwelling of the chief of the tribe. Mr. Atwater watched the proceedings when this mound was destroyed. He states that it contained :—

(1).—" Two human skeletons lying on what had been the original surface of the earth.

(2).—" A great quantity of arrow heads, some of which were so large as to induce a belief that they were used for spear heads.

(3).—" The handle either of a small sword or a large knife, made of an elk's horn; around the end where the blade had been inserted, was a ferule of silver which, though black, was not much injured by time. Though the handle showed the hole where the blade had been inserted, yet no iron was found, but an oxyde remained of similar shape and size.

(4).—" Charcoal and wood ashes on which these articles lay, which were surrounded by several bricks very well burnt. The skeleton appeared to have been burned in a large and very hot fire, which had almost consumed the bones of the deceased. This skeleton was deposited a little to the south of the centre of the tumulus, and, about twenty feet to the north of it was another, with which were—

(5).—" A large mirror, about three feet in length, and one foot and a half in breadth, and one inch and a half in thickness. This mirror was of isinglass (mica membranacea) and on it—

(6).—" A plate of iron which had become an oxyde; but before it was disturbed by the spade, resembled a plate of cast iron. The mirror answered the purpose very well for which it was intended. This skeleton had also been burned like the former, and lay on charcoal and a considerable quantity of wood ashes. A part of the mirror is in my possession as well as a piece of brick, taken from the spot at the time."

About two hundred yards from this tumulus, and outside the circular inclosure was a large mound, supposed to have been the common Indian cemetery. It contained an immense number of human skeletons of all sizes and ages. The skeletons are laid horizontally, with their heads generally towards the centre, and the feet towards the outside of the tumulus. A considerable part of this work still stands uninjured, except by time. In it have been found, besides these skeletons, stone axes and knives, and several ornaments with holes through them, by means of which, with a cord passing through these perforations, they could be worn by their owners.

The vestiges of occupation that have been left by those ancient tribes who raised the earthworks in this region are not of a character that render it possible to form any absolute conclusions about them.

There are, however, in Ohio two large and important mounds built in the shape of animals which may, possibly, have been made for the purpose of indicating the emblems which were adopted by the Indians as their totems. One of these is placed on the summit of a hill overlooking the valley of one of the tributaries of the Licking river, and about three miles from the octagonal inclosure near Newark.

In consequence of its shape, it is called the Alligator. There have been various theories with regard to this strange earthwork, and it has been supposed that sacrificial ceremonies were performed there. I had expected to find this figure to a certain extent excavated upon the surface of the earth, but I observed, upon examining it, that it was a regularly built up mound of considerable size.

The other large totem, which represents a huge serpent, is upon the brow of a hill about one hundred miles to the South-west of the Alligator, above a small river called the Brush Creek. According to the measurements of the earliest surveyors, its length, if extended, is about one thousand feet. It was five feet high in the centre, and had, at that part, a base of thirty feet, which diminished towards the head and tail.*

Upon the slopes of the hills near the Alligator, there are numerous remains of ancient earthworks. One of the most extensive of them was in every respect different from those at Newark, and other geometrically designed works, and seems to have been raised for other purposes, or possibly by a different tribe. Its embankments, which are irregular in their form, are in no part higher than six

---

*Upon an examination of the map it will be seen that the Serpent is placed in the territory west of the Scioto, and that the Alligator is east of that river.

The mouth of the serpent is described as being opened wide. This peculiarity is observable with the serpent carved upon the walls of the Casa de las Monjas at Uxmal.

feet, and are thrown up in such a manner as to inclose the top of a small hill, which is situated a short distance from the Alligator. The area contained within them is about eighteen acres. In the centre there is a small circular earthwork nearly one hundred yards in circumference, and in another part of the inclosure there are two mounds which have been opened. They contained large quantities of ashes and some broken pottery.

There are also other camping grounds near the river. The largest of them inclosed a space exceeding twenty acres, and was surrounded by a low bank evidently thrown up for the purposes of inclosing a temporary encampment. Near the Alligator totem I noticed a singular earthwork made in the shape of a half-moon. The farmers living in the neighbourhood told me that they had opened and destroyed many of the small mounds that had been upon their lands. In all cases they had contained nothing but fragments of rough pottery, together with small heaps of ashes.*

Finally, there remains to be taken into consideration those great earthworks on the hills which have been specially classified as having been undoubtedly raised

---

*The valley below the Alligator is in the possession of a race of Welsh colonists who emigrated from Wales about the year 1802. At that time they did not speak English, and for many years refrained from learning that language.

The church services are held in their town of Granville.

These colonists were prosperous and contented. The majority of them bore the names of Griffith, Price, Lewis, and others which are usual in the seaboard counties of Wales.

The adjacent high lands are called the Welsh hills.

for the purposes of defence, and which entirely differ
from such works as those that were placed upon the
plains. The largest of these camps has been called
Fort Ancient, and it must be acknowledged to be one
of the most important fortified entrenchments that
has ever been constructed in any part of the world.

It is placed upon the summit of a hill over-looking
the Little Miami river about thirty miles above its
junction with the Ohio. The site that was chosen by
the Indians is remarkable for its natural strength
and is, upon three sides of it, almost impregnable.
The hill which is about two hundred and thirty feet
above the valley, is in the form of a narrow promontory having almost precipitous sides except where
it is joined to the plateau. The Little Miami winds
round one part of the base, and some small tributary
streams join it from the other side.

The shape and length of the embankments are
shown in the accompanying plan, which is a reduction
that I have drawn from one that was made in 1843
by Professor Locke of Cincinnati.* It will be observed
that the ramparts follow closely the curves of the
ridge of the hill and that the camp is practically
divided into two parts, the outer division being near
the plain, and the inner one being at the head of the
promontory, where the sides of the hill are the most
steep and inaccessible. The latter was probably
intended as a final stronghold in the event of the
outer work being captured.

The magnitude of the inclosing embankments of

*"Ancient Monuments of the Mississippi Valley," pp. 19.

N

Little Miami River

Fort Ancient

B Mounds

B Embankment extending 1350 yards towards the East, terminating at a mound C

Section of the steep slope at d Embankment

Terrac

289 feet

Riv

d

Scale in yards

0   100   200

the outer camp is astonishing. It is here that the position is most open to direct attack, and no efforts or labour have been spared in carrying out what was thought necessary to prevent capture. No Roman or British encampment that I have seen surpasses this great Indian work. I walked round the entire circuit of the ramparts. They are not less than four miles in length. They follow every curve of the hill and the heads of all the numerous ravines.

The ground of the inclosure is level. At the time of my visit it was covered with forest trees, amongst which were many poplars. Upon the slopes of the embankments there was a luxuriant growth of large beeches and oaks. The quantity of earth that must have been conveyed and thrown up when forming these banks must have been enormous. The ramparts vary in height between ten and twenty feet according to the character of the natural defence afforded by the slopes of the hill. At the approach from the plain they are fifteen feet high and have a base of sixty-three feet. The platform at the top averages five feet wide.

There is no ditch. Nothing could more clearly mark the difference between this fortification and one that would have been made by a white race. An outer ditch is usually considered as not only of essential importance in works of defence, but its excavation supplies the earth required for the ramparts. It seems evident that either these Indians in their method of defensive warfare did not always consider a ditch to be useful, or it is possible that, in consequence of not having shovels or pickaxes, they preferred obtaining earth in some other manner which they found more convenient.

Upon enquiring among the farmers who were occupying the adjacent land, I found that there was a prevalent opinion amongst them that the earth composing these embankments had been brought from a distance and that it had been carried by hand. It was also believed by them that the fort could not have been made by Indians and that it was built at a very remote period by some other race.

When walking upon the top of the broad ramparts I observed that there were no evidences of the excavations that supplied the earth for the formation of the enormous banks. In some parts of the interior there were some shallow depressions, and also several holes which had been made for some unknown purpose, but they could not have provided the quantities required. It is possible, and, I think probable, that the earth was taken from the surface of the land within the inclosure. A shallow excavation made to a depth not exceeding six inches over the whole area of one hundred and forty acres would have given a sufficient supply. The methods of digging the ground, and of conveying the earth must necessarily have been very primitive, and it is surprising that, with all the difficulties that had to be overcome, works of such magnitude should have been raised.

At a gap in an angle over-looking the river the remains of a road, which led down to the water, can still be traced. At the part where this road entered the fort it is evident that it had been paved with flat water worn stones. The ramparts here reach their greatest dimensions, being fully twenty feet high. The appearance of Fort Ancient from this position was very remarkable, and the effect was

heightened by the beautiful foliage of the forest
trees that crowned the summits of these lofty earthworks.

The inner part of the camp was strongly fortified.
High banks were raised across the narrow part of
the enclosure at the centre, and two mounds guarded
the approach.   The road to the outer camp from the
plain was also protected by two mounds, and from
these there ran low parallels for a distance of nearly
fourteen hundred yards.   They then terminated by
closing round another mound which was probably
used for the purpose of a look-out.   Some labourers
at a farm near this position told me that there once
existed other parallel banks connected with the fort,
which could be traced for several miles, but that
these had been destroyed.

There are certain features in the construction of
this fortification which have attracted attention,
but their purpose has not been, and probably cannot
be, explained.   There are not less than seventy gaps
or openings leading out of the embankments.   It
has been supposed that these were intended to allow
the escape of water from the interior.   There is
another theory which has been suggested, according
to which it is thought possible that they were openings made with the object of enabling the Indians to
rush out at several points to repel their enemies, and
that they were fenced by stockades.

It, however, happens that these gaps are sometimes in positions where the slopes of the hill are so
steep as to be practically inaccessible, and at other
places they are on the level ground from which no
surplus waters could drain away.   They seem to

have formed part of the system of fortification, for they occur in the same inexplicable manner at another hill work of defence, built under similar conditions, on the summit of a promontory with precipitous slopes, about forty miles to the south-east of this position, which was evidently built by the same race.

This large earthwork is called Fort Hill, and it is singular in the respect of having afforded to its surveyor the means of forming a judgment upon the question of its antiquity. Consequently it has become possible to establish well founded conclusions with respect to the dates of the construction of earthworks of a similar character.

Professor Locke, in his report on the geology of that part of Ohio, stated that on the top of the wall of Fort Hill stood a chestnut tree six feet in diameter. "Counting and measuring," he observes, " the annual layers of wood where an axeman had cut into the trunk, I found them at nearly 200 to the foot, which would give to this tree the age of 600 years. A poplar tree, seven feet in diameter, standing in the ditch, allowing the thickness to the layers which I have found in like poplars, 170 to the foot, would give nearly the same result, 607 years."*

Accepting the deductions of Professor Locke as being correct, it follows that the period when this hill fort was constructed was not later than the thirteenth century. Admitting that the thirteenth

---

*Second Annual Report of the Geological Survey of the State of Ohio, 1838, pp. 269.

century is therefore the latest age that can be ascribed to works of this type, they may be much older, for the forest trees within the inclosures may have succeeded earlier growths.

It is not possible to form an estimate of the age of earthworks from their appearance,* and it is only by counting the annual rings of trees that happen to have been growing upon them, that any safe theories respecting their antiquity can be adopted.

Looking at the geographical position of Fort Ancient, with reference to the other hill works of defence that are supposed to have been made by the Mound Builders, there are good reasons for assuming that this was their last stronghold, built with the intention of creating a permanent barrier against the attacks of their enemies. In time of war it was a secure encampment, large enough to contain the men, women and children of a numerous tribe. In time of peace it was well situated for the usual requirements of Indians. It was in the midst of a country abounding with game, and was immediately connected with a good navigable river which enabled their canoes to maintain direct communications with the Ohio and Mississippi.

Although, as far as I was able to judge, there was nothing in the principles of construction of the hill defensive works which appeared to be beyond the capacities of a purely Indian race, I invariably found

---

*The earthworks thrown up between Gallipoli and the Gulf of Saros during the Crimean war in 1854-1855 had the appearance of considerable antiquity when I saw them nearly a quarter of a century afterwards in 1878.

that the men who were settled as farmers near the principal entrenchments held the opinion that they must have been raised by a people possessing a superior condition of civilisation to the tribes who occupied the land at the close of the eighteenth century, and who were personally known by many of the early settlers.

It is, perhaps, desirable that these local opinions should not be altogether disregarded, especially when it is remembered that they are supported to some extent by Indian traditions and by the fact that no embankments of a similar formation exist in any other part of North America. It is therefore necessary that the statements of the Indians, respecting the previous occupation of parts of Ohio and Kentucky by men of a white race, should be given a passing consideration.

The Shawnees, who were found to be in possession of this region, informed the European colonists that the ancient forts had been made by white people, who after long wars against the Indians had been exterminated. Their traditions upon this subject were said to have been clear and decided.

On the other hand the statements of the Delawares, who were settled in the Northern parts of the State point to other conclusions. They said that the men who had raised the forts and entrenchments were called the Tallegewi, and that great wars took place between them and the Iroquois. After many years the Tallegewi were defeated and left the country. The Delawares made no allusion with respect to any differences of race or colour between the Tallegewi and the other Indian tribes.

It is much to be regretted that the evidence upon this interesting subject is so vague and obscure. If men of foreign origin had been settled in Ohio before the fourteenth century it would be reasonable to expect that traces of them would have been left there or some remaining indications of their religion. In the reports and letters of the French missionaries, many of whom spoke and understood the language of the tribes amongst whom they lived, there is no mention made of any rumours or traditions of white people having dwelt in this part of America. There were however at a later period, about the middle of the eighteenth century, certain statements made by officers and men who had been made prisoners by the Indians, which, at that time, received much attention. A cavalry officer, named Stuart, said that in the country west of Mississippi he had seen a tribe of Indians who were remarkably white in colour and had reddish hair. He was informed by them that their forefathers came from a foreign land and had settled in Florida, but that when the Spaniards invaded that country they moved to their present dwelling places. A fellow-captive, who was a Welshman, declared that he understood the language of the tribe, as it differed very little from what was spoken in Wales.

Other reports of a similar character were made by men who had lived with tribes occupying lands near the southern parts of the Mississippi valley. It has also been noticed that Indians having fair hair and blue eyes, were living with the Mandans in their settlements near the Missouri. With respect to the statements about Welsh speaking Indians, it is possible that the captives may have been influenced by the belief in the truth of the tradition that ships, under the direction of Prince Madoc, left the Welsh coasts in the twelfth century and landed their crews and emigrants on the eastern shores of the Florida peninsula.*

It is not, however, necessary to account for the existence of large but irregular embankments, such as those at Fort Ancient, by the supposition that the actions of a numerous tribe of Indians were under the influence or direction of men belonging to another race. But it is otherwise with reference to the geometrical inclosures on the plains, for these must have been unquestionally planned by men who possessed a competent knowledge of the methods of tracing mathematical designs.

Take for example the plans of the works at Newark

---

*According to Hakluyt, Madoc " prepared certaine ships with men and munition, and sought adventures by seas; sailing West and leaving the coast of Ireland so farre North, that he came vnto a land vnknowen, where he saw many strange things.

Of the voyage and returne of this Madoc there be many fables fained, as the common people do vse in distance of place and length of time, rather to augment than to diminish: but sure it is there he was. . . . . . This Madoc arriving in that Westerne countrey, vnto the which he came in the yere 1170, left most of his people there, and returning backe for more of his owne nation, acquaintance and friends to inhabit that faire and large countrey, went thither again with ten sailes, as I find noted by Gutyn Owen.

I am of opinion that the land whereunto he came was some part of the West Indies."

Hakluyt's Voyages, vol. iii, p. 21.

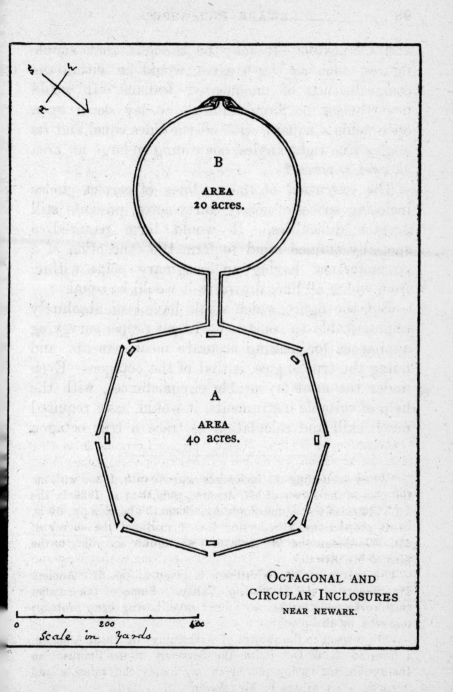

B

AREA
20 acres.

A

AREA
40 acres.

OCTAGONAL AND
CIRCULAR INCLOSURES
NEAR NEWARK.

0   200   400

Scale in yards

and Circleville. It may be thought that simple figures, such as the squares, would be within the comprehension of uneducated Indians. It would nevertheless be found difficult to lay down upon open fields a square, with all the sides equal and its angles true right angles, containing so large an area as twenty acres.*

The execution of the outlines of correct circles inclosing spaces of nearly thirty acres, presents still greater difficulties. It would have required a specially trained mind to form the conception of a circumference having an imaginary point within, from which all lines drawn to it would be equal.

But the figure which would have been absolutely impracticable to construct without proper surveying appliances for making accurate measurements, and fixing the true angles, is that of the octagon. Even under the most favourable circumstances, with the help of suitable instruments, it would have required much skill and calculation to trace a true octagon

---

*When examining the inclosures near Newark, I had with me the plan of the survey of Mr. Atwater, published in 1820 in the 1st Volume of the Archæologia Americana. The plan pp. 66 is, in its proportions, a reduction that I made of the survey of Mr. Whittlesea, but the inclosures are drawn according to the plan of Mr. Atwater.

The survey of Mr. Whittlesea is given at pp. 67 "Ancient Monuments of the Mississippi Valley." Some of the smaller earthworks and parallels no longer exist, having been probably removed by the plough.

With respect to the subject of Archæology in North America, I have to thank Dr. Baird, the Secretary of the Smithsonian Institution, for having placed in my hands the valuable and impartial work written by Mr. Haven.

whose embankments contained within them an area exceeding forty acres. It is difficult to suppose that an accurately designed work of this shape and magnitude could have been planned by Indians, or that the construction of a figure so essentially scientific and unusual, could have been originated by them. It is therefore possible to conclude, that, the geometrical earthworks in Ohio may have been raised by native tribes, acting under the direction of European surveyors, or of men who had received a mathematical education.

Considerations upon the subject of the race and capacity of the builders, have been to some extent complicated by the reports that were made concerning the ages of the trees that grew upon and within the ancient ramparts at Marietta. In the letter of Dr. Hildreth, quoted in the previous chapter, it is clearly stated that trees were growing there which were from four to five hundred years old.

As this evidence is very important it is desirable to examine it with attention. This statement was made when he was attempting to fix an approximate date for the age of a burial mound which was placed near the fortifications. It was at the bottom of this mound that were discovered the ornaments of a sword belt and scabbard. These ornaments were made of copper and plated with silver, and must therefore have been of European manufacture.

The calculation of the age of the trees is probably based upon the results of an examination that took place shortly after the settlement of Marietta during the latter part of the eighteenth century. It was at that time decided by several of the inhabitants to fell some of the largest and oldest trees then growing within the earthworks, and ascertain their ages by counting the number of annual rings contained in them. The operations were executed in the presence of Governor St. Clair and the Rev. Dr. Cutler. Several of the trees were found to have between three hundred and four hundred circles. One tree was carefully examined and Dr. Cutler stated that it contained at least four hundred and sixty-three circles.*

As nothing can be more conclusive as a proof of age than the number of rings found in any tree growing beyond the tropics, this evidence establishes an antiquity for these embankments earlier than the middle of the fourteenth century.

The ages of the trees growing upon the Marietta inclosures do not however enable a date to be estimated for the construction of such works as those at Newark, for the shapes at Marietta are irregular and, according to the survey, do not appear to have been laid down with geometrical accuracy. It is therefore probable that the Newark inclosures were made at some later period.

The fact of a ferule of silver and a plate of iron having been placed with the skeletons in the burial mound at Circleville leads to the conclusion that the tumulus like the one at Marietta was raised since the time of the arrival of the Europeans. On account of its having been placed within the inclosure it was

---

*See the Journal of Mr. Thaddeus Harris, pp. 54, published in Boston in 1805.

originally conjectured that it belonged to the same
people that formed the surrounding embankment,
but the evidence is not sufficient to establish the
correctness of a theory of such importance.

It is difficult to understand what could have been
the object of the Indians in constructing large earthworks in the shapes of squares and circles. Various
theories have been advanced upon the subject, but
nothing that can be considered satisfactory has yet
been ascertained. Upon an examination of the plans
it naturally occurs to the mind to endeavour to form
an opinion as to the reasons which led to the adoption
of these particular forms.

It is probable that these types of inclosures would
be convenient for the habits and purposes of an
Indian tribe during peace, and that they afforded
protection in war. The square inclosures may have
been intended to contain the village, the dwellings of
the chiefs, and the council house. The circles, with
their single opening for approach, which could be
strongly guarded, would in that case be the strongholds in which, during hostilities, would be placed
the women and children. A circular fort, such as
that at Newark, would, under the usual conditions
of Indian warfare, be practically impregnable. In
the event of the outer square being captured it would
have a sufficient area to give the space that would
be wanted for the defending tribe.

The antiquity of these works is a problem that
does not possess all the elements that are required
for its solution. But in consequence of the exceptional system of construction certain inferences can
be determined. It may be assumed that the geo-

metrically shaped inclosures could not have been planned by Indians, and that therefore the square, circular and octagonal works, were constructed at some period subsequent to the landing of the Spaniards in Florida, in the beginning of the sixteenth century.*

If these embankments were raised before that period, it would be almost necessary to admit, that white men possessing a knowledge of mathematics were living amongst the Indians before the discovery of America by Columbus in 1492.

The difficult and interesting questions relating to the origin, civilisation and fate of the Mound Builders, have been the subjects of frequent investigations and of numerous theories. They appear to have inhabited Ohio for many centuries.

---

*Florida was discovered in 1512 by Ponce de Leon, the aged governor of Porto Rico, who was then seeking for the Fountain of Youth, which, according to the statements of the historian of the voyage, was believed to have the power to rejuvenate old men, and restore to them the vigour of early manhood.

An expedition undertaken a few years later, in 1528, by Pamphilo de Narvaez had a disastrous termination. Many Spaniards were left behind, the majority of whom were probably tortured and killed. Others, in accordance with Indian customs, may have been chosen by squaws to be their husbands, and would have consequently taken part in the conduct of tribal affairs.

It is not unlikely that some of these Spanish adventurers, would have taken advantage of any opportunity that may have occurred, to proceed into the interior of the new continent. Due consideration should also be given to the fact that the French may have assisted the Indians in the construction of their forts on the plains, at any period between the dates of their first partial occupation of Canada in 1541, and the final abandonment of their positions in the valley of the Ohio in 1758.

Amongst the various opinions that have been held with respect to the Mound Builders, there is one which attributes their origin to the northern part of Mexico.

Mr. Lewis Morgan, whose works upon the subject of the Indian races have placed him in the position of being a high authority upon all matters relating to them, wrote to me a letter upon the question of their migrations, in which he observed as follows:—" Any opinion as to who were the mound builders must be speculative. It is quite probable that they were village Indians from New Mexico, and having found the climate too severe for their type of village life, retired gradually from the country." Although it has to be admitted that all theories as to the Mound Builders must be necessarily indeterminate, yet nothing has been found amongst the ornaments or weapons that were placed in their burial mounds, which supports the hypothesis that they were different in race or intelligence from the tribes that surrounded them.

CHAPTER VI.

UPON the conclusion of a navigation of the waters
of the Ohio, which had extended over a distance
exceeding nine hundred miles, we arrived at the
mouth of that river, and proceeded on our course up
the Mississippi. Evening was approaching when we
saw a large steamer called the Stonewall, passing us
on her way to New Orleans, crowded with passengers happily unaware of the terrible nature of their
impending fate, and of the event about to happen
before nightfall.

At sunset, all those who were on board of our
vessel, were assembled upon the upper deck, watching the unusual brilliancy of the reflections upon
the water, and the vivid colouring of the clouds
gathering round the setting sun. We then supposed
these effects to be caused by the haze sometimes
observed in the atmosphere during that beautiful
season towards the close of the year, which has been
given the name of the Indian summer. We were
ignorant of the conflagration that was taking place

lower down the river, or we might have surmised
that the glowing tints were possibly caused by the
smoke and flames rising from the burning of the
steamer we had seen earlier in the afternoon.

We were afterwards informed that news had been
received, that a disastrous fire had occurred on board
the Stonewall shortly after we passed her, and the
flames spread with such rapidity, that, although she
was close to the river banks, only thirty-five out of
two hundred and forty passengers were saved. The
accident was caused by the carelessness of a man,
who, when lighting his pipe, accidentally set fire to
a quantity of hay that was carried between the
upper decks as cargo. It was usual to protect the
hay when embarked in this manner, by covering it
with a tarpaulin, but through some inattention this
precaution had been neglected. The Stonewall was
burnt to the water's edge.

As we drew near to St. Louis, we passed the wide
low plains upon which is situated the great Cahokia
Mound. As it was my purpose to make an expedition to that part of Illinois before proceeding to
the upper part of the Mississippi Valley, I went
there a few days after we had landed from the
steamer.

The mound when seen from the plains, stands
out from them in a manner so isolated and prominent, that it seems at the first glance, to be unquestionable that it must have been raised by
human labour; but upon a closer investigation there
are good reasons for believing it to be a natural
formation of the land, shaped originally like a
rounded hillock, and subsequently terraced and

altered in such a manner as to make it appear to be
altogether artificial.   It is ninety feet high, and the
base, if the whole of the irregular and spreading area
is included, covers a space of about nine acres.   The
summit is level, and contains nearly two acres.
Upon this was established a substantial farmhouse,
which I found to be tenanted by a kind and hospitable family, who were evidently in a prosperous
condition, and able to cultivate their land advan-
tageously.

The hillock has been given locally the name of
Monks Mound, in consequence of its having been for
several years the site of a small monastery, belonging
to some of the brethren of La Trappe, who, towards
the close of the last century, emigrated to this
remote spot when the monastic orders were suppressed during the French Revolution.   The monks
used the lower slopes as a garden, and there still
remain the indications of the terraced ground which
was used by them for their solitary walks.   The
Trappists are supposed to have left Cahokia at the
time of the restoration of the Bourbons.   Probably
they returned to France when the Monastery of La
Trappe was re-established, in the reign of Louis
XVIII.

Before the mound was used as a farm there was
on its summit an Indian tumulus.   The farmer

The accompanying sketch of the mounds was taken from the
slope of the Cahokia Mound, at a height of about forty feet
above the plain.   It represents what now remains of these
singular earthworks ; they must originally have been much more
numerous.

taking a practical view of this burial heap, destroyed it and spread the contents over his land.

On the plain below, there exists a remarkable group of circular and platform mounds, which, in consequence of their unusual position and ground plan, demand careful attention. They differ from the earthworks in Ohio, and appear to have been raised by a tribe having exceptional customs and habits of life. The mounds are not surrounded by any embankments, and were entirely unprotected. They were probably raised to make high platforms for the dwellings of the chiefs. One of them was used, at the time of my visit to Cahokia, as the site of the village school-house.

I endeavoured to trace the plan of the ancient inclosure, which contained a group of the greatest archæological importance, but so many of the mounds had been levelled, that it was difficult to form definite conclusions with regard to its shape or extent. It seems to have been an irregular parallelogram, about fifteen hundred yards in length, having at each end a large earthwork or mound, with a wide and well levelled platform on the top. In the centre, there were two conical mounds, which must have been raised in that position for some important purpose. They were each about forty feet high, and appeared to have been so placed as to dominate the mounds forming the sides of the inclosure. The men farming the adjacent plains, stated that there had been a large number of small burial mounds on their lands, most of which had been destroyed. They had found in them quantities of bones and skulls, but no ornaments or stone weapons.

When ploughing the ground, they had seen below the surface, fragments of rude pottery and many flint arrow heads. A large and highly polished stone spear head was discovered near the settlement and given by the finder to the young American lady who was then acting as teacher at the school house on the mound. It was a hard kind of flinty chert, and was a singularly fine specimen of Indian workmanship.*

When I had completed the measurement of the spaces inclosed by the mounds on the plain, I returned to the great mound in order to examine it, and my previous conjecture that it was a natural formation remained unchanged. It was, however, impossible to form a decided opinion upon the subject, for it required a properly executed scientific investigation to be made, before the problem of the construction could be determined. If it should be proved to be artificial, its position and shape as a high platform earthwork, would support a theory, that it was raised by the same race that built the greater temple platform of Cholula, in Mexico.

After quitting the Cahokia mounds and traversing several miles of the plains, where for centuries many generations of Indians had encamped, I returned to St. Louis and embarked on board the Muscatine, a steamer about to proceed to the highest part of the navigable waters of the Mississippi. Sixteen miles above St. Louis we passed the mouth of the Missouri, and observed how its waters, thickly charged with

---

*The school teacher, Miss Maud Osborn, requested me to accept this spear head in memory of my visit.

Indian Mounds, Cahokia.

earth, entirely changed the character of the river into which it flowed. Above the confluence, the Mississippi is a clear, tranquil stream, but after receiving the Missouri it becomes muddy, rushing, and turbulent.*

It had been my intention to have gone up the Missouri to Nebraska, and the ancient hunting grounds of the Pawnees, but there were certain difficulties which made that plan impracticable, so I decided to proceed northwards, and then to cross the prairies of Minnesota, and Iowa towards the valley of the river Platte. I was fortunate in having as a companion on board the steamer, an American judge, who, before being appointed to the post he then held, had been for many years acting as Indian agent to the Sacs and Foxes, and was well acquainted with the habits of the tribes, who were at that time dwelling upon the territories bordering on the banks of the river.

Judge Williams had great sympathy for the condition of the tribes with whom he lived, and he endeavoured to ascertain if it were possible to establish a higher state of civilisation amongst them. He thought that the younger members of the Sacs and Foxes might be educated in such a manner, that with due attention to the nature of the Indian temperament, they could be made capable of taking

---

*The Missouri joins the Mississippi after having pursued a devious course from the Rocky Mountains, for a distance estimated to be nearly three thousand miles, of which the greater part is navigable at that season of the year when its waters are at their highest level.

a sensible part in the conduct of affairs, and become
fitted to fulfil the duties or occupations of useful and
peaceful citizens. The authorities with whom he
consulted, agreed with him as to the utility of the
scheme suggested. Suitable school buildings were
placed upon the reservation, and good teachers
were selected. For a time the work progressed
favourably; the boys were in the first place well
grounded in the English language, and then their
attention was directed to mathematics.

After several years of study, the senior class of
boys had become so far advanced, as to be able to
draw geometrical figures and understand elementary
algebra. The teachers were hopeful, and it was
thought probable, that some of the pupils might
ultimately make such progress as to enable them to
be prepared for Yale University. All the zeal and
energies of the masters, were however proved to
have been useless. One morning the whole of the
senior class appeared at school, dressed and painted
for war. They had thrown off their ordinary clothes,
had put on mocassins and leggings, twisted their
hair in accordance with savage customs and had
stuck feathers in it. The principal asked them what
was meant by this extraordinary conduct. "We
have come to say," they replied, "that we now leave
you; we are no longer boys: we are Indians."
They then, without saying another word, abruptly
left the school and never returned to it.

The experiences of Judge Williams, with respect
to the subject of the higher education of those tribes
of North American Indians, whose territories were
in the upper part of the valley of the Mississippi,

corresponded with what I was told by the French Missionaries placed in charge of the Indian convents in the valley of the St. Lawrence. More than two centuries had elapsed since the work of converting, educating and civilising the Iroquois, Chippewa and Algonquin tribes was undertaken. During that long time there had been no good result. The earnest labours and devotion of their lives to these duties had been unavailing, and the attempts to overcome the wild instincts of Indians were thoroughly unsuccessful. The Judge was of opinion, that, with all Indians, the desire for a free and savage life, became irrepressible upon reaching manhood.

On the plains near the river, there were numerous vestiges of native encampments. At Nauvoo, I was told by a farmer that he opened a great number of low mounds which were on his land, and had found in them nothing but broken pottery and charcoal, but in ploughing his fields he had discovered quantities of arrow heads, and several grooved stone hammers.* Higher up the Mississippi we entered the country once occupied by the Dakotas, who in the seventeenth century were considered to be a

---

*Nauvoo was once brought into prominent notice in connection with the Mormons, as it was here that they built their first great temple.

Judge Williams had personally known Joseph Smith, the founder of Mormonism, and Rigdon his chief colleague. Joseph Smith, he said, was an illiterate man, but, was remarkable for a kind of shrewdness combined with great insight into character.

Rigdon, who had been formerly a Baptist preacher, was well educated, and was generally employed in obtaining converts and

most brave and powerful tribe, having superstitious customs and tribal regulations of an unusual nature.

One of their minor methods of warfare was noticed by the early explorers on the prairies through which we were passing. It was the custom with wandering bands of this race, if surprised by a larger body of enemies and thus unable to make an open resistance, to dig wide, shallow pits, in which they placed the women and children, and obtained a certain amount of protection for themselves. These excavations were scooped out with great rapidity, the men and their families using for this purpose knives, tomahawks and wooden ladles. This method of digging the ground, may probably have been similar to that adopted by the Mound Builders in raising their ramparts. War pits were also made by the Hurons when retreating from the Iroquois. When coasting the north shore of Lake Superior, I was shown on the map the positions where several of these places of refuge and defence had been observed.

---

explaining to them the meaning of Smith's visions and the doctrines of the new religion.

He described Brigham Young, with whom he was also acquainted, as being a person of determined character, with a domineering manner.

When I was at Salt Lake City, in the following December, I had a long interview with that able and astute leader of men.

Within twenty years from the time when he conducted the flight of the Mormons across the deserts from Nauvoo to Utah, he had succeeded in establishing a highly satisfactory condition of good order and prosperity throughout the territories under his government; and controlled, with unquestioned authority, a community consisting of one hundred and forty thousand people.

We saw at night upon the bluffs, the fires of Indian camps; it was thought probable that these Indians, whose villages were situated far towards the West, had come to this part of their ancient territory, for the purpose of performing certain forms of worship before one of the large detached granite boulders, situated on the plateau near to their tents. On the following evening, as we steamed slowly through Lake Pepin, we looked with much interest at the high steep promontory, upon whose summit the love-distracted maiden Winona* sang her death song, and then leapt from the edge of the cliff and was dashed to pieces on the rocks below, within sight of her tribe who were assembled near their tents on the shore.

The Muscatine terminated her long upward voyage against the swift stream, at the city of St. Paul's, nineteen hundred and forty-four miles above the mouth of the river, a few miles below the great falls of St. Anthony, and near the confluence of the Minnesota. All this region was at one time, the principal

---

*As I looked at the cliff and the reflection of its shadow in the calm smooth waters of the lake, I recalled to mind a similar scene viewed from the deck of H.M.S. Racer when passing at sunset the promontory of Cape Leucate, in Santa Maura, the classical site of Sappho's leap. There is a special interest attached to the fate of Winona, for it proves that Indian girls of Dakota birth are capable of higher degrees of sentiment with regard to their marriage, than those believed to exist among other tribes. She was not permitted for some tribal reason to marry the man she had chosen, and preferred death to marriage with the warrior to whom she was assigned by the command of her parents.

gathering place of the branch of the Dakotas, called
Sioux, and near at hand was the cave where their
annual council meetings took place. To this place
were also brought for burial, the bones and skulls of
their dead, whose bodies had previously been placed
upon scaffolds, and exposed to the influences of the
winds and weather.

Upon a bluff overlooking the Mississippi, there
are still to be seen a strange group of large mounds,
whose purpose has not been ascertained. The examination of them has failed to afford the slightest
clue by which any theory or conjecture can be safely
established. Soon after my arrival I went there to
examine them with particular attention, for I had
observed certain peculiarities in their shape and
position, which resembled portions of the defensive
hill works of the Mound Builders. Mr. Hill, a
member of the Historical Society of St. Paul's,
accompanied me, and pointed out those mounds
which had been opened, and carefully inspected by
competent observers. It has been supposed that
they were the burial places of the Sioux during long
periods of time, and it was hoped that some discoveries would be made of antiquarian importance.

The largest of the mounds was first examined, but
nothing was found in it. There were no signs of
burials near the slopes, and at the base, contrary to
expectation, there was not found any indication of
a fire having been made, and there was no charcoal.
In another conical mound, although no bones were
seen, there was in the centre a hollow space which
contained several pieces of charred wood. A comparatively low platform mound was then opened. Two

skeletons were found buried near the surface, but from their position and state of preservation, they were considered to be late interments ; nothing else was found within. Finally a large mound, situated upon the extreme edge of the bluff, was thoroughly excavated, and in this there was found, as in the previously opened conical earthwork, a small hollow space in the centre. In consequence of these negative results, it was not possible to form any conclusions as to the object of Indians in raising these exceptional works. I thought it not improbable that it might have been their intention to use them, either for raised dwelling places, or for defensive inclosures which had not been completed.

Their position is almost impregnable ; the mounds are not placed separately but are closely joined together, so that they form a kind of embankment. The outer slopes are so close to the edge of the cliff, that they are practically a prolongation of the steep slopes, and thus present a singular parallel with portions of those embankments of Fort Ancient which overlook the valley of the Little Miami. The similarity in the methods of placing the mounds, is made additionally obvious from the fact, that there are numerous springs issuing from the upper parts of the bluff, which flow down as rivulets into the river below. There are altogether fifteen mounds on the top of the promontory ; the largest of them is about twenty feet high.

Upon our return to St. Paul's, we heard that a band of Sioux had come into the neighbourhood, and were encamped amongst the woods on the opposite side of the river. As I wished to see these Indians, I

crossed over to the settlement of Mendota, and after
a walk of a few miles, saw their tents pitched close
to the borders of a small lake. I was greeted with
a loud noise of barking from their dogs, who were as
numerous outside the camp of the Sioux as they
usually are around the dwellings of the Kurds in
Asia Minor. After overcoming some preliminary
hostile difficulties with these yelping curs, I received
a silent and not pressing welcome from the Indians,
who were mostly squaws and children, the men
having gone away temporarily upon some expedition.

It was getting dark, and the women were making
preparations for supper. Good fires were burning
brightly in the centre of the wigwams, the kettles
were hung over them, the water was boiling, and the
interiors were cheerful scenes of enjoyment. The
life within and without, was similar to what may be
seen in an English gipsy encampment in the New
Forest in Hampshire. There was something singularly attractive in the habits of life amongst these
wandering nomads, and the warmth and comfort
inside the tents, was in pleasing contrast to the cold
and wintry aspect without. This simple and natural
state of existence, has unquestionably a great charm
for those whose natures are essentially Bohemian.
It is not surprising that Indian lads, accustomed to
this kind of life, should feel wearied and cramped
by the trammels of civilization. It is natural that
they should long to get away from the confinement
and irksome training of school, and return to the
freedom and independence of their savage hunting
and wandering instincts.

There lived at the adjacent town of Mendota, a

CHIPPEWA ENCAMPMENT.

SIOUX ENCAMPMENT.

half-bred Indian, of French and Sioux parentage named Faribault, with whom I became acquainted. In his youth, he had. dwelt with his mother in the villages of the Sioux, and spoke their language. In manhood, he had acted as an agent and trader for the tribes, and passed much of his life in constant communication with them, and possessed an intimate acquaintance with their superstitions and religious ceremonies. This kind of direct personal knowledge, can only be obtained by a man whom the Indians consider as being one of themselves, in consequence of his having had an Indian mother belonging to their tribe. It was the custom of the Sioux, when they encamped in this part of the country, to meet at his house, and several of them happened to be there when I was present.

Faribault, like all Indians, was usually very reticent, but when he noticed that I took much interest in matters relating to the habits of his tribe, especially such as were connected with their religious beliefs and customs, he became frank and outspoken. He told me of his own various strange personal experiences, and was particularly earnest when he mentioned some of the most remarkable of the rules relating to their fasts and sacrifices. The Indians, who were usually standing near us listening to what he said, would occasionally, from time to time, signify their assent to his statements by harsh grunts of approval.

Amongst the superstitions mentioned by him, none caused more attention than those connected with the worship of their Spirit rocks. One of these, which has always been considered to be an important

Manito, happened to be on the plateau above
Mendota, and the Indians directed me to the spot
where it was placed. I found it to be a huge granite
boulder, which had probably been deposited there by
the moving waters or icebergs, during that remote
period when they were travelling southwards from
the sub-arctic latitudes. As it had no geological
relation whatever with the sandstone ground upon
which it rested, the Sioux might have conjectured,
that it had been dropped from the clouds. To
ignorant savages, unversed in the mysteries and
conclusions of scientific geology, no other explanation
could have been satisfactory. It lies upon a level
space of land, upon the top of a bluff, commanding
magnificent views over the valleys of the Mississippi
and Minnesota. The confluence of these great rivers
can be seen, and the steep water-worn cliffs below
the falls of St. Anthony.

Whilst standing upon the promontory, and looking
at this wide prospect, I was joined by a priest, who
had been fulfilling his duties at a neighbouring
settlement. We remained near the Spirit rock,*
looking at the solitary mass of granite, glittering in
the sunshine, and thought that it was not surprising
that the Indians believed this strange rock to be the
manifestation of a great unknown power, and should
have invested with supernatural attributes what
must have seemed to them to be marvellous.

The boulder is polygonal in form, and stands about

---

*The accompanying illustration is drawn from a pencil sketch
made by the author near this spot.

SPIRIT ROCK.

CONFLUENCE OF THE MISSISSIPPI AND MINNESOTA.

seven feet high above the ground. In the other
dimensions, it averages a thickness from nine to
twelve feet. It is composed chiefly of grey granite,
and its weight must exceed seventy tons. Faribault
said that, when he was a young man, wandering
bands of Sioux occasionally came to this Spirit rock
and encamped near it. They usually stopped about
a week, but sometimes during a whole moon. It
was their custom during this period to continually
offer sacrifices, dance round the stone, and paint it
with various colours, red, blue or white. Finally,
before taking down their tents, they covered it with
their best furs or skins, and left them there as propitiatory offerings.

The falls of the Mississippi were also worshipped
by the Indians, through whose territories that great
river flowed in its upper course, and the manner in
which adoration was made to the Power, which was
manifested in the movements of these cataracts, is
well described by Captain Carver, who visited them
with one of the chiefs of the Winnebagoes in 1767.
The chief in the first place, addressed a brief invoca-
tion to the Manito, and then he made his offerings.
In this instance he gave everything he possessed,
that was valuable, including all his ornaments,
together with his pipe and roll of tobacco. He
concluded his acts of devotion* by asking the Great

*"I was greatly surprised," states Captain Carver, "at behold-
ing an instance of such elevated devotion in so young an Indian,
and instead of ridiculing the ceremonies attending it, as I
observed my Catholic servant tacitly did, I looked on the prince
with a greater degree of respect for these sincere proofs he gave

Spirit to give them his protection, a bright sun, a blue sky, and untroubled waters. I visited the spot near which the chief must have stood upon that occasion. Much had been changed in the succeeding century, but the wild and tumultuous character of the falls, and the noise and foam caused by the rushing waters, are still very impressive.

From Mendota I proceeded towards the north-west, in the direction of the Minnesota as far as Mankato, with the intention of crossing the prairies southwards towards Nebraska. It was also my purpose to visit the Winnebagoes at their reservation. This tribe had been removed from their lands near Lake Michigan, and settled a few miles from Mankato; but upon my arrival at that town, I was informed that they had been again moved to a reservation further west, to give room for the occupation of the land by the numerous emigrants from Europe, especially those thrifty, hard-working agriculturists, who came from Sweden and Norway. The new settlements in this part of Minnesota were still in an alarmed condition, in consequence of the memory of the massacres that had taken place a few years previously, when the Sioux rose in rebellion, and committed a grave series of atrocities upon the white inhabitants.

At the conclusion of the war, thirty-eight of the chief perpetrators of cruelties upon the unoffending

---

of his piety; and I doubt not, but that his offerings and prayers, were as acceptable to the universal Parent of mankind, as if they had been made with greater pomp, or in a consecrated place." *Travels in North America*, pp. 62.

white people, were condemned to death and were hanged. The events that took place upon that occasion were described to me by an eye-witness, as having been exceedingly repulsive, in consequence of the defiant shouts and gestures of the prisoners. Hanging is a form of execution particularly disliked by Indians, because they consider that it is ignominious. The war was caused by a belief, spread among the tribes, that they had been treated with great injustice. They declared that they were not allowed to remain in possession of their lands, and that the treaties which had been made with them, had not been fairly carried out. The savage desire for revenge was aroused, and barbarous acts were committed by the Sioux, whilst they were in a state of passionate excitement.

On a terrace overlooking the waters of the Minnesota, close to the spot where the Sioux had been executed, I met a half-breed Indian, who was known to have seen some of the unmerciful deeds that had taken place. I asked him to give me an explanation of the reasons that had caused the Sioux, most of whom had led peaceful lives, to suddenly avenge themselves in this brutal manner. He said, that whatever may have seemed to be their character, all these Dakotas had an inveterate hatred for the pale faces, who had deprived them of their lands, their hunting grounds, their freedom, and all that made their lives tolerable. After a pause, he observed in a harsh angry tone, that the women and children were killed, because, in cases such as these, it was a rule with Indians, to not only kill all the men, but also all who could become men or give birth to men, and that it was their object to secure the total extermination of their enemies.

I afterwards met, near the lands which had been occupied by the Winnebagoes, one of those waifs of civilization, who prefer the adventurous freedom of the Indians to the ordinary forms of existence among the whites. He was a Virginian by birth, and had left his home at an early age to join the Apaches, whose hunting grounds were near the borders of New Mexico. He lived with them for several years, and then, desiring a change, he had joined a band of Chippewas. He was given by them the name of Ara-po-gai-sik or Day Catcher, because he was first observed when approaching their camp at daybreak. I found him to be a man of considerable intelligence, and conversant with the habits of the tribes with whom he had dwelt.

It is unusual to find men of English descent electing, by their own wish, to entirely live with Indians. It seems to be different as regards the French or French Canadians, who appear to have certain instincts in their nature, which enable them to conform readily with the domestic customs of Indian life.

The subject of the claims of the Indians to the possession of their ancient hunting grounds, was brought to the notice of the United States Government during the time I was at Washington, after my return from Yucatan in the summer of 1870.

A large deputation from the Ogallallas, a warlike tribe of Sioux, who dwelt on the prairies to the west of the Missouri, came to the city for the purpose of making a statement of their grievances, with regard to their lands. They declared that the treaties concerning them had not been faithfully carried out.

The deputation consisted of the principal chief, an Indian named Red Cloud, who held a great reputation as a brave and daring warrior, and. with him were Brave Bear, Rocky Bear, Red Dog, and other chiefs, who were also well known for their courage and fearlessness, which they had shown upon several occasions in fights upon the plains. Several men of the tribe accompanied them.

I happened to see those Ogallallas frequently, under various circumstances; they had that power, which is characteristic with thoroughbred Indians, of assuming when thought necessary, a reserved and dignified manner. Red Cloud, especially, maintained the deportment consistent with his position as the hereditary chief of his nation.

The speeches delivered by them in the presence of the Commissioner of Indian affairs were remarkable as proving that they possessed great natural oratorical abilities.   The description of the events occurring in their territories, and the unfair treatment which they considered they had received, were expressed with much force and poetical imagination.

Their appeals were, however, unavailing. It was made clear to them, that it was not possible, that small numbers of Indians could be permitted to retain possession of extensive grounds, to the exclusion of the necessities of an advancing civilization, and that they must accept the fate which was inevitable, and accustom themselves to be confined within reservations of a limited and definite area.

The Secretary of the Interior, told the Sioux that the existing things were changing, and that they might as well try and keep back the winds with their hands, as to prevent these changes.

CHAPTER VII.

IT was getting late in the year, when I commenced
to cross the prairies of Minnesota and Iowa. The
higher plateaux were in many places already covered
with snow, upon which we saw numerous tracks of
wolves. The long icicles upon the graceful little
waterfall of the Minne-ha-ha, indicated the approach
of a severe winter, and flocks of wild geese were
flying towards the upper lakes.

For many miles the surface of the land looked
black, in consequence of the prairie fires that had
burnt the grass, during the latter part of the
autumn. On the eastern borders, near the rivers,
we passed some scattered villages, chiefly occupied
by emigrants of Welsh or Scandinavian origin ; but
towards the interior the land was too wet and
exposed for the purposes of cultivation. Here and
there, on the plains, we saw the lonely huts of
adventurous squatters, who obtained a precarious

living by supplying the wants of those who passed near them, on their way towards the South. At one of these dwellings situated upon the open plain, twenty miles from the nearest village, we halted after a long journey over a dreary country, forming the watershed of the streams that flowed east or west into the valleys of the Missouri and Mississippi.

The hut was occupied by a man, who, with his wife and family, had been settled in this remote region for several years. As there was no timber to be obtained in the neighbourhood, he had built the walls of his house with wide, thick slabs of turf, which made a good protection against the storms of winter. He possessed one hundred and fifty acres of land, of which he only cultivated the small portion he had been able to preserve from the ravages of prairie fires. The difficulty of guarding the homestead against this danger, had caused him to feel much anxiety, but he said that he had, at last, discovered an effectual method of preventing any damage being caused, as far as his crops and buildings were concerned.

He saw upon one occasion, that the grass was burning on the verge of the southern horizon, and the flames appeared to be advancing rapidly in the direction of his farm. It occurred to him to try the plan of running two plough furrows in parallel lines between the edge of his land and the approaching fire. He made them about twenty yards apart, and then burnt the grass, thus leaving a bare space of blackened earth. The flames advanced upon their onward course, destroying everything before them until they reached the outer furrow, when they were stopped by there not being any grass for fuel, and as they could not leap over the intervening space, the fire passed to the right and left, leaving the farm in the centre untouched. The prairie around this squatter's home, was wild and dreary.

The track led us over a region which had been shaped into hollows and undulations, caused by the action of numberless streams and rivulets which had cut their way in all directions. There were also many small depressions which contained pools of water. We observed in all these ponds numerous erratic boulders of various sizes. The majority of them were small, but others were of considerable magnitude, and must have weighed from fifteen to twenty tons. They were usually composed of red, green, and dark grey granites, similar to those I had seen on the surface of the country to the south-west of Lake Superior.

The boulders were usually standing detached on the ground near the edge of the water, but sometimes they were heaped together in a pile in the middle of the pond. Upon an examination of the positions of the strange aggregations of stones which had been moved from their original place in the north to this plateau, the impression was conveyed to the mind that these smaller boulders may have been dropped during the period when icebergs were floating over the land. It seemed to be probable that some of the icebergs were stranded, and had left on these spots the cargo they had carried away from higher latitudes.

Upon other parts of the level prairie where the land was dry, there were many isolated masses standing up in their places upon the surface, in the same manner as the Spirit rock near Mendota. It was remarkable that these boulders, which were often very large, were not embedded in the soil, but appeared to have remained in the positions in which they had been deposited. Some of the larger ponds contain quantities of wild aquatic plants, which yield a kind of rice—the same which was frequently mentioned by the French exploring missionaries in the seventeenth century—by the name of La Folle Avoine. This wild rice was gathered by the Dakotas and Chippewas, and stored by them for food in time of scarcity.

As we approached the boundaries of North Iowa, we found that the winter had set in earlier than usual, and the prairies were covered with several inches of snow. The aspect of the country, upon which the only marks of life were the footprints of animals, was exceedingly desolate. The horizon was sharply defined by the white edges of the land against the sky, and the curvature of the earth was thereby made distinct. The land seemed to fall away from the eye at a distance which looked very near. On plains of this perfectly level character in these latitudes, the actual true distance of the horizon—as seen by a person of average height standing upon the ground—would be about three miles ; but in consequence of the conditions of light upon the surface of the snow, it appeared to be less, and the borders of the round line of horizon seemed to confine us within a small circle. This effect was particularly noticeable when the sun rose and touched the eastern parts of the curvature, the sky at that time in the morning being clear and cloudless.

The weather became daily more severe, and at last we had to encounter a hard gale of wind from the north-west. Suddenly one afternoon, a sweeping snow storm overtook us, and in a few hours all vestiges of the track were lost. Our position became perilous, as nothing could be seen which would help us in the slightest degree as a guide, and enable us to steer a straight course. The sky was gloomy and dark with snow clouds, and the prairie was as bare as the open sea.

The night was approaching, and matters were beginning to be serious, when the coach was stopped by striking against some concealed obstacle, and the horses swerved round. After gazing upon the fresh snow for a few seconds, the driver said that it was practically useless to attempt to follow the track, as it was impossible to make out its direction. It was evident that there was not the slightest reason for making any endeavours to follow one way more than any other, and we had the dangerous prospect before us of having to pass the night under circumstances of great hardship.

Fortunately it was suggested, that we might try the experiment of maintaining a line of progress by attending to the point from which the wind came. It had been observed that, when we were going along the straight track, the wind was upon the right hand, nearly abeam, and it was considered possible that if we could manage to keep it upon that bearing, we ought finally to arrive at our destination. The driver thought that this plan did not offer much prospect of success, on account of the scattered boulders and the rough nature of the country. He

however decided to do what was proposed, and started
forward.   An unforeseen difficulty soon arose.   The
horses having no track before them to follow, kept
constantly swerving to the left to avoid the wind,
and it required much skill and energy to keep their
heads pointed in the right direction.

The obstructions we had to encounter, caused
us much anxiety, for we were exposed to a
bitterly cold gale, and the storm blew against us
with a severity that was unendurable.   It was with
no slight pleasure that, just before the night, we saw
upon the verge of the horizon ahead, the lights of
the town where we intended to stop.   When we
arrived there, it was found that the roads had
become almost impassable, in consequence of the
great depth of the snow that had fallen in a few hours.

As the prairies of Western Iowa had thus become
a vast white table-land, whose ground was hidden
from view, I crossed the Missouri as soon as possible
and proceeded to the interior of Nebraska where the
storm had not taken place and the surface of the
land was still in its autumnal condition.   I stopped
at various places in the valley of the river Platte
and, at one of the newly formed settlements, obtained
convenient quarters in the house of a man who had
passed the greatest part of his life with the Pawnees,
a tribe of Indians who have always been considered
to hold an exceptional position with respect to their
religious observances and language.

He had lived in the tents and was well acquainted
with their habits of life, and like all other men whom
I had met who had been much in contact with the
Indians, occupying the country west of the Missis-

sippi, he had been impressed by the reality of their
personal faith in supernatural manifestations of power
for good or evil.

I was much interested in ascertaining the existence
of certain facts which seemed to show analogies between these Pawnees and the race who under the
name of Toltecs or Aztecs had migrated from some
unknown country into Mexico. It has not hitherto
been explained how it happened that this tribe who,
as far as is known, have always lived in this region,
placed in the centre of the continent, should possess
a language which is absolutely different from that of
any other race of North American Indians, and that
they should have been, for a long period of time,
surrounded by powerful tribes with whom they could
never have held any spoken communications. Mr.
Albert Gallatin, a learned American ethnologist,
draws attention to their singularly isolated position.
He states that "they speak a language altogether
different from that of the Sioux tribes or of any
other Indians known to us."*

They do not appear to have been a numerous race,
for, when their territories were first explored, it was
estimated that, including men, women and children,
their numbers were under seven thousand. At the
time that I passed through the ancient hunting
grounds in Nebraska, their descendants (of whom
there were said to be about three thousand) were
gathered together in a reservation north of the
Platte. I saw a few of them near the banks of that

---

*Archæologia Americana, Vol. II, pp. 128.

river, and some others who had committed a series of ferocious acts on the plains and had carried off several scalps. They were captured, imprisoned and condemned to death. These men were wild-looking savages who stalked restlessly round the cells in which they were confined like intractable and untameable animals. Those I saw wandering near the Platte had, for some unknown reason, dressed themselves in war paint. Their eyes were encircled by broad bands of red ochre. Their faces were covered with blue stripes which in their outlines resembled the tattoed lines of the Maoris in New Zealand.

The natural colour of the Pawnees I met was rather darker than the skins of the Sioux and Chippewas. The men were of more than the ordinary stature and were powerfully built. Their heads were broad and massive and all of them had remarkably high cheek bones.

The early explorers, sent by the Government towards the West, did not learn much about the superstitions of the native tribes, but it is mentioned in the Report of the Expedition to the Rocky Mountains in 1819-20 that the Pawnees, then living near the forks of the river Loup in the valley of the Platte, had originally a custom, which was believed to be annual but was no longer followed, of offering a human sacrifice to the Great Star.

The victim was always a prisoner that had been captured in war.

Mr. James, one of the members of the exploring party, stated that the star to which the sacrifice was made, was the planet Venus. It is probable therefore that this ceremony had some connection with the

worship of the sun, as the Indians, who were accurate observers of all natural events, would have
noticed that Venus, both as a morning and evening
star, appeared to govern the movements of the greater
light, and either announced its approach at dawn or
followed its departure at sunset.

The Pawnees and the Dakotas are the only North
American tribes known to have had the custom of
killing human beings, for the purpose of presenting
them to their gods as propitiations in time of distress, or as thanksgiving offerings after successful
wars. The sacrifices made to their gods of war by
the Aztecs were probably introduced into Mexico by
that fierce race. The last human sacrifice offered by
the Pawnees occurred in the year 1837, and in this
case it is believed that the offering was made to the
spirit who caused the land to produce fertile crops.

A young girl of fourteen years of age had been
captured during a war with the Sioux, and it was
decided that she was to be killed and sacrificed to
this particular Manito. The strange character of
the method of immolation arrests attention. The
girl was carefully secured upon a frame-work made
of light poles, raised a few feet above the ground.
When she was in the right position for the sacrifice,
a fire was kindled beneath, but before the flames
had actually begun to touch her, and precisely at
the moment when it was perceived that the fire was
sufficiently strong to begin to burn her, she was suddenly killed by a flight of arrows.* She was then

---

* In Chapter xvii it will be seen that the Aztecs or Toltecs in
Yucatan, also, in certain cases, killed the victim by a flight of
arrows.

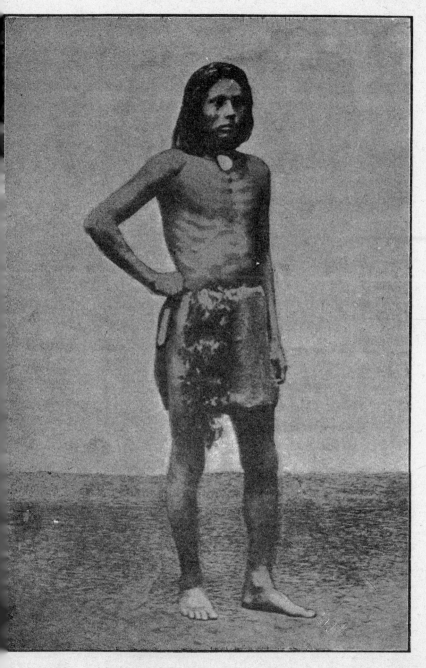

Sha-to-Ko (Blue Hawk). A Pawnee.

taken down from the scaffolding and the flesh was cut into small portions and taken away into the fields, where the blood was sprinkled over certain parts of the land which had been planted.

The fact of a sacrifice so important as that of a girl on the verge of womanhood being made to the god believed to have power over all matters relating to the growth of corn and other vegetable produce, proves that the Pawnees cultivated the earth to a greater extent than other tribes. Their neighbours, the Dakotas, were more exclusively a hunting race, and their human sacrifices, as far as has been ascertained by events that have happened within the past century, were usually made for the purpose of propitiation in the more solemn forms of Sun-worship, or of appeasing the anger of evil spirits or demons when manifested by storms of lightning and thunder.

My host told me that during the time he had lived amongst the Pawnees he had not seen anything in their observances which led him to suppose that they had any kind of belief in a future state beyond this world, or in any absolutely over-ruling Power. The few ceremonies performed by them were apparently propitiations of the various supernatural Manitos who, they considered, had influence over them either individually or as a tribe. One of their most frequent practices consisted of offering incense to them in the form of tobacco smoke, and they invariably presented it in the same manner by throwing the first whiff upwards towards the sky, the next downwards to the ground and then to the right and left. He had also observed that when this act was finished, each Indian seemed to mutter some brief ejaculation or prayer.

With respect to their superstitions he thought that they were practically spiritualists, and believed in the presence of unknown and unseen influences below, above or around them, having each in their own separate degree powers of good or evil. He mentioned an event which had happened within his personal observation.

A Pawnee during a violent storm was injured by a flash of lightning. The tribe were convinced that this misfortune had been inflicted upon him as a direct punishment for some wrong deed he had committed, or that he had in some way, by his own conduct incurred the displeasure of the god of Lightning. As a consequence of this belief, he was avoided, and compelled to live apart, as a man placed under a curse or malignant influence.

These Pawnees had the reputation of being cruel to their prisoners, and in that respect had the same usages as the Iroquois who tortured the captives and then burnt them at the stake.* All North

---

*One of the best authenticated instances of this custom of torturing prisoners was witnessed by a Mr. James Smith who, during the time that he was a captive amongst the Delawares, was present when the English prisoners taken after General Braddock's defeat were brought into camp by the Indians.

He states that, upon that occasion, about a dozen of the prisoners were stripped and tied to stakes, tortured with fire-brands and burnt to death.

The ferocity of the Indians towards their captives after battle was well known to the British and French commanders, and was one of the difficulties that attended their employment as allies.

American tribes appear to have similar habits
when their savage natures are aroused by bloodshed
and war, but it is also acknowledged by those who
have had an intimate knowledge of them, that
under other and milder conditions, they possess

There is a subject indirectly connected with these Indian
customs in war which may here be considered. It is that of
cannibalism.

Investigations into this question lead to the conclusion that
there is no evidence to show that any of the North American
tribes were in the habit of following this revolting custom
except under rare circumstances during the prosecution of a
serious war.

I only know of two instances, seen and recorded, of Indians
devouring human flesh. In both cases it is evident that the
acts were committed in accordance with the usages of hostile
tribes when engaged in war.

The first case is mentioned in a report made to his superiors, by
the French missionary, Father Roubaud, who accompanied the
Indian allies of the French troops during the operations against
the British forces in 1757.

An English captive, who was believed to have been an officer,
was cooked and eaten by the Ottawas under circumstances singularly repulsive. The Father Roubaud, who was present and
witnessed part of the proceedings, was horrified by what he saw,
and finding that he could do nothing to check the tribe in their
savage feast was forced to withdraw to his tent.

The other instance occurred after the capture of the garrison of
Michel Mackinac by the Chippewas. Mr. Alexander Henry, the
same person who, at another time, undertook the mining operations on the shores of Lake Superior which are mentioned in a
preceding chapter, was a captive. He states that one of the
white prisoners was killed and divided into five parts which were
cooked in five kettles and then eaten at a special feast.

Mr. Henry was of opinion, from what he observed, that this
food was taken with repugnance. An Indian told him that what
he saw was done to inspire the warriors with courage.

qualities of an affectionate nature, which are shown in their domestic lives. An event occurred not far from the settlement which exemplified their attachment to their children.

The only child of a Pawnee and his wife died and was buried in a grave dug in the open prairie near a spot where a small band of Indians had temporarily erected their tents. In the grave with the child were placed all the things which had belonged to her, including her mocassin shoes, her plate and cup and her trinkets. Her father had in his possession a good set of sleigh bells, said to be worth seventeen dollars which he had intended to sell to one of the white men in the neighbourhood, but after the death of his daughter he said that he was happy because no one had yet bought his bells, for he was consequently able to give them to her, and they were put by the child's side and buried. The father and mother then built round the grave a wooden fence to keep the wolves away, as the Pawnees were going to move their tents to a distant part of the country. This fence was shortly afterwards destroyed by a prairie fire, and the place of the grave is not now known.

These fires are becoming less frequent and, when they occur, are attributable to carelessness. I happened to see one of them sweeping over the plains near the river Missouri, my position at the time being at right angles to the line of its direction. A high wind was blowing from the South-west and the tall grass was bent over in such a manner that the flames instead of going with the wind towards the North-east, caught the tops of the grass and consequently travelled steadily to windward in the teeth

PAWNEE WOMAN.

of the gale. The smoke rolled away to leeward in dense clouds and the flames leapt upwards on tongues of fire to heights of twenty or thirty feet. The movement forward was like that of the rapidly advancing crest of a breaking wave. I estimated the length of the front of the fire to be nearly two miles.

When wandering over the wide Iowa and Nebraska plains, many problems present themselves to the mind with regard to their formation and existing condition. Of these, none are so perplexing to the farmers as those which relate to the absence of trees. Several theories have been mooted and many conclusions have been adopted, and thought to be rational, but as a rule they cannot be accepted as being altogether satisfactory. One of the most general opinions, is that the treeless state of the land has been caused by the destructive effects of fire. Another opinion is that which attributes the greatest counteracting influence to the nature of the soil.

One of the most careful investigators into this subject was the accomplished geologist Mr. J. W. Foster, whom I met at Chicago, and who was at that time President of the American Association for the Advancement of Science. He told me what had been the results of his work, and accompanied me to parts of the outlying Illinois prairies, to examine the character of the earth near the surface. He had, a short time previously, carried out a series of experiments relating to the physical geography of the Mississippi valley, and had given his attention to the composition of the upper formation of the prairies on both sides of the river.

He had arrived at the conclusion that the absence of trees upon them was not caused by fires or by the character of the ground, but was the consequence of the conditions of rainfall, temperature, climate, and exposure, all acting in a direction opposed to that natural order of things in which trees would be inclined to flourish.

On the way south from Mankato, I observed that the banks of the Des Moines river were thickly timbered, and that on the borders of the various rivulets which had cut their way through the ground to a considerable depth, there was usually a flourishing growth of trees, chiefly consisting of oak, black walnut, basswood, and maple varieties. In all these instances the trees were sheltered, but on the exposed prairie immediately adjacent the ground was bare, and without a vestige of any signs of trees or shrubs. In that particular region it seems therefore probable, that the exposure to gales of wind sweeping over the plateau, may be the principal cause of trees not being able to take root and live.

There are, however, other prairies equally bare of timber which are not so exposed. Upon those situated near the water shed or dividing ridge of the tributaries of the Missouri and Mississippi, it may be the quantities of water lying permanently within a few feet below the surface which prevent any growth taking place. No single theory seems to explain the facts, but from my own observation, I am inclined to think that the chief deterring influence is the nature of the soil.*

---

*When I was at the village of San Domingo del Palenque in Central America, Dr. Coller, a resident there, told me he had carried out, during several years, a series of investigations

There is an unexplained problem respecting the growth of trees in certain parts of North America, which has received much local notice. My attention was directed to the subject when I was in the neighbourhood of Lake Simcoe in Upper Canada. An Englishman, who had established a homestead there and made clearings in the forests, told me he had observed that after the old trees had been felled, new shrubs and timber of an entirely different character grew up in their place. There was nothing in the nature of the surrounding woods which, to his mind, could account for the change, as there were no trees of the class that had taken root existing in that part of the country.

A similar alteration in the order of succession of forest growths was reported by the geologists employed by the Government in conducting the early surveys of Michigan. They stated that large tracts of land, originally covered with pines, had been succeeded by a second growth consisting of white birch, aspen, pine and hazel. In this case the primeval forest had been destroyed by high winds and after-

---

to ascertain the reasons for the existence of large green savannahs in the heart of the adjacent forests. He had formed the conclusion that those open spaces were caused by the exceptional character of the ground which, he said, differed from that upon which the trees grew. The similar openings amongst the forests in Ceylon called patenas, are, I believe, also supposed to be the effect of the nature or poverty of the land.

It is noticeable that the forests usually skirt or surround savannahs in sharp well-defined outlines like an enclosing barrier, in the same manner as the meadows, formed by the consequences of the action of beavers, occur in Michigan.

wards burnt.   It was supposed that where clearings
had been made by fire, changes of the above nature
occurred, but no suggestions were given as to the
manner in which these new and strange growths
established themselves.

Near Ishpeming, I saw that in all cases where
forest openings had been made by the action of fire,
luxuriant masses of dense raspberry bushes occupied
the land ; and it was said that where the woods were
cut down by the axe bushes of another class, bearing
different berries, sprang up and flourished.

In other parts of the North-west, variations in the
succession of forest trees have been seen to occur ;
and usually there seems to be some connection between the type of the new plants and the methods
by which the clearings have been made.   As a general rule there are very few birds to carry seeds or
pips from distant regions and therefore it is possible
that in places where the ground has never for many
centuries been previously disturbed and where the
thick forest has been for the first time removed, and
sunlight and fresh atmospheric conditions are admitted upon the land, new circumstances arise which
are favourable to the development of dormant life.*

---

*After my return to England I happened to discuss this sub-
ject with Colonel Yule, who had just then completed his work of
editing the Travels of Marco Polo.   He told me that when he
was in Burmah, Lord Dalhousie, who was at that time Governor-
General of India, sent him into the interior to visit the forests of
Aracan.

He found within them several large clearings, and observed
that the new growths were of a different character from the old

Before leaving the valley of the Platte I made several excursions on the plains for the purpose of examining two of the most extensive of those singular groups of mounds which have been called prairie-dog villages. The largest of them was situated about two hundred miles west of the Missouri and three miles north of the Platte. It occupied a space exceeding fifty acres, which was covered by the rounded heaps of earth and pebbles thrown up by the little marmots when excavating their burrows. These creatures, when they are sitting on the tops of their mounds in a watchful attitude keeping a sharp look out around them and holding their paws before them, resemble a colony of ground squirrels. When I was at a certain distance from them they maintained continuous and defiant sounds like the shrill

---

trees and were invariably bamboos. He also saw amongst the mountains many deciduous trees which were quite bare of leaves whilst their branches were covered with brilliantly coloured flowers.

Upon another occasion Dr. Rae, who had passed much of his life in the Hudson Bay Territories and became known by his discovery of the relics of Sir John Franklin's expedition, mentioned to me that he had frequently seen that when trees had been uprooted, raspberry bushes sprang up in their place thus showing that their seeds must have been in the ground. Dr. Joseph Norwood, Assistant Geologist, in his report of the survey of the region west of Lake Superior, undertaken in 1847, states that from facts which had come under his observation, he was led to believe that, " if after the clearing of the pine forests, the annual fires cease, a growth of oak springs up in some places and aspen in others." (*Owen's Geological Survey*, pp. 296). In British Columbia the ancient forest pines are often succeeded by cedars or alders.

yelps of puppies, but upon a nearer approach they suddenly disappeared down their holes.

The existence of these isolated groups of burrowing animals, dwelling together in communities, was made the subject of observation by the expeditions sent by the United States Government to explore these regions, and it was reported that it was not unusual to find rattlesnakes living in the same holes as the prairie dogs. Captain Stansfield, the leader of one of these exploring parties, stated that the holes were generally guarded by a rattlesnake, and that when the hand was about to be thrust into the hole to draw out the prairie dog which had been shot at, but had got into its burrow, the ominous rattle of the reptile was heard within.

Twenty years had elapsed since that time, and many changes had taken place in the conditions of animal life upon these plains. I thrust my stick down various holes but there were no rattlesnakes in them. I afterwards heard that in these districts the reptiles, which had been so numerous, had disappeared. Another group of these village communities which I examined was placed to the south of the Platte. Although it covered a comparatively small area it was more fully tenanted and the dwellings were closer together, each mound almost touching its neighbour. One of the young occupiers of this village had been captured and tamed by a squatter living near the settlement in which I was then stopping. As it rarely happens that the habits of these marmots can be regularly observed, this creature's actions were noticed with great curiosity.

It was the daily habit of this prairie dog to sit

PRAIRIE AND BOULDERS, NORTH IOWA.

PRAIRIE DOGS, NEBRASKA.

(THE MOUNDS ARE ABOUT EIGHTEEN INCHES HIGH.)

for hours upon its haunches, with its fore-paws held
steadily in front of him, continuously maintaining
a careful watch upon everything that was happening.
I observed that although the method of sitting was
that of the squirrel tribe, the shape and appearance
of the body was of a different type, and like that of
a large guinea-pig. The most attractive point about
the little animal was its keen manner of keeping
guard like a sentinel. Nothing seemed to escape
its vigilance.

When the fact of rattlesnakes living in the same
holes as the prairie dogs was originally made known,
there were several theories advanced upon the
subject ; but, in the absence of any direct evidence
as to the nature of the apparent alliance or friendship, nothing could be positively proved. It was
however subsequently discovered that young marmots were occasionally found inside the bodies of
rattlesnakes which had been killed near the mounds.
It is therefore probable that the reptiles used the
burrows for their winter residences, after having
expelled the previous inhabitants.

Nothing is more surprising than the effect of the
movement of civilisation westwards upon the number
of the animals who were accustomed to exist upon the
prairies. The explorers who passed through these
waste lands in the beginning of the nineteenth century, reported that the surface of the country,
especially near the river Platte, was often blackened
by immense herds of bisons. Fifty years later when
I went over the same ground no buffaloes were to
be seen there, and they no longer frequented that
part of Nebraska. The rattlesnakes have also almost

disappeared in consequence of the introduction of animals that were hostile to them.*

The manner by which this destruction of the snake tribe has been carried out, was brought to my notice when I was crossing Lake Erie. Near the west shores of the lake there were several islands which had been infested with reptiles to such an extent as to make it dangerous for men to land upon them. A resident who had lived for many years upon the adjacent shore, and who happened to be on board the steamer when we passed near one of the largest of the islands, told me that in order to clear the ground a large number of hogs were landed upon it, and within a short time the island was made perfectly safe. It was observed that they rushed

---

* The subject of the destruction of snakes is mentioned by Mr. Murray, in his " Travels in North America."

When passing through a ravine in the territories of the Pawnees he observed, " I never should have believed it possible that so many rattlesnakes could have been assembled together as I saw in that ravine. I think there must have been nearly enough to fatten a drove of Missouri hogs," and he adds in a note. " It is well known that in the Western States where rattlesnakes are still plentiful the hogs kill and eat them ; nor is their bite formidable to their swinish enemy, on whom its venomous fangs seem to produce no effect. It is owing to this well-known fact that families resident in those districts conceive that hogs-lard must be a kind of antidote to their poison, and frequently use it (I believe successfully) as a remedy." (*Travels in North America, by Hon. Charles Augustus Murray, Vol.* ii, *pp.* 42.)

An Englishman who had a large farm in West Virginia, told me that the hillsides were cleared of the snakes, which had previously infested them, by turning out pigs upon them.

A similar result took place in Minnesota and upon the prairies east of the Missouri.

immediately forward and when close to the snakes they dropped upon their knees and commenced to devour them with the greatest avidity. The darting of the fangs upon them did not seem to have the slightest injurious effect. It is therefore probable that this strange invulnerability of the hog is due to the thickness of its hide, and the close stiff bristles which prevent the penetration of the poison.

On the prairies, the explorers mention their having seen, besides buffaloes ; deer, hares, wolves, eagles, buzzards and ravens. I saw several herds of antelopes and a few wolves : one of them belonging to the coyote species was observed in the evening to be prowling round the huts of settlers at the forks of the Platte. It was caught and forthwith dispatched. It was a good sized wolf with a thick coat of shaggy iron-grey hair and looked fierce and savage. On the banks of the southern branch of the river near this spot I joined an American companion in an expedition to look for prairie grouse. We found them amongst the brushwood in considerable numbers, but the birds were wild and it was difficult to get within range of them. The Platte at this part was nearly three thousand feet above the sea.

On the desert, at a height of seven thousand feet, I saw antelopes grazing upon the prairie grass which was growing abundantly and afforded ample supplies of food for them. Wolves were also on these plains skulking in the vicinity doubtless hoping to appease their hunger before many hours had elapsed. These wide and lofty table lands were the ancient hunting grounds of the Dakotas and Cheyennes.

It was getting late upon a fine winter's evening
when our coach crossed the brow of a hill and we
caught sight of the calm blue waters of the Great
Salt Lake surrounded by snow-covered mountains.
It was a quiet scene of singular beauty.   The skies
were brilliant with the glowing effects caused by the
rays of the declining sun.   It was nearly dark when
we arrived at the City of the Mormons and our horses
were pulled up at the door of an attractive little inn
which Brigham Young had provided for the accommodation of strangers.

After quitting the prosperous lands of Utah on my
way to California I stopped in the centre of that
part of the American desert situated near the borders
of Oregon and bounded on the west by the ranges
of the Sierra Nevada.   It was my object to visit a
tribe of Shoshones who were then encamped in the
neighbourhood. I found them dwelling on a dreary and
exposed plateau in the midst of a region covered with
small black volcanic stones and fragments (or flakes)
of obsidian, with which an old arrow head maker
was busily engaged fashioning the rude weapons
required by the tribe.   It was the middle of December.   The winter was cold, and the country around
looked bleak and desolate.

The Indians were in wigwams made of saplings or
withies, bent over in such a manner as to form the
shape of a semi-circle or a low rounded beehive.
They resembled, in their construction and size, the
temporary huts used by wandering bands of Chippewas upon the shores of Lake Superior.   The
interiors of these rude and miserable lodges were
not inviting.   Squalor, dirt and gloom were present
to the eye, and influenced the mind.

INDIAN, SALT LAKE VALLEY, UTAH.

The men differed to some extent from all other Indians that I had seen, and were in appearance like the Asiatics in the southern Provinces of China, and had not the massive heads and aquiline features of the Dakotas or Pawnees ; they were also of a more debased type. This, however, may have been the result of many centuries of struggles against starvation and exposure to the severe weather that must be experienced in the deserts upon which they wander. Outside the main part of the encampment there was a small group of wigwams, which I found to be occupied by Utes, a tribe even more degraded and wretched than the Shoshones.

The Utes, or Digger Indians, have always been considered to be the lowest in civilization of all the American tribes. It has been thought that they may be the descendants of outcasts, but this opinion does not seem to be based upon sufficient evidence. There are good reasons for believing that they are allied in race and language with the Shoshones, and they are apparently treated by them on terms of friendship and equality.

The Diggers have been given that name in consequence of it being their custom to live chiefly upon roots, or whatever other food they can obtain by digging. They also find a scanty support from grass, seeds and locusts. They have been occasionally met wandering in Utah in a naked and half-starved condition. It is not possible to imagine human beings to be in a lower or more harsh state of existence. Misery and want do not however appear to influence the natural buoyancy and cheerfulness of these nomads. Possibly their freedom, the constant occupation of searching the hills and deserts for subsistence, and their unconstrained life, give them compensation for the hardships that they are forced to endure.

There is only one other race that I have seen living under similar conditions of continuous want and wretchedness, with whom the struggles for bare existence are equally severe.

That unfortunate people are the Fuegians, who wander in search of food upon the rugged coasts of Tierra del Fuego.

When passing through the Straits of Magellan in H.M.S. Pearl in January, 1877, we saw several families of the natives in Churruca Bay occupying wretched wigwams, placed close to the water's edge.

Some of them embarked in their canoes and came alongside to ask for food and tobacco. They appeared to be in a half-starved and emaciated state, and were sustaining life upon mussels and edible roots. The medical officers of the ship measured the men, as I wished to ascertain their size and weight as compared with the Patagonians dwelling upon the opposite shores of the Straits. It was found that the height of these Fuegians was between four feet nine inches and five feet two inches. The average stature was under five feet. The measurements round the chest were comparatively large, being thirty-four to thirty-five inches.

We afterwards anchored in Gregory Bay, Patagonia. As soon as we were observed, a numerous tribe of Patagonians rode down to the beach, and pitched their tents opposite the ship. Several of the chiefs came on board and subsequently allowed themselves to be weighed and measured.

It was ascertained that their average height was five feet eleven inches, and their chest measurements averaged forty-four inches. Their weights averaged two hundred and thirty-two pounds.

The contrast in the physical condition between the Patagonians and Fuegians is extraordinary when it is considered that only a narrow channel of water, easily traversed by canoes, separates them. It is probable that the Utes, Shoshones and Fuegians may have been forced by adverse circumstances to retreat to the inhospitable regions in which they live. No race would willingly accept or undergo such unchangeable hardships.

CHAPTER VIII.

North American Indians.—Diversity of Languages.—The Iroquois.—Dialects.—Descent of Iroquois chiefs through the
female line.—Pagan Indians.—Belief in a Great Spirit.—
Ceremonies. — Dakotas. — Superstitions. — Dreams. — Fasts. —
Sun-worship. — Medicine men. — Customs of mourning by
widows.—Supernatural influences.—Lightning.—Transmigration.
—Worship of Spirit rocks.—Serpent worship.—Human sacrifices.
—Burial customs.—Method of curing sickness by steam.—Note
upon analogies between the customs of the Indians, Maoris,
and the natives of the Sandwich Islands.

It is expedient with respect to the condition of the
North American Indians, to take into consideration
some of the circumstances relating to their languages,
customs, and superstitions; particularly such of them
as may appear to have remote analogies with the
observances of other races, or with the more advanced state of civilisation that existed in the
fifteenth century, among the tribes who had conquered the aboriginal inhabitants of Mexico, Central
America, and Yucatan. It is also especially necessary that a brief investigation should be directed to
certain exceptional forms of the Indian faith in the
influence and power of the unknown gods by whom
the Dakotas believed themselves to be surrounded
and who were propitiated by acts of severe personal
suffering and penance.

In the Northern continent there are two principal facts which attract the attention of those who are thrown into contact with the Iroquois, Chippewas and Dakotas. The first of these which comes under notice is the extraordinary number and diversity of their languages, and afterwards, upon a more extended acquaintance with the customs of these Indians, the strange and most grave nature of the higher character of their ancient religion. With regard to the differences of the languages my attention was first called to this circumstance by M. Cuoq, who, when I visited the Missionary establishment upon the shores of the "Lac des deux Montagnes" in Canada, was in charge of the converts. M. Cuoq was a learned philologist and had published a volume of studies upon the Indian languages.*

The assemblage of Roman Catholic converts brought together at the Mission was composed of two tribes, who spoke different languages which were so absolutely distinct that they were unable to converse with each other. One of these groups were Algonquins, whose ancestors originally dwelt to the north of the St. Lawrence, the other was formed from the Iroquois who came from territories bordering upon the southern banks of that river. M. Cuoq, when conducting the religious services, preached to them in their own languages alternately. It is not surprising that these scattered remnants of the two great tribes whose languages were radically dissimilar should still (although they have lived as

---

* "Etudes Philologiques sur quelques Langues Sauvages de L'Amérique," Montreal, 1866.

neighbours for several generations) be unable to understand each other. It is, however, a different matter when the conditions are considered under which the original Iroquois language has become changed into the six languages spoken by the Senecas, Oneidas, Cayugas, Onandagas, Mohawks and Tuscaroras. The extraordinary manner in which the Iroquois language has thus become separated is especially noticeable at the Canadian reservation of those tribes situated near the banks of the Grand River.

According to the traditions of the Iroquois it appears that the nations were composed originally of one large tribe, all of whom spoke one language, and that they dwelt on the southern shores of Lake Ontario. It is stated that they became too numerous for the land which they occupied, and a great council was held to consider what steps should be taken to establish themselves in such a manner as to have hunting grounds sufficiently extensive to enable them to obtain supplies of food. After long discussion it was decided to disperse and to divide into communities. But, in order to prevent disaster from the possibility of being conquered by their enemies when thus separated, it was arranged that they should dwell near each other and thus be able to unite for the purpose of war. It happened, in consequence of this dispersion, that the language gradually became so greatly changed that the tribes were unable to understand each other, and in a period comparatively brief, six distinct dialects were formed which in the course of time became practically new languages.

When these Iroquois, who had been our allies in war, were gathered together and placed upon lands within the Canadian frontier, it was found expedient by them to make one of the dialects a language, which might be so far understood by the six nations, as to be employed upon all occasions when they had to perform their ceremonies, or carry out any purposes which they had in common.

Upon the occasion of my visit to their reservation, I was accompanied by two Indians respectively of the Seneca and Cayuga tribes, both of whom spoke English intelligibly. I asked the Seneca what was the dialect they had chosen to be their language when the Iroquois were assembled together. He replied, that it was the Cayuga, because they believed it was the original language which had been spoken by all of them, and the six nations at the Grand River had learnt it sufficiently to enable them to understand what was said when they met at the Council house, but, for all ordinary purposes, and amongst themselves, each nation spoke its own dialect. With reference to this subject of variations in language, it is evident that amongst the North American Indians, who are scattered over such a large extent of country, the differences in the spoken tongues of the tribes must, in many instances, be caused by the fact of there being no written language, and of their being divided into races, kept apart by wars. It is therefore to be expected that great changes would occur within comparatively short intervals of time. With tribes originally belonging to one nation, these would rapidly become formed into dialects according to the manner in which the

tribes moved into other hunting grounds, and became
settled into distinct tribal groups. But after making
all due allowances for these conditions, it still remains
difficult to understand how so great a number of
languages have become established amongst a comparatively small population. At no time, since the
discovery of America, have the total numbers of
Indians within the regions now forming the United
States, exceeded five hundred thousand men, women
and children. In 1829, it was estimated that the
Indian population slightly exceeded three hundred
and thirteen thousand. In 1850, according to the
census, the total numbers were four hundred
thousand.*

The most remarkable fact with regard to the
Iroquois tribes is that, after having had one original
language, they should have become unintelligible to
each other, although they lived in close proximity.
Their territories were within the limits now occupied
by the State of New York. With the Dakotas and
Chippewas, whose territories are adjacent, the conditions are different, for these languages have no
relation with each other, and the most careful
researches have failed to trace any connection
between them. The Chippewa dialect belongs to
the group of languages classified as Algonquin.
Dialects belonging to that original stock are spoken
by the Chippewas, Ottawas, Illinois, Shawnees, and

---

*In the Encyclopædia Americana (1886), the total Indian
population is said to be (exclusive of Alaska) 264,369. The
Dakotas are stated to number thirty-one thousand.

all the New England tribes.   The Dakota language
is at present known to be spoken in thirteen principal dialects, and several sub-divisions. The Iroquois
is exclusively confined to the six dialects spoken by
the six nations assembled in their reservations.

The history of the dispersion of this race seems to
establish the fact that Indian languages can, within
a comparatively short period, be so greatly altered
as to become practically distinct. This has happened
with a nation whose separated tribes have always
remained at peace with each other and have united
for common defence, or for the prosecution of a war
against powerful enemies. With savage nations
whose original languages are essentially dissimilar,
the constant wars which take place between them
possibly introduce elements of change which would
influence very considerably the spoken dialects of the
opposing tribes. It was a frequent custom after the
conclusion of hostilities for the conquerors to incor-
porate in their tribe the women and children of those
whom they had vanquished. Thus a new dialect
would be introduced amongst them, and the two
languages would necessarily become blended. A
succession of wars would cause a continuance of
variations of language, and thus it would gradually
come to pass that dialects would be formed not only
greatly differing from each other, but most difficult
to trace to any positive origin.

The Iroquois were not only exceptional in having
a fixed system of confederation which enabled them
to combine their forces in a manner which increased
their fighting strength, but they also had special
customs with regard to their chiefs. It was estab-

lished amongst them as an unalterable regulation that their hereditary descent should be in the female line. This unusual system has attracted much attention. When I was at their reservation I asked my Indian companions for an explanation of the manner in which this was carried into effect in ordinary practice, for it seemed to involve difficulties with regard to intermarriage between the respective nations, and I wished to hear some direct evidence upon that subject.

The Seneca said : " Our children always take the rank of their mothers and join their tribe ; thus I, a Seneca, not a chief, married a Cayuga woman the daughter of a chief and my son is therefore a Cayuga and will be a chief of the Cayugas." Another Indian said : " I live with the Cayugas and my father was a Cayuga, but I am an Onondaga because my mother was an Onondaga woman."

Whilst I was talking with these men, and passing through the villages of the Oneidas, Senecas and Tuscaroras, I observed that there was no church or any building set apart for religious purposes and I asked the Seneca how this happened, as in the other Iroquois reservations that I had seen, the church usually was in a prominent position near the centre of the settlement. He said that I was amongst men who were called Pagan Indians, and that the Grand River Iroquois were divided into two classes, Christians and Pagans. The former were settled upon a part of the lands a few miles distant. He also told me that they always kept themselves distinct from the converts, and were careful to follow their ancient belief and maintain, as far as possible, the ceremonies and religious customs of their ancestors.

I asked a Cayuga, who had joined us, and who was one of the leading men of his tribe, if he would tell me to what extent, and in what form, their Pagan worship was practised. I also mentioned, that I wished for information with regard to the Iroquois belief in a Supreme Being. It was ascertained by the Jesuit missionaries, that a belief in one over-ruling Power was found to exist among them, and in this respect they differed from all other American Indians, with whom it seemed to be conclusively ascertained, that their worship only consisted of propitiations of the various powers that they believed had influence for good or evil in connection with matters around them. It was found by the priests, that the chief obstacle in enabling the savages to comprehend the meaning of their teaching, was the want of capacity in the minds of the Indians to understand the nature of a Power who controlled all movements of the heavens and earth. It was consequently interesting to meet an Indian who could intelligently explain this unusual peculiarity of the Iroquois belief.

This Cayuga, in reply to my questions, said, "We all believe in the Great Spirit whom we call How-wan-ni-yu, and we have four feasts in every year made to him. Those at the New Year and at the Harvest time are the greatest. We meet at the Long House* dressed, as was the custom in former times,

---

*The Council building on the reservation was called the Long House, not on account of its size or shape, but in accordance with an ancient tradition.

with skins and feathers, and have our faces painted.
In the middle of the room we place our offerings
of wheat, fruit, tobacco, and flesh, according to
what we can give, and the season of the year.
Round this pile of offerings we have a dance. After
this is over, our principal chief makes a speech and
tells us about the goodness and nature of How-wan-
ni-yu. Then we have another dance, after which
another chief makes a speech, and so on, until all
the speeches are finished. Then all the offerings
are divided amongst us and the meeting ends."

I asked the Indians if they had any other kind of
worship or prayer. They said they had nothing
more, and that the dance to How-wan-ni-yu was
not considered by them to be a prayer, but was
meant as an acknowledgment of the goodness of the

When the separation of the Iroquois took place, it was
decided by the Council that the expression Long House was
to be used as a symbol, that the nations were theoretically
under one roof, which extended over all the lands occupied by
them. In pursuance of this theory, certain tribes were given
particular duties. The Senecas had to guard the gates looking
towards the sunset, and the Mohawks were to watch the
approaches to the gates placed in the direction of sunrise.

As far as it is possible to form conclusions, with respect to
the state of the Indian tribes in the sixteenth century, it appears
that the Iroquois, in consequence of their league, had attained
to a comparatively advanced state of warlike capacity, and had
organised methods of conducting a campaign.

They also formed regular alliances, and made treaties which
they faithfully executed.

In their treatment of captives they were cruel and barbarous,
but they possessed in the highest degree the qualities of courage
and endurance.

harvest. I found a difficulty in obtaining from these Iroquois any definite opinion with regard to their ideas of the nature of How-wan-ni-yu, but at last the Cayuga said abruptly : "We consider him to be the maker of all things upon the earth, and we know nothing more about the matter." There were, originally, various ceremonies performed by the tribes in connection with the appearance of the first new moon of the year, and there were also tribal dances after any success in hunting or in war, but these are no longer performed. One of the new moon ceremonies was the sacrifice of a dog by fire, and the ashes were scattered over the ground as an offering.

Upon leaving the reservation, it was not possible to feel otherwise than regret that it had become the fate of the descendants of a powerful nation of warriors to be penned within these restricted limits. Men, women and children, were leading aimless and useless lives. They were pensioners upon Governments which would gladly escape from the duties and expenses which the existence of these Indians demand, and who are, in many cases, victims to the temptations offered to them by the habits of modern civilisation.*

---

*I should here mention that, when I was at Boston, I was much assisted in making investigations into certain characteristics of the North American Indians by Mr. Francis Parkman, whose researches upon all subjects relating to the condition of the aboriginal tribes in the sixteenth and seventeenth centuries, have placed him in the first rank of the historians of that period.

Mr. Parkman was personally well acquainted with the Dakotas, amongst whom he had dwelt for nearly two years.

The Dakotas and the Iroquois have always been considered as the most powerful and warlike of the aboriginal races of North America. Both of these tribes also possessed, certain religious customs relating to the mental and physical training of their youthful warriors, which were intended to strengthen their characters, and to give them the power to endure privations and suffering with fortitude. The Dakotas carried into effect their observances to an extent far beyond that of any other race. Their superstitions and religious ceremonies, with reference to this system of preparing the foundations for the establishment of the qualities required to enable a Dakota to fulfil his duties as a courageous and honourable member of his tribe, are most characteristic, and appear to be invaluable elements in the formation of the qualities required by a race dwelling in wild and desolate lands, surrounded by enemies, It was an invariable rule with all the Dakotas, that the youths upon reaching manhood, should pass through a probationary period of fasting. This was done for the purpose of enabling each young Dakota to obtain a knowledge of the spiritual world by which he was surrounded, and to learn, by the revelations that

---

He, on several occasions arranged, in the kindest manner, that I should meet those who were interested in the native races. Upon one of these occasions I met Mr. E. G. Squier, whose original surveys of the ancient earthworks in Ohio were published by the Smithsonian Institution.

The introductions given to me by Mr. Parkman to the distinguished archæologists, Mr. Lewis Morgan and Professor Daniel Wilson, were also most useful.

would be made to him in dreams, the nature of
the Manito which would influence his thoughts and
actions during his life. The fasts were always performed in solitude, far away from the tribe, and frequently continued for a considerable time. It was
supposed that towards the latter part of this probation, his dreams would give him an insight into
the mysterious conditions of life and nature that
appeared to be supernatural, and that he would
discover the god, animal or other object to which
he was especially linked and which he was to propitiate by sacrifices.

It was an essential part of this early endurance of
trial and abstinence, that it not only should be performed in secret, but that for the remainder of his
life the Indian should hold his faith in silence, and
never communicate to others what his dreams had
revealed to him. Thus far this early initiation into
the mysteries of the unknown world had practically
the effect of establishing the mental character, and
was a form of training which impressed upon each
Indian a separate individuality. Upon the conclusion of the probation of fasting and solitude, the
youths had each to pass through trials of their
physical endurance, and had to suffer various tortures
to prove themselves to be capable of becoming
warriors, and to show their manhood by their power
of bearing pain with unflinching fortitude.

When I was in that part of the continent which
for long periods of time had been occupied by the
branch of the Dakota race called Sioux, I endeavoured to ascertain the nature and practice of
these customs as far as they were known by the

existing Indians. In prosecuting these researches
into a subject so interesting and exclusive, I was
fortunate in meeting with a man so well informed
upon all matters connected with these Indians as
the half-breed Faribault. He had lived with the
Sioux for many years at the time when they had
possession of lands bordering upon the banks of the
Mississippi, and had been present, on several occasions, when their most serious superstitious ceremonies were performed. Amongst these were the propitiations made to the sun, a form of worship which
was more rigidly and earnestly practised by the
Dakotas than by any other nation in North America.

Sun worship existed amongst all the Indian
tribes dwelling in the Mississippi valley, particularly
with the Natchez in Louisiana, but the manner and
the ceremonies differed, and with none of them were
the painful personal sufferings and penances, undergone by the worshippers, so great as they were with
the Dakotas. An instance of the severity of this penance occurred in the year 1849, when Faribault was
living with a Sioux tribe encamped on the western
shores of the Mississippi, near Prairie la Crosse.
"An Indian," he said, "dreamt that he had incurred
the displeasure of the Great Spirit, and that it was
necessary to appease him by sacrificing to him everything that he valued, and also to perform penance by
undergoing the utmost pain that he was able to
endure. A scaffolding was raised near the camp,
consisting of two upright poles—of sufficient length
—which were firmly fixed in the ground. These
were connected near the top by a cross pole. When
this was completed the Indian stood up and, shortly

before daybreak, a cut was made within the fleshy parts of each arm near the shoulders through which was passed a rope. Cuts or holes were then made in the breasts and other ropes were pushed through them. The cords were then tied to the stakes in such a manner that the arms were suspended by them. The breast ropes were secured in a position such as to allow that a certain portion of the man's weight was held by them. His feet were allowed just to touch the ground. His dog was killed and placed in front of him together with his blanket, cut into strips, his feathers, his ornaments, and all that he possessed.

"When these preparations were made the Indian waited for the rising of the sun, and directly it appeared above the eastern horizon he threw his head back and fixing his gaze upon it commenced dancing. His friends at the same time maintained an incessant beating of a small drum. The dancing continued throughout the day, the Indian moving his position as the sun moved and taking care always to keep the sun in his front and to gaze steadfastly upon it without shrinking from its full light. After sunset he remained watching the western sky throughout the night. In the morning he turned round towards the dawn and when the sun appeared, was immediately cut down from the scaffold and fell exhausted upon the ground."

This act of sun worship is frequently performed, and the Sioux firmly believe that if they do not obey the dream which points out to them this duty, serious misfortunes will happen to them and their families. Instances have been known of men being able to endure long periods of torture, and young Indians, when passing through the early trials of their strength, will frequently remain for hours entirely suspended by ropes rove through their flesh. It is not possible to estimate the actual personal suffering thus inflicted upon themselves by these North American Indians, by the standard of what would be felt by more sensitive and more highly organised races. I have seen Chinamen endure with stolid indifference, tortures that would cause Europeans to feel the utmost agony.*

The Dakotas had another form of sun worship, which is still practised by some of the tribes in the West, but which appears to be chiefly intended as a tribal thanksgiving or rejoicing. A pole is raised in the centre of the encampment and upon it are placed figures of birds, beasts and reptiles. The Indians dance round this pole during the day taking

---

*In the prison at Omaha I saw three Pawnees named Blue-Hawk, Yellow-Son and Tall-Wolf, who had endeavoured to commit suicide in order to avoid being hanged. One of them, I think it was Blue-Hawk (Sha-to-ko), had managed to conceal a long piece of hard wood, one end of which he had rubbed down to a sharp point. He was employed in pushing this through his body, between the ribs, when he was observed by the warder and prevented from completing his purpose. Another prisoner had removed a brick from the floor and was trying to fracture his skull with it. All of them had torn away portions of their skin and cut themselves in many places with small fragments of glass which they had obtained secretly. The warder told me that he had taken every precaution to stop these desperate attempts of the Indians to destroy themselves. They seemed to be able to bear these self inflicted wounds without showing signs of distress.

care to keep their faces towards the sun. Shortly
before sunset the figures are shot at until they have
all fallen upon the ground. After this there is
another dance which ends when the sun sinks below
the horizon. The ceremony is then concluded.

Sickness is, with the Dakotas as with the
Pawnees, considered to have been sent as a punishment for some wrong deed that has been committed
either by an individual or by the tribe. I was told
by Faribault that whenever a Sioux found that he
was suffering from illness he sent for the medicine
man,* who, upon his arrival, would immediately pro-

---

*The supernatural powers attributed to the "medicine men"
are not worthy of attention, except so far as they illustrate the cre-
dulity of Indians, and show the influence of certain methods of
imposture upon them. Their tricks are usually of a kind which
are perfectly within the capacity of an ordinary juggler.

Their pretension of possessing the power of making rain is
however a subject of a different nature.

This particular act is chiefly remarkable because there is no
form of imposture which can be so readily detected. Nevertheless the Indian tribes throughout the western parts of North
America usually have "Rain makers," in whose powers they
appear to have confidence.

I met in California a young Englishman who had been living
for several months with various tribes near the coast, between
British Columbia and New Mexico.

He told me that he had been present upon an occasion when
a successful attempt at rain-making occurred. The event took
place upon a promontory in the southern part of California.

The tribe wanted rain, and their rain-maker declared that he
could obtain what was desired. He proceeded to make upon
an adjoining hill, a large bonfire which was kept well supplied
with fuel and gave out dense volumes of smoke. The fire was
kept burning for over twenty-four hours, and then the efforts
of the rain-maker were rewarded by a good and sufficient
fall of rain. Here, as elsewhere, the Indians employed fire
and smoke as agents for producing rain.

ceed to ascertain what evil act the patient had done, and would then take the requisite measures to drive out the evil spirit representing the nature of the offence. It is assumed that the offence committed by the sick person has some reference to a man, woman or animal. The medicine man, who pretends to have the power of second-sight, looks steadily at the patient, until he declares that he can see the inner demon that torments him. After certain incantations, he makes out of clay an image of the creature which is causing the sickness, and then shoots at it until it is shattered. It is expected that this act will cause the devil to depart. If this method of cure fails, other images are made, as it is then assumed that more than one evil deed has been perpetrated. Finally, if all these remedies are unsuccessful it is pronounced that the patient must perform a penance. This usually consists of a long fast, and is considered to be a personal matter strictly confined to the relations that exist between the Indian and the Manito under whose guidance he believes himself to be, and which has been ascertained during the period of the great fast performed in his youth.

It was the custom with the Sioux, whenever the head of the household died, for the women to mourn for a year. One of their chiefs had died a few years before I was at Mendota, and Faribault, who had known him intimately, went to the settlement to see the widow. He found her engaged in the occupation of cutting deep gashes in her arms and legs. She had, in her hand a rounded scalping knife and with this weapon she was striking herself and inflicting wounds from which blood was flowing. All the furniture and mats had been removed from the tepee or tent, and she was sitting upon the earth. At the conclusion of the time of mourning it is usual for the women to go to their friends or join some other household, and the old tepee is then thrown down and left in a heap upon the ground.

At the time that Faribault was speaking about these customs, there were present several Sioux, who had come from their encampment, and were listening to him. When he had finished his narrative, I took the opportunity of asking these men some questions about the belief of the Sioux, with respect to lightning and thunder, as I had heard that the Dakotas held some especial opinions upon these manifestations of supernatural power. One of the beliefs attributed to them was that lightning was a stone, and it was difficult to understand what could be their reason for holding such a strange belief. They said, in answer to my question, that lightning was certainly a stone, and that they knew it was so because they had seen it, and it was very hard and like a rock. Possibly the Indians had seen the fall of some aerolites, or they may have observed the effects of lightning after it had struck the earth. They state, that sometimes a small hot stone is found near the roots of a tree that has been injured by a flash of lightning.

I asked Faribault, whether any of the tribes with whom he had lived, appeared to have any belief in one supreme Great Spirit. He replied, that, as far as he had been able to judge of this matter, the Sioux held this belief vaguely, but, that it did not influence their actions. The Dakotas have a Pagan custom of investing animals, hills, mountains, and all remarkable natural manifestations of unknown powers with especial spirits of good or evil influence, each demanding different forms of worship and propitiation. They have also—under certain conditions—a belief in the transmigration of souls into animals. They consider that this takes place when an Indian has been guilty of some act of cowardice or treachery. In such a case, his spirit is supposed, after death, to go into some animal or to take its form, and then it is sometimes believed that it haunts the neighbourhood of the camp. The superstitious nature of the Sioux is often strangely affected by traditions respecting these wandering spirits, and when under this influence, it is said by the half-breeds living amongst them, that they seem to possess the power of seeing supernatural things.

There was an instance of this mentioned as having occurred a few years previously. A Sioux died : it was known that he had dreamed that, after his death, he would enter the body of a bear, and would then wander round the tents of the tribe. After his death, an Indian looked out at daybreak, and declared that he saw upon an opposite hill a large grey bear. Upon hearing this rumour the tribe assembled, and many of the men imagined that they saw it. After this appearance there was a universal dread of the bear. It was frequently seen, and the Indians were careful to avoid meeting it. During the time that the tribe were encamped in this part of the country, south of the Minnesota, the bear was occasionally seen prowling over the hills. One

of the chiefs was asked by a white man, who was
trading with this tribe, why it was not killed, and
he was told, that it was because it contained the
spirit of a dead brother.   There was no doubt in the
minds of the Indians about the reality of the vision.
They were positive in declaring that they saw the
bear, and would point it out to the half-breeds
staying in the camp, who could never see it.
This power of seeing what is to other men unseen,
is stated to be possessed by many of the Dakotas,
and is probably, in a great measure, due to a highly
sensitive condition of mind, caused by their long
periods of self-imposed abstinence.   Faribault said,
that Sioux, when travelling the country, will
suddenly start and tremble, and point to something not visible to the half-breeds, and declare
that they see the form of the spirit that they dread.

The dreams and fasts of the Dakotas, and the
time passed by them in solitude, explain much that
is strange and exceptional in their nature.   It is
thus intelligible how it happens, that the young
Indians have such an earnest and vivid belief in the
spiritual nature of the unknown and mysterious
world, and that they invest with supernatural
attributes the mysterious powers which surround
them.   It must seem natural to them, that thunder
and lightning, sun, moon, mountains, and rivers,
should be considered as manifestations of powerful
spirits, that require to receive worship and sacrifice.
What, however, is not so obvious, is the cause which
impels them to worship large rocks and stones,
which cannot, by any stretch of the imagination, be
supposed to possess active powers of good or evil.

Upon this subject I asked the Indians for their explanation, saying, that I supposed they did not directly worship a stone, such as that near Mendota, but the spirit who had placed it there. Faribault said, that this worship also followed upon dreams, and the Indians, who were present, concurred in his statement. It sometimes happens that a Sioux, in his dream, instead of seeing the image of the sun or some animal, will see nothing but one of these large Spirit rocks. It is thus conveyed to his mind, that this is his god, by which his actions and fate are to be governed during his life, and to whom he must offer sacrifices.

The whole tribe will occasionally take part in the worship of a boulder.* A dreamer, usually in this case, a man who is supposed to be gifted with prophetic power, dreams that it has become necessary to propitiate some unknown spirit. Then if he afterwards dreams of one of these boulders he acquaints the tribe with the nature of his dream, and the camp is immediately moved to the neighbourhood of the particular stone that is to receive sacrifices. This worship of Spirit rocks continues to take place. There is a large rounded mass of granite on the west bank of the Mississippi, lying upon the prairie a few miles below Lake Pepin, which is still visited by wandering bands of Sioux. It had been painted a bright red colour. When passing near the spot where it was situated, I saw the fires of the encampment of Indians who had come there to perform their ceremonies.

*See Chapter VI.

Amongst the various superstitious customs of the Dakotas, none are more singular than those which are related to serpent worship, and I listened with attention to the opinions of the Sioux upon this subject. They said that with serpents, as with other animals, the sacrifices made to them were entirely a personal matter, depending upon the nature of the dreams and upon the special kind of affinity that an Indian might believe himself to possess with them. With regard to rattlesnakes the methods of propitiation varied, for it happens that some of the men of a tribe find that they have a power of fascination over these reptiles. Others are aware of a feeling of dread of them, and consequently act differently. Usually a snake worshipper, upon meeting a rattlesnake, carefully clears and smooths the ground and places upon it his offering. He then fills his pipe with tobacco, lights it and turns the mouth-piece towards the snake, holding the bowl in his hands. He then makes his request.* But, said the Sioux, these things are done in secret and very little is known about them. Each Indian, especially concerned, knows how and in what manner to offer his sacrifice.

There is necessarily a difficulty in comprehending the depth or extent of the belief in the supernatural powers of the gods ruling over them, as understood and acted upon by ignorant and savage natures, such as the Dakotas, whose opinions have been

---

*The offerings are sometimes made to appease the angry spirit dwelling in the serpent.

Occasionally the Dakotas sacrifice a dog to it.

formed after they have undergone long periods of
fasting and suffering. An event occurred in a tribe
then dwelling near the banks of the Minnesota,
which proved that these Indians believed that their
gods took a direct part in the government of the
world beneath them, and manifested their anger by
punishing those men who had offended them, unless
a sufficient sacrifice was made as a propitiation. This
event was reported in the year 1852, by Mr.
Prescott, who was residing amongst the Sioux.

His letter ran as follows :—

"St. Peters, *January* 26, 1852.
" Sir,
" I mentioned an instance of human sacrifice
amongst the Sioux, but I did not know for what
cause at the time, but since I have found out the
cause of the sacrifice.

" There came up a terrible thunder-storm. The
lightning was flashing and falling in every direction
about the Indian's lodge, and the Indian thought
the lightning or thunder was angry with him, and
was about to kill him ; so the Indian took his gun
and shot his own son, and offered him as a sacrifice
to the thunder, to save his own life." *

Amongst the Indian races occupying the Northern American continent, the Dakotas and the
Pawnees are the only tribes who are known to have
had the custom of sacrificing human beings to their
gods. It is of importance to remark that these two
races dwelt in neighbouring lands, and had customs

---

* " Indian Tribes of North America." Vol. IV. pp. 51.

which point to analogies with the Toltecs and Aztecs, in Southern Mexico, and the Mound Builders in Ohio. With the Dakotas human sacrifices were the greatest of the propitiations to their angry gods. It was known that Faribault had dwelt with a tribe of the Sioux upon an occasion when one of these sacrifices occurred, and I asked him to give me a detailed account of the proceedings that then took place, for cases of that serious nature rarely happen, although some centuries earlier, when tribal wars were frequent and perilous, it may be conjectured that they were numerous.

Faribault said that, at the time when this human sacrifice occurred, he was living with a band of Sioux belonging to the Sissiton tribe, and they were encamped near the west shores of Lake Pepin. "They had come to the conclusion that, for some reason which they did not comprehend, a curse was upon them. Everything seemed to go wrong. Game was scarce and hard to kill, and there was much distress and sickness. Fastings and the usual sacrifices seemed to be of no avail, and nothing removed the evil influences which surrounded them. Finally an Indian, not a chief, but a man who was an orator and a prophet, had it made known to him by a dream what propitiation was required. This man had three daughters. The youngest of them was twelve years old; she was a beautiful child and her father's favourite. He dreamt that, to appease the Great Spirit, it was necessary to sacrifice this child. In the morning before sunrise, he awoke the girl and told her to go out of the tent, wash herself and then put on her best dress and all her ornaments. He then called the tribe together and told them his dream. When they had heard what he declared they removed the tents to an adjacent camping ground and remained there until he joined them. He was then left alone with his daughter. He told her that in his dream he had seen the Great Spirit who had commanded that she should be sacrificed. His daughter accordingly stood up, and facing the sun, began to sing her death song, which was a kind of hymn. At noon, when the sun had risen to its highest point in the sky, he killed her."

The Sioux stated that after this sacrifice everything prospered, sickness ceased, game became abundant and all went well with the tribe.*

The burial customs of the Dakotas were, in several respects, distinctive. The dead were placed upon an open frame work or scaffolding, which, when the tribes were encamped upon the prairies, was raised a sufficient height above the ground to be out of the reach of wolves. Ultimately the bones were taken to the tribal burial places. It is not improbable that the Mound Builders had similar usages. §

---

*The remaining daughters were alive when I was in Minnesota. One of them was married to a man of the tribe. The other was the wife of a white man, who, Faribault said, was employed as a drummer at Fort Snelling.

§With many of the Dakota and Chippewa tribes there existed a custom of placing upon the scaffolding a wand which was painted red, blue and white. They believed that the spirit of the Indian had to cross a river over which was a long log of wood. Upon reaching the opposite bank, the spirit met the spirits of his enemies. To one of them he would show the red, to another the blue, and finally he pointed to the white and then all enmities ceased.

The Sacs and Foxes who dwelt on the lands near the southern borders of a part of the Dakota territories had different customs. Judge Williams told me that, when he was residing amongst them, it was their practice, when burying a man, to fix two upright posts. The body was placed in a sitting position on the surface of the ground with the back resting against one of the posts, and the feet touching the other. It was then covered over with earth.

The methods followed by the Dakotas and Chippewas in curing illness by the use of steam appear to be of very ancient origin, and evidently are the same as those that were described by Clavigero as being practised by the Aztecs in the towns of Mexico. They are also adopted by the Shoshones in the deserts of Utah. Amongst the Dakotas a low circular wigwam is made about four feet high. The frame is usually covered with buffalo skins in such a manner that no steam can escape. A small opening is left through which the patient can crawl in. In the interior of the wigwam some sand is put upon the ground. Stones which have been heated by fire are then pushed in under the wigwam and placed upon this sand, together with a jar of water. The patient then pours the water upon the stones until the interior is filled with vapour or steam.

When the Jesuit missionaries surveyed the shores of Lake Superior in 1669, they reported that the savages in preparing their meals, used a pail made of birch bark, which contained water. Hot stones were thrown into this until the water was raised to a temperature which was sufficiently high to cook

BEAR SKIN.   ROCKY BEAR.

RED DOG.

CHIEFS OF THE OGALLALAS.

(DAKOTAS.)

their food. This custom was similar to that which was followed by the Maoris in New Zealand.

It is hazardous to attempt to form any conclusions, based upon analogies, respecting the habits and superstitions of savage races, but with regard to the Maoris and the Dakotas, there are circumstances which require that a passing notice should be given to them.

The New Zealanders, like the Dakotas, placed the bodies of the dead upon platforms or high scaffoldings. After a certain time the bones were scraped and gathered together, and taken to the burying place.

The Maoris also had much faith in dreams, and believed that it was chiefly through them that they received communications from their gods. It was also usual for widows to show their grief, upon the death of their husbands, by cutting themselves with sharp instruments.

The Sandwich Islanders, who are believed to be of the same race as the Maoris, used, in cases of sickness, a steam bath in the same manner as the Dakotas.

In 1878, I met a number of Maoris in the valley of the Waikato, in the northern island of New Zealand. The men and women differed from the Malay type, and resembled, in many respects, the North American Indians. I am of opinion, that at a remote period, there must have been a communication between the aboriginal natives of the Sandwich Islands, and the Indians dwelling upon the western coasts of North America.

CHAPTER IX.

In the forenoon of the third day of January, the
"Golden City" commanded by Captain Lapidge, left
San Francisco for the Central and South American
Pacific ports.

We had on board, as passengers, several members
of the Austrian mission, originally embarked in the
frigate Danube under their chief Rear-Admiral Baron
Petz, with instructions to make commercial treaties
with China, Japan, Siam, Guatemala, Chili and other
Spanish-American States. This part of the mission
had been detached to visit Guatemala and it was arranged that upon the completion of their duties in
Central America, they should rejoin the frigate in the
Southern Pacific. Dr. Scherzer, the author of the
narrative of the voyage of the Novara, and who had
also published the journal of his travels in Central
America, was placed in charge of this service. He
was accompanied by Baron Herbert and Baron

Ransonnet, acting as secretaries. I had already met
these members of the staff and it was a mutual
pleasure to find that we were proceeding to the same
regions.

Soon after leaving the harbour we approached the
rocks upon which great numbers of seals were seen.
They watched our movements with attention, and in
reply to the sound of the blows of our paddlewheels
upon the water, bellowed at us defiantly.

The " Golden City " passing the Seal Rocks.

We at first steered a course near the shore, but
finding that there was a heavy ground swell,
we kept about four miles out from the land, a distance sufficiently close to enable us to have a good
view of the Californian hills. One night, large beacon
fires were reported to be observed on the heights of
the southern extremity of Lower California. The
course was consequently altered towards a small bay
within Cape San Lucas, and a boat came alongside
conveying passengers. It was very dark and the

signal fires threw a fitful glare upon the sea and our
ship, at intervals.   As we followed the line of the
coast, the scenery became very grand as we approached the mountain ranges of Mexico.   The
weather was fine, the sea, rightly called Pacific, was as
smooth as glass, and there was an effect of atmosphere which gave a marvellously beautiful colouring
to the slopes and valleys of the mountains.

Several days after our departure from San Francisco
we entered the little land locked harbour of Man-
zanillo.   When rounding the point we disturbed several flocks of pelicans.   They gathered speed with a
few flaps of their great wings and then swept over
the water noiselessly without further effort, altering
the direction of their flight until they were sheltered
from observation by some intervening rocks.*   Man-
zanillo is one of the seaports of the city of Mexico,
and communicates with the capital by a road leading
to Colima and Guadelajara.   Near the village there is
a shallow lake called La Laguna de Cuyutlan, in
which exist an extraordinary number of alligators.

-----

*The albatrosses in the Southern ocean which, like the
pelicans, are birds of great size and weight (I have measured
some which exceeded twelve feet across the wings) maintain for
hours an equal height above the level of the sea.

In the high latitudes south of the Cape of Good Hope and the
Crozet Islands there is always a strong gale blowing, and consequently by a very slight and imperceptible movement or inclination
of the wings the albatrosses obtained the necessary pressure
which enabled them to rise, descend, or maintain their hovering
position.

In the case of pelicans moving rapidly in a perfect calm, the
method by which they maintain their height in the air is not so
easily understood.

After our ship had anchored, some of the passengers went to look at this quiet reptile-infested
lagoon, which is separated from the sea by a narrow
strip of land. Captain Lapidge told us that a few
years before our arrival, there had been a long continuance of westerly winds, and these together with
an unusually high tide caused the sea to flow over
the isthmus into the lagoon. Numerous alligators
then came out from it and crossed over into the bay
where they were immediately attacked by sharks,
which abound on this part of the coast. He said
that a fearful combat took place and for several
days the bay was deluged with blood.

It had become dark before we returned from the
lagoon, and we passed through the Indian village
situated near its banks. The women were busy
grinding, on rounded granite slabs, grains of maize;
or cooking various herbs and vegetables in small
earthern pans. The interior of their huts contained
one room. The ground was usually bare, but in
some instances a few mats were laid down. The
exterior was formed of long upright poles or sticks
closely bound together. The roofs, which were high
and sloped steeply downwards, were made of brushwood and palm leaves.

During the night we continued our voyage near
the Mexican coast, and on the morning of the 10th
entered the harbour of Acapulco. In the crowded
market place we saw a strange medley of races,
Indians, Negroes, Ladinos, Mestizos, and Pintos who
afforded ample occupation for the artistic talents of
Baron Ransonnet. The Indians were of moderate
stature and of a dark swarthy colour, their faces

were broad, and their hair was long, heavy and very black. All had peculiarly restless eyes. We were interested in looking at the Pintos, a numerous race of Indians inhabiting the hills of this part of Mexico, who are given that name in consequence of the coloured spots on their skin. Some of them were merely spotted, others had their feet or hands almost white and of a disagreeable livid tint. In several, the dark red skin of the face was completely covered with white round spots. These spots always begin as blue marks and develop into sores, which afterwards heal into these indelible white scars. The Indians say that this kind of leprosy is inherited. In all other respects they were perfectly healthy.

At midnight on the 13th, we arrived off San José de Guatemala. Captain Lapidge lowered a boat and put us on board the nearest vessel, which we afterwards found to be a North German barque called the Gelert. Although the sea was smooth she was rolling heavily. The Golden City also gave some deep lurches, and it was difficult to get in or out of the boat. Baron Ransonnet left us with the intention of proceeding to Panama. Finally Dr. Scherzer, Baron Herbert, and myself, made the best of our position and slept—or endeavoured to sleep—for the rest of the night upon the deck of the Gelert.

The view from the barque when the sun rose above the horizon, was of a character not to be forgotten. The great range of volcanoes which, commencing in the North in Alaska, runs like a backbone near the Pacific Coast through the entire length of the American continent to the southern limits of Patagonia, is here very remarkable. The great mountains of Agua and Fuego, rising respectively over twelve and thirteen thousand feet above the sea, were immediately opposite to us. The volcano of Pacaya was on the right, and, on the left, were the distant volcanoes near the Lake of Atitlan.

Our landing was accomplished without difficulty, and in the forenoon we left San José for the capital in an open carriage, with three good horses harnessed abreast. The road ran in a straight line through the forest which covered the low tropical plain, extending for a distance of forty miles from the sea to the base of the hills. Occasionally we passed the huts occupied by the mixed race descended from African negroes and Indians, who have been given the name of Zambos.

It would be difficult to account for the existence of a race of African descent, dwelling near the Western coasts of the Pacific, if we did not possess the statements of the Spanish historians, and their explanation of the circumstances which necessitated the introduction of negroes for the purpose of working in the mines or plantations, and to take the place of the Indians who died in great numbers in consequence of the severity of their treatment by the conquerors. The features of these Zambos, resembled those of the aboriginal race of Indians, but the hair was like that of the negroes on the West coast of Africa.

At the village of Masagua, we saw several Indians who had come down from the hills. They were men of unusually diminutive stature, all of them being under five feet in height, but they were well-formed, muscular and active. The town of Escuintla was reached after sunset, and towards midnight I went

to the Plaza to see the numerous groups of Indians,
who were resting there for the night on their way to
a church festival that was going to be held several
days' journey eastwards. The moonlight was extraordinarily brilliant, and the Indians evidently considered that its influence was dangerous, for they
carefully avoided it, and sheltered themselves amongst
the trees, or within the deep shadows cast by the
walls of the church. The platform in front of the
beautiful façade of that building, was surrounded by
colonnades of palm trees. Beyond, but seemingly
close at hand, were the gigantic forms of the twin
volcanoes of Water and Fire.

Before daybreak we arrived at the village of
Amatitlan, situated on the borders of the lake of
that name near the base of the volcano of Pacaya,
and in the morning we saw before us the plateau
upon which stands the city of Guatemala, five
thousand feet above the sea. Gradually we found
that we were accompanied by Indians belonging to
the various villages near the road, who were on
their way to the market place, carrying on their
backs heavy loads of wood, crockery and vegetables.

As we approached the gates of the city, our horses
increased their pace, and the scene became very
animated. Hundreds of Indians joined us from all
directions, and ran by the sides of our carriage.
The bells of the numerous churches were ringing for
prayers. We passed the castle, the market place
crowded with Indian women selling their wares, and
the cathedral. Priests and sisters of mercy were
hurrying along the streets ; groups of soldiers carrying old-fashioned muskets, were lounging near their

barracks. Our horses became excited and broke
into a gallop, and finally, with great noise and speed,
we drove up to the doors of the Hotel Aleman, and
were soon installed in comfortable rooms opening
into the central court or patio, which forms such
an agreeable feature in all well-arranged Spanish
inns.

Soon after our arrival Colonel Miguel Garcia y
Granados, one of the Government officials, called
upon Dr. Scherzer and gave us a vivid report of the
political condition of the Republic. The Indians of
the provinces between Guatemala and the Mexican
frontier were in rebellion. A large force of them
under the leadership of an Indian, named Serapio
Cruz, were marching towards the city, and a battle
between them and the Government troops was
imminent. He also mentioned some interesting facts
with respect to the late President Carrera. Carrera
was a remarkable instance of native capacity. He
was an uneducated Indian of obscure birth who, by
sheer force of character, energy, and courage, was, at
an early age, placed at the head of large bodies of
Indians during the various revolutionary outbreaks
which succeeded the declaration of Independence
from Spain. Finally he became President of the
Republic and governed the people with such obstinate
determination and firmness of will that, in a few
years, he was able to place the whole country under
a steady system of control. In doing this he was
assisted by the fact of being an Indian and having,
consequently, great personal influence over the natives. He also received the support of the priests
for, like all Indians, he was extremely fanatical.

Colonel Garcia told us that Carrera always had on his writing table a toy representing Louis Philippe with his hat in his hand. This toy had a rounded base and was so weighted that, when it was touched, it rolled backwards and forwards, and would thus represent Louis Philippe constantly bowing hat in hand. Carrera when engaged at his official work would frequently make the toy move, and then would say to those that stood near him "It was in that way, by too much bowing, that Louis Philippe lost his throne, I shall take care that I do not make the same mistake." Carrera was not only supported by the priests, but also by the Spaniards, who knew that he alone could keep the Indians in subjection. Latterly he spoke much of the Indian chief Cruz, and said that he was the only man in the State who was to be feared.

During our residence in Guatemala, I was fortunate in having the acquaintance of Don Francisco Gavarrete, who held a post under the Government and was well informed upon all subjects relating to the Indians. He was also, I understood, the proprietor of some of the lands within which were the sculptured monoliths and idols of Quirigua. At the Museum in the city there was a good collection of Indian antiquities which had been found within the territories of the Republic, including several idols from Copan and Santa Cruz del Quiché. When examining these I was accompanied by him and he directed my attention to certain objects of importance. Many of them were well carved and it was clear that the sculptors were able to work and shape the hardest stone with accuracy and skill.

There was a small idol, made of hard green stone, which had been found hidden behind the high altar of a church near the town of Gueguetenàngo. Dr. Scherzer, who during his travels in Central America, had learnt much about the religious customs of the natives, told us that the priest of a church situated amongst the hills near Atitlan had noticed an Indian girl, who was one of his parishioners, showing an unusual fervour in her devotions, and he tried to find out the cause. He, at last, discovered that she had buried an idol in the ground close behind the church beyond the altar, so that although she appeared to be praying to what was before her in the church, she was actually addressing her requests to the idol outside. This priest considered that his Indians were by nature idolaters and that it was not practicable to prevent them from returning to their ancient habits. Señor Gavarrete said that in the Department of Vera-Paz the Indians had still the custom of erecting somewhere near the churches small idol-houses in which they kept the image of a saint. To this they offered sacrifices of meats and flowers, and at certain seasons they were accustomed to keep watch or guard at the door throughout the night.

It is more than strange that nothing has been discovered in the course of the explorations of the various ancient sites in this part of the continent, which throws any light upon the methods employed by the Indians, for the purpose of carving and shaping granite, green marble, and hard lava. No mason's implement of any kind has been found. A few copper chisels appear to have been used for some purpose which is unknown. They could not appar-

ently have been of much service in working stone,
for the edges were rounded and the metal was soft.
This question as to the system adopted by the
Indian sculptors in producing such excellent work,
is as inexplicable now as it was to the Spaniards in
the sixteenth century.

Señor Gavarrete asked me to accept a fine obsidian spear head which had been found amongst the
ruins of Quirigua. This black volcanic glass is
admirably adapted for cutting and wounding purposes. I had previously picked up in an ancient
earth-work outside the city, several fragments of
the same substance, which had evidently been placed
on the edges of wooden daggers or swords which inflicted jagged and dangerous wounds. Obsidian
knives were used by the Aztec priests when offering
human sacrifices to their gods. The spear head was
in form and in the method followed for chipping
the mineral into the requisite shape, similar to the
large arrow heads made by the Indians in the
western parts of North America, where obsidian is
obtained near the volcanic ranges of the Sierra
Nevada.

During the latter part of the month numerous
groups of Indians passed through the city on their
return from the pilgrimage to Esquipulas. The
festival of the church at that place occurs annually
on the 15th of January. It is estimated that upon
an average over eighty thousand Indians are present
upon that occasion. Esquipulas became an important shrine in consequence of a wooden crucifix, black
from age, having been found buried in the ground
near that town. It was supposed by the Spaniards

that it must have been lost by one of their missionary priests when passing through that part of the province at some early period soon after the conquest. This black crucifix was placed in the sanctuary, and from some cause which has not been ascertained, it was soon held in the highest veneration by the natives.

Indians assembled there in great numbers from all parts of the country, and travelled great distances in order to be present at the festival, and to take part in the performance of the religious ceremonies.

At the Cathedral in Guatemala we frequently saw the pilgrims kneeling before the shrines and showing much devotional respect to certain images. These natives were invariably grown up men and women. They journeyed on foot, carrying with them their provisions and water-gourds. They seemed to be desirous of avoiding all contact or conversation with others. Their conduct was quiet and unobtrusive. It was their custom to pass silently through the city. At the doors of each church they stopped for a few moments, and then entered and knelt before the altar. After the completion of these acts of worship, they proceeded on their journey across the plains towards the huts and villages scattered over the slopes of the distant hills. They never halted in the street, or took any part in the daily movements of the inhabitants.

The pilgrimage is also undertaken by Indians from the distant regions of Central America. Many of them traverse hundreds of miles. There is something in the devotional nature of these ignorant aboriginal people which escapes the comprehension

of those who observe them.   I noticed that the
Indians varied considerably in stature and complexion.   The men who dwelt among the Cordilleras
seemed to be of a finer race than those who were
settled on the plains, and were much darker in the
colour of their skin.

The most attractive spot in the city was the
market place.   Within the square, crowds of people, Indians and Ladinos, were daily assembled, all
of them buying, selling and carrying on the ordinary traffic, with a silence and listless indifference
which was in strong contrast with the life and
animation of the cities in the United States.   It
was a constant pleasure to observe the movements
of the younger Indian women, who in their appearance and demeanour, were far superior to the
men.   This difference arises from their habits and
employment.   The women have a certain kind of
dignity in their manner, caused, in a great measure,
by their usage of carrying water jars and pans of
crockery poised upon their heads.   They therefore
walk slowly and hold themselves upright.   This
custom which begins from early childhood, and forms
part of their daily life, has the result of giving them
good figures and a particularly graceful movement.

The men, on the contrary, have a crouching appearance, caused by the method in which they have been
accustomed, from boyhood, to carry their burdens.
They relieve the pressure of the weight on their
backs by means of a broad band passed over the
forehead and thus, by bending forward, the load is
made less oppressive.   The men and boys consequently contract a stooping posture, and this pre-

sents an unfavourable contrast to the women, whose bearing is precisely the reverse. There is another circumstance which has its influence in shaping the figures of the women. They carry all small things on the open palm of the left hand, which is thrown back and held well raised up. In fact the same causes which affect the appearance of the Indians in North America are present here, but with the difference that there it is the squaw who contracts the stooping and bent figure, through carrying her children and other burdens, and it is the man who maintains the upright figure and dignified manner.

On the plains a few miles to the west of the city, in the direction of the village of Mixco, there is a large and extensive group of ancient Indian mounds of whose construction or purpose nothing is known. They have never been scientifically examined and I was not able to ascertain that any plans had been made of them. No author has alluded to them unless by a mere passing notice, and yet they seemed to throw more light upon the question of the Toltecan or Aztecan migrations than any other remains of ancient antiquities. Possibly no previous traveller in this part of Central America had also seen the mounds of Cahokia, near the eastern banks of the Mississippi, or he could hardly have failed to have observed that their resemblance is so great, and indeed so evident as to place it almost beyond doubt, that the builders of the mounds at Cahokia were of the same race as those that dwelt on the plains of Mixco.

As it would be highly improbable that any nation would migrate from lands abounding with means of food, comfort and warmth to what must have been, at that period, the comparatively inhospitable regions of North America, the tribes that constructed these mounds must have originally migrated from the valley of the Mississippi.

I was employed for several days in making a rough survey of this Indian settlement and took measurements of the inclosure. The ground plan was made in the form of an extensive and irregular parallelogram about twelve hundred yards long and five hundred yards wide. The mounds upon the sides of the greatest length vary in their dimensions. Some of them are very large and exceed forty-five feet in height. The most important are those platform earthworks at each end of the inclosure upon which may have been placed the principal communal buildings, or the houses of the Caciques. There was also a mound of an exceptional shape, situated in the interior which, from its position, may have been intended for purposes similar to those that existed within the embankments of Fort Ancient in Ohio.

When Carrera was President of Guatemala he wished to know for what object these mounds were built, and he therefore gave orders that one of the largest of them should be thoroughly examined. It was ascertained, contrary to expectation, that it was not a burial place. The only thing found in it was a large and well carved granite grindstone of the same shape as those at present used by the Indians for grinding maize. The results of Carrera's excavations appeared to establish the conclusion that the mounds were chiefly raised for the purpose of placing dwellings upon them; and this is also, I was

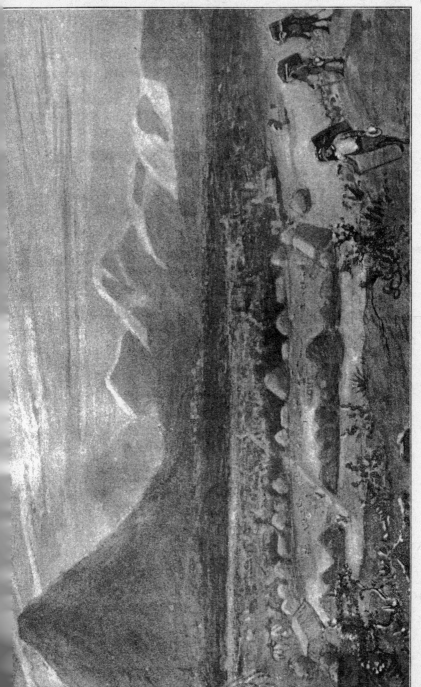

ANCIENT INDIAN MOUNDS NEAR GUATEMALA.

informed, the opinion of the natives living in the neighbourhood.

In the meanwhile from day to day the capital had been disturbed by rumours of the movements of the advancing insurgents, and it was difficult to make any decided plans with regard to my journey in the interior. It was considered by the Government authorities that it would be highly imprudent for me to attempt to pass through the disturbed provinces, as the natives were known to have become unsettled and excited. It was therefore with great satisfaction that I heard that the Indians were coming near and that a decisive battle was imminent. The President Don Vincente Cerna had taken all proper precautions, and had placed the troops under the command of his most able officer, General Solares.

On the twenty-third of January we were informed that the rebels were approaching, and that an action between the forces was expected to take place immediately. Baron Herbert and myself then went into the adjoining country with the hope of obtaining a distant view of the operations. In the afternoon we heard the firing of guns from the castle announcing to the people that the Indians were defeated, and, to prevent there being any doubts upon the subject, messengers arrived from General Solares bringing with them the head of his opponent. This practical method of assuring the inhabitants of the success of the Government troops had a good effect. It was afterwards made known that the Indians had been surrounded at an early hour and taken by surprise whilst they were amongst the ravines. Serapio Cruz fought desperately but was killed and decapitated.

Thus ended the Indian rebellion, and a period of considerable local anxiety.   A political revolution is an event which may be expected to occur frequently in Spanish-American republics, but a rising of Indians in rebellion or, as it is called, a " Guerra de Castas" (war of races), is a far more serious matter, as was proved by the occurrences that happened at the time of the revolt of the Indians in Yucatan, in 1847, when their war cry was " Death to all Spaniards."

At a dinner given at the English legation upon the evening of the conclusion of the insurrection, the subject of the state of the Guatemalan provinces was considered, with reference to the expediency of my intention to travel alone through the disturbed districts.   Many of the members of the foreign legations were present.*   It was thought that the Indian population near the Mexican frontier and amongst the remote parts of the Cordilleras would be, for some time, in a restless and excitable condition, and might be inclined to show their revenge for what had lately happened, by killing any white man who should attempt to pass through the country or who should by misadventure fall into their power. I was however informed by a Spaniard who understood the character of the native races that, although

---

*The foreign residents living in Guatemala, included Mr. Corbett, our Chargé d'affaires ; M. de Cabarrus, chief of the French legation ; the Duke and Duchess de Licignano, Dr. Wynne, Mr. and Mrs. Hague, Mr. and Mrs. Hockmeyer, and M. Hardy: to all of whom I was indebted for much kindness and hospitality.

this opinion was true with respect to Spaniards, an Englishman would probably travel over the Cordilleras with safety. I accordingly lost no time in completing my preparations for the journey.

There was a difficulty in obtaining a good ambling mule, without which long rides over a rugged country would be necessarily fatiguing. Fortunately the Duke de Licignano, who was residing in Guatemala, was willing to part with one of his trained mules, and it was with great satisfaction that I saw this well-bred animal brought into the courtyard of the inn, and placed under the care of my guide.

I received from the Government an official passport or letter of recommendation to the Corregidors under their jurisdiction, which I hoped would be of service as far as the frontier.

Mexico was reported to be temporarily in a lawless condition, but I expected to find upon my arrival within its boundaries, that the authority of the republic was sufficiently established to enable me to proceed without any serious obstacles to the ruins of Palenque.

CHAPTER X.

At daybreak on the thirtieth day of January, my
Indian guide Anastasio, reported that the mules were
ready. He had filled the saddle-bags with a good
supply of provisions, together with a store of native
chocolate, and had otherwise made due arrangements
for the mules in the event of any mischance happening to them. We then proceeded on our way to the
town of La Antigua Guatemala. Baron Herbert
came with us for several miles, and Mr. Hague
proposed to accompany me for a day's journey and
see me safely started on my road.

When we came near the Indian mounds, I halted
for a short time to take a sketch of them from some
rising ground whence a good view could be obtained.
On the left rose the Volcan de Agua. In the distance could be seen the village of Mixco, and on the
right were the Sierras, stretching far away towards
the North, looking well-defined in the clear atmosphere of a bright and sunny morning.

At Mixco we stopped for breakfast, and were

joined by the cura of the parish, who was an agreeable and well-informed man. Mixco is especially interesting to Englishmen on account of its having been the curacy of our fellow countryman, Thomas Gage.* He was appointed there in December, 1629, and had the charge of this and some adjacent parishes for about seven years. He then left Guatemala and returned to England. Beyond the village we obtained a view of the Lake Amatitlan. We then passed San Lucas, and reached La Antigua Guatemala in the afternoon.

Upon our arrival we called upon Padre Martinez, and asked him to show us the ancient cathedral. It was in a ruined condition, and at the time of our visit the nave and aisles were occupied by cattle. In the centre of the roof we observed the emblem of the imperial arms of Austria, the double-headed eagle, which fixed the date of the erection of the building as being in the reign of the Emperor Charles V. There still remained within the shrines many fine wood carvings, and it could be seen that the ornamentation of the interior must have been in accordance with the artistic abilities of the Spanish architects of that period. After leaving this fine example of one of the earliest churches in Central America, we looked at the ruins of the palace and government buildings. It was evident that the ancient Guatemala, before it was destroyed by earthquakes, must have well deserved its repu-

---

*Author of " A New Survey of the West Indies," published in 1648.

tation of being, next to Mexico, the most flourishing city in the New World.

Close at hand and dominating the ruins, are the lofty twin volcanoes of Agua and Fuego (Water and Fire). The former in 1541, caused the destruction of the first town established by the Spaniards, which is now called La Vieja Guatemala. The manner in which that capital was overwhelmed and destroyed, was so exceptional, that it is desirable that the events which then occurred should be brought into consideration.

It was stated by a Spanish resident who was present on that occasion, that although the rain-fall had been abundant during the year, there was nothing in the other atmospheric conditions to give any reason for anxiety. But on the 10th of Sept., 1541, two hours after sunset, a mass of water suddenly issued from the crater of the nearest volcano, and rushing down the slope of the mountain with great velocity, immediately swept away the greater part of the town. This inundation was accompanied by the shock of an earthquake. During the night the disasters caused by the rapid waters are described as having been terrible. The torrents, with which were mingled masses of detached rocks and the trunks of uprooted trees, carried away everything before them. Amongst those who perished was Doña Beatriz de la Cueva, the widow of Alvarado, the conqueror of these southern provinces.[*]

---

[*] "Relation of what happened by the Will of God, on Saturday, the 10th of September, 1541, two hours after sunset in the town of Santiago de Guatimala." Ternaux-Compans.

CATHEDRAL AND SQUARE, LA ANTIGUA GUATEMALA.

The Spanish inhabitants formed the belief that this unusual disaster must have been caused by movements of a miraculous nature, and that the eruption of a volcano throwing out floods of water was a punishment inflicted upon them on account of their sins. They thought that evil spirits had been permitted to cast loose upon them the penalties of fire, water and earthquake. Bernal Diaz who a few years afterwards resided at La Antigua Guatemala, gives in his History of the Conquest a vivid but imaginative description of the horrors of that night, based upon statements made by the bishop of the diocese. He reports that during the tempest great stones were rolled down the mountain and into the city by numbers of demons (muchos demonios,) and that many people heard shouts, yells, and voices, and saw two monstrous black men moving in the rolling waters, calling out, "Forsake everything, for the end of all things is at hand."*

Various theories have been suggested in explanation of this outburst of water from the volcano. It is supposed that the crater may have contained a large volume of water, which after the excessive rainfall of the year exerted such pressure as to burst open the inclosing sides and that the contents were suddenly set free. If this theory is accepted as being correct, it must be granted that the interior of the crater was sufficiently compact to enable it to be water-tight, and consequently

---

*Historia Verdadera de la Conquista de la Nueva España escrita por el Capitan Bernal Diaz del Castillo, uno de sus Conquistadores.

capable of becoming a small reservoir or lake. It is
possible that the Volcan de Agua may have been for
a long time extinct, and that consequently the
sides of the interior of the crater gradually became
impermeable. Under ordinary circumstances the
materials of which volcanic cones are formed, would
not be capable of retaining great quantities of
water.*

---

*The substances thrown out from craters frequently differ in their
character. Judging from the composition of the surface of portions of the land near the Guatemala volcanoes, especially upon
the slopes of the barrancas, it is evident that large quantities of
pozzolana were ejected. One of the latest eruptions that has
occurred was at the Island of Santorin in the Grecian Archipelago
in February, 1866. I was present when the new volcano emerged
from the sea.

The inhabitants of Santorin, upon seeing volumes of steam and
smoke issuing from the waters of the bay, apprehended some
serious peril to be imminent. They feared the possibility of their
town being overwhelmed by an eruption of ashes, and made
a request that a ship of war should be sent to the spot to render
any assistance that might be necessary. I immediately went
there in the "Racer" and remained until all fears of danger
had passed away.

The crater of the volcano, afterwards called Aphroessa,
rose slowly from the surface of the water, and it was possible to
observe the nature of the interior during the intervals between
the eruptions. There was no lava or pozzolana, but only large
cinders which, as they issued from the crater, were thrown into
the air, and then fell upon the outer slopes, thus gradually
forming an island.

It was a very remarkable scene; during the day there were
heavy volumes of smoke and constant rumbling sounds, as the
pent up forces below the mouth of the crater were gathering
strength to throw forth the mass of cinders that closed them in.
At night the glare caused by the reflection of the fire of the interior upon the dense clouds immediately overhanging it was

I believe that the destruction of La Vieja Guatemala by the action of a vast torrent of water issuing
from a volcano is the only instance that is known of
such an extraordinary event, and it can be well
understood how it happened that the superstitious
residents in that capital felt assured that such a
catastrophe must have been the work of demons and
the powers of darkness. The second city was placed
in a position where there was less liability to injury
from any eruption, but it suffered so constantly from
the shocks of numerous and successive earthquakes,
that it was abandoned after having been occupied
for more than two centuries. The present capital
was established in 1775.

The Volcan de Fuego is still occasionally active,
and not many years before I passed near it, flames
and dense volumes of smoke were reported to have
come out of the crater, but no serious eruptions have
taken place in this century. In the last century
several occurred, and upon one occasion the city was
enveloped in complete darkness during the greater
part of the day. At the present time the volcanoes

---

very vivid. The surface of the surrounding waters was over-
spread by running tongues of brilliantly coloured flames. The
island was composed of cinders and ashes, whose porous nature
could never permit any lodgement of water upon them. I
examined several of the craters of the extinct volcanoes on the
islands adjacent to Aphroessa, and there was no instance of any
small pond or collection of water existing within them. The interior of the Volcan de Agua, possibly contained a thick sub-
stratum of water-bearing pozzolana.

An account of the volcanoes of Santorin was given by Sir
Charles Lyell. "Principles of Geology." Vol. ii, pp. 70.

look down upon the ruined cities with grandeur and
repose.

On the morning of our departure from La Antigua
Guatemala, we rode through the Plaza and passed
near to the ancient palace of the Spanish governors,
the public buildings, and the cathedral.   All these
ruins looked beautiful in the clear light of dawn.

As the sun rose we began to ascend the hills.
When we reached the summit I stopped for a few

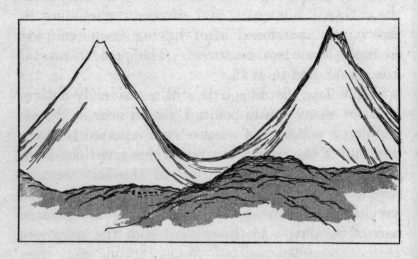

Volcan de Agua.   Volcan de Fuego.

minutes for the purpose of observing, towards the
south, the lofty cones of Agua and Fuego whose
graceful outlines were clear and distinct in the
atmosphere of a deep blue tropical sky.   In the forenoon we reached Chimaltenango, which was once a
place of importance but is now becoming deserted.
Beyond this town we followed a track leading to the
village of Comolapa, and had to descend an abrupt

and deep ravine, which crossed that part of the
country. We then rode up a long hill and passed
near several groups of oak trees, whose leafless
branches were made gay by clusters of brilliantly
coloured orchids.

Upon arriving at Comolapa, I obtained a room in
a little inn, where we arranged to remain for the
night, having already accomplished a distance of
nine leagues. The parish priest, Padre Rodriguez,
proposed that I should join him at supper, at which
meal there also appeared a Mexican, travelling on
his way to Guatemala from the frontier, and who was
able to give me some useful intelligence about the
roads and the political state of the country in the
province of Chiapas. The Padre spoke with earnestness about the difficulties he had to overcome
with regard to the teaching of the Catholic doctrines.
He said that there were more than two thousand
Indians under his charge. They attended church as
a custom, and seemed to take part in the services,
yet, he was certain that in their hearts they retained
a faith in their ancient worship, and that they had
shrines concealed amongst the mountains where they
kept their idols. He had also found, by experience,
that there was the greatest repugnance amongst
them to all attempts at education, and no children
would attend school after they were seven or eight
years old.

We looked at the interior of the church. Some
of the wood carvings at the altars were well designed
and executed. Over the western porch there was a
large coat-of-arms, with lions as supporters. In
this district a great number of the Mexican allies,

who accompanied Alvarado in the conquest of Guatemala, were given lands, and many of them, during
the early periods of the Spanish occupation, were
men of considerable wealth ; but their descendants
and their families have now disappeared or have
become merged into the aboriginal population.

On the following morning we proceeded on our
journey to Patinamit. We passed a high mound,
situated near the path, which in shape was like that
of Grave Creek, in Virginia ; but it was not so large.
Its height was about fifty-five feet. Augustin proposed that we should take a short cut, in consequence
of which we lost our way, lengthened the ride by
over two leagues, and had to descend and ascend a
profound and precipitous barranca. On the sides of
the track we saw many ferns, and passed clumps of
mountain firs and other trees belonging naturally to
high altitudes. We were riding over a country at an
average height of seven thousand feet, and following
steep and rough tracks, which tried the prudence of
our sure-footed mules to the utmost. At noon we
reached Tepan Guatemala, and were received at the
convent by Padre Viatoro. The remainder of the
day was passed in examining the ruins of ancient
Patinamit, the chief city of the Kachiquels, a tribe
of the same race as the Quichés.

Patinamit is placed upon the summit of a height
separated from the rest of the world by a steep
ravine, which, except at one narrow point, so completely encircles it as to make it practically a kind
of detached island. The site resembles that of Fort
Ancient, and the earthworks are nearly as large as
those upon that great fortified hill. It is supposed

that the palaces and temples of the Kachiquels were built upon this plateau, but nothing of them can now be traced. There are a few mounds from ten to thirty feet high, and there are several heaps of large loose stones, evidently taken from the ravine. The position must have been exclusively chosen for the purposes of defence, for it is almost impregnable to assault. The surrounding barranca is, in several places, perpendicular for a depth of over two hundred feet. The slopes are composed of a firm volcanic substance, consisting chiefly of pumice, pozzolana, ashes and stones.

It has been stated* that, in Patinamit there was, during the rule of the Kachiquels, a small building, in which was kept a kind of stand formed of a substance resembling glass. The judges sat round this building and heard the causes brought before them. In the ravine below there was a black transparent stone, in looking into which, could be seen the representation of the punishment to be awarded. It was also consulted in time of war. Upon my return to the convent, I asked the padre if he knew anything about this stone, which might have been an unusually large fragment of obsidian, such as would have been found in this region, formed of matter thrown out from the craters of volcanoes. He said that he had never seen it, and did not know whether it still existed. He wished me to understand that he did not take any interest in the past history of the parish, but devoted his attention to

---

* " History of the Kingdom of Guatemala," by Don Domingo Juarros, translated by J. Baily, Lieutenant R.M., pp. 384.

his work amongst the numerous Indians placed under his care.

Upon the morning of our departure, whilst the guide was saddling the mules, I went out to the platform in front of the convent walls, to look at the wide and distant views which it commanded. This outer court was placed well above the ground. On the top of the steps which led up to the platform, stood Padre Viatoro, dressed in his robes, and receiving the homage of his Indian parish-ioners as they passed beneath him on their way to their daily work. I had already become aware that the influence of priests of the Dominican Order was exceptionally great amongst the Indian tribes in the Cordilleras, but I had not hitherto observed the actual evidence of their personal power over the minds of the aboriginal race. The events that were taking place before me, were extremely strange and characteristic. Each of the Indians, as he went by, bowed down towards the earth, and waited to receive a blessing. Several women who had requests to make, knelt and remained in that posture. All of these meek, simple and ignorant natives seemed to look upon their priest as a being of a far superior nature to themselves, and Padre Viatoro by his imperious manner, did not permit them to suppose that he could be approached otherwise than with the greatest respect and deference.

As we proceeded on our journey, I stopped my mule in order to take a final glance at the convent, and saw the tall erect figure of the Dominican sharply defined against the sky, whilst men, women and children were still passing before him. In the far distance were the ranges of the Cordilleras, and close at hand was the great stronghold of the Kachiquel conquerors, who, many centuries earlier, held the ancestors of this submissive race under their subjection and cruel tyranny. It was a scene in all respects so remarkable, that it remains fixed upon the memory.

Our path to the hamlet of Las Godinas led over hills and plains, until we arrived at the edge of a barranca which we had some difficulty in crossing. This great chasm was about one mile wide at the top, and was more than a thousand feet deep ; it crossed the level country for several miles. The sides were almost perpendicular for the first three hundred feet of descent, and then sloped sharply downwards. Our path was narrow and, in the places where it curved round the projecting precipitous banks, looked dangerous, but the mules went forward without hesitation. As it seemed to be unadvisable to attempt to guide my mule, I adopted the plan which I thought to be the most safe, and dropped the bridle over her neck, and she was thus left free to choose the road. I soon found by experience, that complete confidence could be placed in her wise and cautious judgment.

Upon reaching the bottom we rode for some distance up the valley, and then ascended to the level of the plain. After a short ride across the open country we came to another equally steep barranca which had to be crossed. This chasm I estimated to be nearly twelve hundred feet deep. The sides were composed of volcanic ash, pozzolana and blocks of lava. The nature of the violent influ-

ences that must have been at work in the production
of the ravines, which have thus separated these
plateaux has yet to be fully investigated. With
regard to the theory that they were caused by earthquakes, it may be observed that those around Tepan
Guatemala must be approximately twenty miles
from the nearest volcano.

At noon we reached Las Godinas and halted at a
rancho to get breakfast, and to give our mules a feed
of sacate, which is an excellent and nutritious fodder
composed of the stalks of maize. At this hamlet
were assembled a large number of Indians who had
come there from the adjoining highlands. The
men were in many respects like the North American
Indians. They were of a deep copper colour, and
had black hair, and large, well shaped noses, broad
faces and peculiarly long upper lips. Their eyes
were round, black, furtive and restless. They be-
onged to the Kachiquel tribe, and spoke a dialect
of the Quiché language.

After a few hours' rest we proceeded. Suddenly
we opened upon a magnificent view. Two thousand
feet below us was the great Lake of Atitlan, five
thousand feet above the sea. It was a bright, calm,
sunny afternoon, and the still waters, reflecting the
colour of the sky, were as blue as a sapphire. On
the opposite shore, overlooking the lake, was the
Volcano of Atitlan, eleven thousand, eight hundred
feet high, and beyond was a continuous chain of volcanoes stretching westwards towards Quezaltenango.
As we descended the hills the points of view kept
changing. It would be difficult to surpass these
marvellously beautiful combinations of lake and
volcanic mountain scenery.

In the afternoon we reached Panajachel, and after having found a place of shelter for the mules, I asked the way to the house of a lady to whom I had a letter of introduction. The envelope bore the address of Doña Aña Gertrudio Leon de Montalban. I was told that I should find her at home, and that I was to make inquiries at the small grocer's shop in the main street. Accordingly I went to the shop and asked the old woman behind the counter, who was at the time employed in selling tallow candles, if she could kindly tell me where Doña Aña de Montalban was to be found. She said "Señor, permit me to look at the letter," and putting on her spectacles, she gazed at the envelope, opened it and slowly read what was inside. After having grasped the meaning of the writing, she smiled and said—" I am Doña Aña and this letter is written by a very good friend of mine, and Señor, my house is very much at your service; if you will wait for a few minutes until I have closed the shop, I will give you a room, the cook shall prepare a supper this evening, and I hope you will make yourself as comfortable as the poor means at my disposal will permit."

Panajachel was crowded with Indians. It was the day of the festival of the Patron Saint of an adjacent church, and they had all been to there present offerings and light their candles at the shrines. In the evening numerous Indian women dressed in white passed through the village, carrying candles home to place before the altar of their own house idol.

The cura of the district, Padre Pedro, asked me

to join him, after his duties were concluded, and talk about the events of the day. The Padre was evidently a capable and zealous priest. He had the reputation of having studied the character and language of his Indian congregations, and of being acquainted with their habits and traditions. I was therefore glad to have an opportunity of obtaining from such a good authority some well founded information respecting the reports of sacrifices to the lake and volcano.

Father Pedro said that the ancient custom of sacrificing maidens at Atitlan, was also followed at the mountain near Quezaltenango. Whenever the rumbling noises were heard, threatening an eruption, a maiden was offered as a sacrifice to the angry god by throwing her into the crater. There used also to be performed some sacrificial ceremonies connected with the worship of the goddess of the lake, but he did not know what were the customs upon those occasions. The Abbé Brasseur de Bourbourg relates, in his notes of a journey through S. Salvador, that the lake of Xilopango was originally consecrated to the goddess of water, and that in each year, when the maize was about to ripen, four young girls were sacrificed.

It was reported that, in some remote districts, sacrifices were still offered, but this is very doubtful. The Padre observed that the Indians at Panajachel, and in the villages bordering on the lake were excessively superstitious. In their houses or huts they usually had a room or space set apart for the abode of their saint's image. This image would sometimes be carried to the parish church and be left there for a time, and then would be taken back to the house again with ceremonies and lighted candles. I mentioned to the Padre how I had noticed that the Indian women here had a habit of talking together in a low tone. He said this was chiefly owing to the dialect of the Quiché language which was spoken in this district, in which many of the sounds were expressed like a whisper.

At day-break Augustin was at the door with the mules, and my kind hostess prepared for me a cup of chocolate which she said would fortify me for the journey. We then left for Sololá, and soon were watching a glorious sunrise. The lake of Atitlan is irregular in its shape. According to my travelling map it has a circumference exceeding thirty miles. The most remarkable features are its great depth, and the almost perpendicular cliffs on the northern side which seem to be of volcanic formation. The deep blue of its waters is possibly owing to their depth, and the rarefied state of the atmosphere at this altitude. Our road led us through several villages containing chiefly Indian populations, and then we ascended a long and abrupt hill. As the day advanced we were joined by bands of Indians with cargo mules, travelling to the market.

Sololá is the chief town of the Department, and the Corregidor was good enough to add some recommendations to my government letter. We stopped there long enough to rest the mules, and then proceeded on our way to San Tomas, eight leagues distant. Upon reaching the upper slopes of the hill I dismounted, in order to visit some Indian farm buildings that occupied several acres of rising ground near our path. Although there were evidences of what may be called comparative wealth, these Indians—like all others that I had seen—only possessed a single hut with one large room in it. Men, women and lads were all busy ; the boys cleaning and spinning wool for their black ponchos or cloaks, and the women, as usual, engaged in grinding maize and making tortillas.

We followed a steep ascent. The path was cut into broad steps, up which my excellent mule clambered with the utmost ease and rapidity, and in a manner which brought back to the memory many rides amongst the Druse villages in the mountains of the Lebanon. Upon reaching the summit of the sierra, I turned the mule's head round to enable me to look at the lake and the group of volcanoes beyond it. It was then a scene of great beauty, but at some remote period in the world's history, it must have been a centre of great volcanic violence and devastation.

Our track led, in an almost straight direction, over hills and across valleys, maintaining an average altitude of about seven thousand feet. In this region orchids were numerous. On the edge of one of the lofty plateaux overlooking a narrow valley, I stopped to look at and sketch a tall wide-spreading pine, upon whose branches these plants were growing with the utmost luxuriance. The orchids in this part of Guatemala are constant to a certain altitude which, as nearly as can be estimated, is about six thousand five hundred feet. They exclusively prefer to dwell upon the branches of oaks and pines, and always cling to such as are strong and full-grown.

The manner of their habits in selecting the trees upon which they desired to settle, was eccentric. Thus, with respect to the pines, they chose those that had broad, spreading branches, and avoided those whose branches grew upwards. They adopted the same rule with the oaks. In no instance did I see orchids growing upon any trees except oaks and pines ; all others were left bare. But even when the groups seemed to be all well suited for their purpose, they would select certain favourites, and upon the branches of these they would abound, giving life and colour to them, and leaving the neglected trees dark and gloomy by contrast. The majority of the orchids were green, but sometimes they were of a bright rose colour, and these when seen, as we then saw them, clearly defined against a deep blue sky, gave a brilliant colouring to the foreground. They added much to the pleasure of our day's ride. They were gay, capricious and beautiful.

San Tomas stands high and commands wide and extensive views of the sierras. Upon reaching the plateau we rode through the village, and finally stopped at the gate of the convent within whose walls we were received by Padre Hernandez. He afterwards proposed that I should look at his church and the altars.

There was much in the interior that had a special interest, in relation to the obscure subject of the ancient faith of the Quichés, the great tribe that possessed the dominant power in this part of Central America at the time of the Spanish Conquest, and whose descendants are believed to dwell in this

secluded part of the country. There was no religious service taking place or about to be held, and
there was nobody present within or without; but the
nave and chapels were illuminated with numbers of
candles. The church was large and there were several
side altars. In front of each of them rows of lights
had been placed. Down the length of the nave
there was a long thick block of wood in which were
fitted sockets for holding candles. There were also
quantities of offerings placed before each image, or
whatever emblem the Indians chose to worship.

" For in these matters," said the Father," I do not
interfere, and in fact, I have no power or authority
whatever within my own church. The Indians
come and go as they please, light their candles, hold
their own services before the altar, and frequently
take one of the saints out of the church, and carry
it away to some hut where, for several days, they
will perform musical ceremonies before it, and then
the saint will be brought back to its proper altar."

Padre Hernandez, although he had lived many
years with these Indians, had not been able to obtain
the slightest positive knowledge of what they
really believed. All that he knew about the subject
was, that they were very superstitious and devotional. He said that in many cases in the sierras,
they had their places of worship where they kept
idols, and at certain seasons of the year went to
make offerings, and also to sacrifice animals to them.

After a stroll through the village, I went to the
Plaza, in the centre of which were assembled the
Alcaldes and other parish dignitaries. They were
sitting round a wood fire, discussing some urgent

matters of local interest. As I had not hitherto
stopped in a populous district or village entirely
peopled by Indians, and controlled by native
Alcaldes, I decided to join the group. I received
an Indian welcome from these Quichés, by not being
noticed and was given a place in the circle in silence.
I soon became interested in listening to their extremely harsh and guttural language, and in observing
the types of the men, all of whom were Indians of
leading families.

It was a fine night. The new moon was low in
the horizon. The planet Venus was just beneath
it, and immediately above was Jupiter, a rare and
beautiful conjunction, looking bright and sharply defined in the clear atmosphere of this elevated table
land.

When the discussion came to an end I left the
Alcaldes engaged in toasting tortillas over the embers
of the fire, and returned to my host at the convent.
It had been the fate of Padre Hernandez to
have passed the best years of his life in the vain
endeavour to get these Indians to understand the
tenets of his faith, but he had latterly given up, as
useless, all these attempts and left them to follow
their own wills. One great and unexpected difficulty he had found impossible to overcome, in consequence of the imperfection of the Quiché language,
was his inability to convey in equivalent terms the
ideas he wished to explain. He also experienced
another serious hindrance in the execution of his
duties. His parish was extensive and contained
several villages which lie amongst the sierras, remote from each other ; and as the Quiché is an un-

written language, and there are consequently no
grammars or dictionaries to create a fixed standard,
words are forgotten, sometimes their meaning becomes changed or they are differently accented or
applied ; and thus, in the course of time, the dialect
of one village differs from another.

I observed to the Padre, that, on the way from
Sololá, I had noticed that the Indians contrived to
live in an isolated manner. He said this was always
the case with them. They were naturally inclined
to keep much apart. Those who lived amongst the
mountains had their huts at considerable distances
from each other, and the villages maintained but
little communication ; as a natural consequence the
language was always changing. "All these Quichés,"
he said, " are becoming extremely ignorant. They
keep no record of time or events, and do not seem
to take interest in anything except the dull pro-
cedure of their daily lives."

The Padre had found it impossible to feel in any
degree assured, that he understood the private
feelings or political views of these Indians. He considered them to be apparently indifferent to what
was passing around them, and yet capable of being
aroused in a very sudden manner, and of acting
together for some common purpose. Their enthusiasm for anything relating to their superstitious
devotion to the images was however very evident.
One of the things which he thought to be inexplicable, was their extraordinary veneration for the
rite of baptism. They seemed to attach some
peculiar importance to this ceremony, although the
Padre did not think that what was in their minds

had any reference to the Church tenets. In all matters connected with religion, the Indians had become quite independent. They came from afar to make offerings of blossoms and leaves, lighted candles before the altars of those saints they wished to honour, and then silently returned to their huts.

In the morning, before leaving San Tomas, I was interested in observing in the crowded Plaza, some of the characteristics of this once powerful Indian race. The men were of middle size, strongly built and of a swarthy copper colour. Their noses were large and remarkably broad at the base. Their eyes were dark and wild. In features many of them resembled the Sioux. Their voices were loud and the language disagreeably rough. The women had soft voices and were very gentle in their manners. They reminded me of the Coptic women of Lower Egypt, in their method of carrying their pitchers of water. There was the same graceful attitude, and slow and steady walk. What perhaps, added to some extent to the resemblance was the long blue dress, and the little turban-shaped mat placed on the head to receive the pressure of the weight.

CHAPTER XI.

Barrancas.—Santa Cruz del Quiché.—Padre Andres Guicola.—
Ruins of Utatlan.—Report of Don Garcia de Palacio upon
human sacrifices to the gods in Central America, Statement of
Bernal Diaz, about the sacrifices in Mexico.—Burning of the
Quiché Caciques at Utatlan.—Worship of idols by the Quichés.
—Sierras.—Gueguetenango.

THE journey from San Tomas to Santa Cruz del
Quiché was made unexpectedly fatiguing, in consequence of the difficulties placed across our track
by the numerous barrancas which traversed the
plains. Several of these ravines were of considerable depth, and their slopes were abrupt. It was
satisfactory to realize that we were travelling in the
dry season, and the footing for the mules was therefore fairly secure.

Upon our arrival at the village, I rode onwards
to the convent steps where I was met by Padre
Andres Guicola, who was unfeignedly delighted to
see me. He said that he was glad to welcome me,
and talk to somebody who was not an Indian, and
was particularly pleased to hear that I was an
Englishman, for he was a Biscayan, and had been
born and bred near San Sebastian, and had listened
to the traditions concerning the great Duke of
Wellington, and memories, on the part of the ladies,

QUICHÉ INDIAN.

(HOLDING THE OFFICE OF ALGUAZIL.)

of the brave officers of his army. It added much to
the pleasure he felt in receiving me, to know that his
guest was the son of one of those officers, who had
not only been present at the operations in Biscay and
on the French frontier, but was also severely
wounded at Albuera, a battle held in great respect
by all patriotic Spaniards.

His isolation amongst these secluded mountains,
must have been repugnant to the nature of this kind
hearted and genial padre. He told me that he had
been living in his parish twenty-one years, having
been appointed in 1849, and during that long time
regularly fulfilled his duties amongst his Indians.
He declared, in answer to some questions that I
asked with reference to the adjacent ruins of Utatlan, that he knew but little except from what he
had read in the history of Juarros. The friars of
the convent wrote some observations about them,
and also possessed some documents relating to the
ancient customs of the Quichés, but these were destroyed during the revolution of 1829, when the
churches and convents were sacked. Consequently
no records existed.

The view from the Convent was magnificent,
commanding towards the north-west the ranges of
the Cordilleras, and towards the south-west the
hills near Quezaltenango. The lofty plateau upon
which it stood, was nearly seven thousand feet
above the sea. It is upon three sides severed from
the outer world by a steep barranca which almost
surrounds it. The ruins of Utatlan, the ancient
capital of the Quichés, were about one mile distant,
and were evidently placed in such a manner as to

take the greatest advantage of this ravine, in order
to form a stronghold, which according to the conditions of Indian warfare must have been practically
impregnable.

After having obtained some local information
respecting the structures that I wished to examine,
I crossed the plain and entered this fortress, which
once held the reputation of being one of the greatest
of the Indian cities. I was prepared to see much
that would be of the highest interest, because no
change had taken place within its walls since the
time when it was destroyed by Alvarado, in 1524.
The site has never since that period been occupied
or in any way disturbed. Upon making a slight
preliminary survey of the position, it was evident
that it had been chosen for a fortified inclosure, in
the same manner and for the same purpose as
Patinamit. Both fortresses resembled in their character the defensive encampment of Fort Ancient in
Ohio.

Utatlan is, with the exception of its narrow
approach, surrounded by ravines. In consequence
of the ground being thus confined, the original
extent of the city can be easily ascertained, and it is
therefore indisputable that the population maintained
within the ramparts could never have been numerous. It is however observable that it must have
contained buildings, temples, and sacrificial altars of
considerable magnitude. The sites of many of these
were still apparent and their ground plans could be
traced. Portions of the walls were also standing.
Parts of the altars were covered with a strong thick
cement.

After having walked round the exterior of the fortress, I made a series of measurements of the spaces covered by the courts of those structures which were supposed to have been temples or places set apart for the purposes of religion and instruction. I observed that some of the ground plans were similar in their proportions to those that I had noticed within some ancient earthworks near the modern city of Guatemala.

The pyramidal altars or Teocalli had, in their forms and constructions, their platforms and places for idols, many points of resemblance with others that were known to have existed in Mexico.

The rectangular courts in front of the altars, were possibly the quadrangles within which the ceremonies connected with human sacrifices were performed. Nothing is absolutely known with respect to the sacrificial customs of the Quichés, and the allusions to them in the Quiché manuscripts are not definite. It is, therefore, fortunate that there exists a statement made to the King of Spain in the year 1576, upon the condition of the country and the customs of the Indians in the districts presided over by the government of Guatemala, which describes in considerable detail what happened amongst the Chontal and Pipil Indians dwelling in the south-eastern parts of the province. It was made by the licentiate Don Garcia de Palacio, and with respect to the subject of these human sacrifices, there has been nothing written which gives so full and evidently accurate an account of those remarkable ceremonies. The Report is so valuable and instructive, that it is desirable to quote what immediately relates to them. Palacio, after describing the country near lake Uxaca, says :—

" Three leagues from this is the village of Micla, where anciently the Pipiles Indians of this district performed great devotions, and came to offer their gifts and hold their sacrifices ; as likewise did the Chontales and other adjacent Indians of differing languages. They had in their sacrifices some particularities different from other places, and had *Kues* and *teupas* of great authority, of which there are yet large signs and indications.

" Besides the Cacique and usual chief, they had a Pá-pa* whom they called *Tecti*, who was dressed in a long blue robe and wore on the head a diadem, and sometimes a mitre worked in different colours, and at the top of this a bunch of very fine feathers, from some birds that there are in this country, which they call Quetzales.¶

" He commonly carried in his hand a staff like a bishop, and all obeyed him in whatever related to spiritual matters. Next to him, the second place in the priesthood was held by another who was called *tehu a matlini* who was the chief wizard and most learned in their books and arts, and who declared the auguries and made prognostications.

---

*Bernal Diaz states that " Pá-pa," was the name given by the Indians in Yucatan to their chief-priests. The Spaniards were much surprised to find upon their arrival in America, that the Indian chief-priests were called by the same name as the Pope of Rome. " Kues" were temples or altars.

¶ Quetzales are birds with bright green plumage, having their tail feathers of great length, and are found chiefly in the highlands of Guatemala.

" There were, besides these, four priests who were called *teu pixqui* dressed in different colours, and with robes down to their feet, black, green, red and yellow ; and these were of the council in the matters of their ceremonies, and were those who assisted in all the superstitions and follies of their heathenism.*

" There was also a majordomo who had the charge of the jewels and ornaments of the sacrifices, and who took out the hearts of those that were sacrificed, and performed the other personal things that were necessary ; and besides there were others who had trumpets and heathen instruments to convoke and call together the people to the sacrifices that were going to take place."

Palacio states that the rising sun was worshipped and that there were two idols, one representing a man named Quetzalcoatl and the other a woman named Itzqueye and that to these all the sacrifices were made. There were two special ceremonies which took place, one at the commencement of the winter and the other at the beginning of the summer, when two boys between the ages of six and twelve were sacrificed. Palacio then describes the sacrificial customs in war :—

" The high priest, the learned wizard, and the four priests met together, and ascertained by their

---

* Palacio's Report was published for the first time in the original Spanish by Mr. E G. Squier, in 1860. As it is important that the author's meaning should not be misunderstood, I have translated it literally, as far as this is possible, considering that it is written in the Spanish of the 16th century.

sortileges and witchcrafts whether they should have war or if any one was coming against them, and if the sortileges said yes, they called the Cacique and captains of war, and told them how the enemies were coming, and where they should go to make war.

"The Cacique summoned all his warriors, and went out in search of the enemies, and if they gained the victory in the battle, the Cacique dispatched a messenger to the high priest, and informed him upon what day he had succeeded, and the sage examined unto whom the sacrifice should be made. If it was to Quetzalcoatl the ceremonies lasted fifteen days, and upon each day one of the Indians of those that had been captured in the battle was sacrificed ; and if it was to Itzqueye the ceremonies lasted five days, and upon each day an Indian was sacrificed.

"The sacrifice was performed in this manner. All those who had been in the war came in order singing and dancing, and they brought those that they had to sacrifice, with many feathers and *chalchivetes*** on their feet and hands, and with strings of cacao upon their neck, and the captains conducted them in their midst. The high priest and priests together with the people went out to receive them with dances and music, and the caciques and captains presented to the high priest these Indians for the sacrifices, and then they all went together to the court of their *teupa*, and they danced all the above said days and nights.

---

* Carved and polished ornaments made of hard stone of green colour.

" In the middle of the court they placed a stone like a bench, and upon this they placed the Indian that was to be sacrificed, and the four priests held the Indian by the hands and feet. The majordomo then came out with many feathers and covered with bells, with a stone razor in his hand, and opened the breast and pulled out the heart, and when he had taken it out he threw it upwards towards each of the four cardinal points, and the fifth time he threw it in the middle of the court directly upwards, thus declaring and giving to the god the reward for the victory. This sacrifice was made in public, so that every one both small and great could see it."

It is interesting to turn from the customs described as occurring in the remote town of Micla, to the events that happened in the city of Mexico, several hundreds of leagues distant. It was late in the afternoon of a summer's day, in the year 1521. The Spaniards had been repulsed in one of their most important attacks on the enemy, and had been driven back over the causeway after suffering serious losses; Cortes was wounded, and sixty Spaniards had been captured, together with many of their Indian allies. In accordance with the Aztec superstitious rites, these captives were at once conveyed to the Teocalli of the war gods.

Bernal Diaz, who had taken a prominent part in the battle, states that " during the retreat, they frequently heard the great drum resounding with a deep and dismal noise." At last the Spanish troops reached a place of comparative safety, where they were secure from the enemy's attacks, and out of reach of stones and arrows, and then, Diaz says,

"Sandoval and Francisco de Lugo, and Andres de Tapia with Pedro de Alvarado, were each relating what had happened and what orders Cortes had given, when the drum of Huitzopotli again began to sound, together with kettledrums, shell horns and other instruments like trumpets, and these sounds were horrible and dismal, and we looked at the summit of the highest Kue, and we saw our companions who had been captured in the rout, and that they were being carried up by force, and with blows and thrusts, and being taken violently to be sacrificed, and when they had reached the top at a place where was the shrine in which were the accursed idols, we saw that many of them had feathers put upon their heads, others were made to dance before Huitzopotli, and after they had danced they were thrown on their backs on the top of the sacrificial stone, and then they cut open their breasts with flint knives, and pulled out their beating hearts and offered them to the idols that were in that place. The bodies and feet were thrown down the steps below, where other Indian butchers were waiting, and who cut off their arms and legs, and then flayed the skin from their faces, and tanned them like glove skins with the beards on, and kept them to show at their festivals and when they had their drunken feasts. In this manner were all sacrificed; they devoured the legs and arms, and the hearts and blood were offered to the idols.* These cruelties

---

*Diaz observes that Guatimozin—who, after the death of Montezuma had become the Emperor of the Mexicans—sent the hands and feet of the Spaniards that had been sacrificed, together with

were seen by the whole camp, and by Pedro de Alvarado, and Gonzalo de Sandoval, and all the captains, and we said amongst ourselves, thank God that I was not carried off to-day to be sacrificed."*

In the whole range of American history, there is nothing which more vividly strikes the imagination than the scenes described by the Spanish conquerors during the siege of Mexico. The human sacrifices and the subsequent cannibalism, represent the most revolting acts of superstition that have ever disgraced human nature.

It is strange that, although so much has been recorded of the Aztecs and their customs, no clear

---

the heads of the horses that had been killed, to the Indian chiefs who had formed a league of alliance with Cortes, and sent them messages to the effect, that the remaining Spaniards would soon be conquered, and that consequently those chiefs should submit to the Aztec power and send ambassadors to him. In the meantime, human sacrifices took place daily in the great temple, accompanied by the dismal sound of the drum, the discordant noises of the shell trumpets, and the horrible shouts and yells of the Mexicans. During the night large fires were kept burning on the platform, and on each night several Spaniards were sacrificed.

These ceremonies lasted for ten days, until all the captives had been sacrificed ; and during this time the Mexicans made frequent and furious attacks upon the troops. Diaz relates, that the Indian soldiers told them that they were wretched creatures who would soon be all killed, and that their flesh was disagreeable to taste and bad to eat. " Vuestras carnes son tan malas para comer."

The last Spaniard who was sacrificed was Christobal de Guzman.

*Bernal Diaz, Historia Verdadera, chap. clii.

account has been given of the shape and dimensions of their Teocallis within the city of Mexico. We have only very doubtful representations given of them. Taking these as the best available guides it is evident that the altars in Utatlan were built upon similar principles, following upon a smaller scale the same general structural plan and proportions. Utatlan was considered as one of the most important places in Central America. According to the historian Juarros, it held a rank only second to the capital of the Aztecs.

Alvarado conquered the city in April, 1524, and he states in his official Report to Cortes, that in consequence of the natural strength of the place, and the depth of the ravines which prevented a general action, he had decided to destroy it. He gave directions to burn the chief caciques alive, to set fire to the town and completely reduce it to ruins, for it was so strong and dangerous, that it was more like a stronghold of bandits than a town of citizens.*

A curious circumstance is mentioned by him as happening during his march against Utatlan. On the way, and near some rising ground, he saw the Indians sacrifice a woman and a dog, and he says that his interpreters told him that this act meant defiance. This statement is remarkable because it has always been supposed that dogs were not found amongst the Mexicans. Bernal Diaz observes that

---

* First Report of Pedro de Alvarado to Cortes, dated Utatlan, 11th April, 1524.

these dogs were of small size, that they were used for food, and did not bark.

Before leaving Utatlan, Alvarado placed in office as chief of the Quichés, an Indian named Sequechul, who was according to the laws of that race the next in succession. From this time nothing more was known of the Quichés, until the licentiate Alonzo de Zurita, passed this way about the year 1554, in the execution of the duty assigned to him by the command of the king, to report upon the condition

Approach to Utatlan from the plain.
Height of mound is about 30 feet.

and customs of the Indians, both before and after the conquest. Zurita was informed that, before the conquest, the Quichés had three chiefs. The first had over his seat or throne three canopies of feathers, the second two, and the third one. He says that the city had at one time contained several kues, (small pyramidal altars) dedicated to idols, but that they were then in ruins, and the successors of the caciques were in the utmost poverty.

I passed over the ground where Alvarado's camp
had been pitched, and where the caciques were sen-
tenced to be burnt. Certainly the sixteenth century
witnessed most extraordinary scenes of cruelty and
carnage in this unhappy country. At this distance
of time it is difficult to understand what could have
been the reasons which impelled the Spaniards to
burn the Indians in such numbers. Many of them
were consigned to the flames for disobedience to
orders, others upon suspicion of treasonable designs
against the conquerors, others for being discovered
worshipping their ancient gods, or for not conform-
ing to the new religion. Perhaps the most inexplicable of all these cruelties is what happened soon
after the conquest of the city of Mexico. Cortes,
upon his return there after his expedition to Honduras, heard that during his absence, there had been
a rising of Indians in one of the distant provinces, a
sort of local rebellion which had been suppressed.
Upon his making inquiries as to the cause of this
disaffection, the principal inhabitants of the province
came and reported to him that the Spaniards under
whom they had been placed had burnt alive eight of
their principal chiefs, five of whom died on the spot,
and the remaining three a few days afterwards, and
although they had demanded reparation and justice
it had not been granted to them.*

Later in the century all the penalties of the In-
quisition were established, but it was found that the
results of these acts to enforce the Spanish rule, and

---

* See the 5th letter of Cortes, to the Emperor Charles V.

to convert the Indians were unsatisfactory. The
Indians fled to the hills and forests, and would not
obey the orders to form communities or villages and
thus be exposed to such cruelties. Finally the
punishment of burning alive was abolished, and the
milder punishment of whipping at the post was introduced and has remained. It is at the present
time the customary method of punishing the natives
for any default or misconduct.

In considering this subject of the treatment of the
Indians at the time of the conquest, due weight has
to be given to the influence of the priests, their
enthusiasm, and their intense desire to convert the
natives by persuasion or by force. The well known
inveterate hatred of the Indians towards their conquerors, a hatred which still exists, was a dangerous
element always present and to be guarded against
by adopting severe measures of repression. The
good fortune that had attended the operations of
Cortes and his handful of Spaniards in the conquest
of this region, was doubtless in a great measure due
to the condition of the country, and the never ceasing
tribal wars. Cortes and his generals were consequently always able to obtain the assistance of
numerous allies who were glad to seize any opportunity of destroying their enemies. But when the
conquest was completed and the Spaniards had the
lands distributed amongst them, and the system of
encomiendas was adopted, it became necessary, at
all hazards, to prevent any combinations of Indians
against them, and to put down or crush out with
unmerciful firmness the slightest tendency to rebel
against the iron and cruel rule under which they

found themselves to be subjected. Many risings
were quelled, all tendency to insubordination was
punished, and the Indians remained under control.
But this result was only obtained after these unfortunate tribes had been subjected to the most
astonishing severities that have ever been inflicted
by a civilised race of conquerors.

At the convent at Santa Cruz, Padre Guicola
spoke much about his parishioners. He said that
he was impressed with the conviction that the
Quichés in many respects still followed their old
idolatries, and worshipped their idols secretly. He
thought that he had discovered that certain Indians
were " sacerdotes " to these idols, and that in some
manner which he had not been able to find out,
they, amongst themselves, maintained their ancient
priesthood.

The accommodation for strangers was more monastic than I had expected to find. My cell contained
nothing but a wide hard board placed upon four
legs, and there were neither hooks nor posts to
which I could hang my hammock, consequently it
was not practicable to make convenient arrangements for securing comfortable quarters at night.

Before my departure I had a conversation with
the Padre about the history of the convent, and the
work that used to be carried out by the monks.
Some of the descendants of the caciques of Utatlan
were educated by them, and the traditions of the
origin and migrations of the Quichés were composed
by them, whilst they were still capable of remem-
bering what had been related concerning their
early history. The most important of the manu-

scripts is stated to have been written in 1544, by the
son of one of the Quiché caciques, who took part in
the operations of war at the time of the arrival of the
Spaniards. The Padre was not well acquainted with
the subject of the past history of his convent, and
like the other priests that I had met in the Indian
parishes, his attention was almost exclusively directed to his duties, one of the most significant of
which, in the opinion of his Indians, was the performance of the rite of baptism.

I asked him what was the best track to follow in
crossing the sierras, and he made inquiries for me.
Several of the inhabitants of the village said, that
in the remote parts of the hills I wished to cross,
the paths were not well known, and might be found
to be impracticable, and there was the danger of
meeting scattered bands of rebels. Augustin however informed me, that he had learnt from several of
the natives, in whom he could place confidence, that
we need not expect to meet with any serious difficulties, and that in the event of being uncertain
about the right direction, we might rely upon coming
across Indians who would guide us. My large
Government map was of no use in the matter, as
nothing was marked upon it except ranges of mountains. Meanwhile to guard ourselves against possible
trouble, I gave directions that we should take with
us a sufficient supply of food for ourselves and the
mules, and thus we started upon our road, without
feeling any hesitation with regard to our future
proceedings.

In the forenoon we came to a halt amongst the
mountains, and Augustin, who was proficient in his

knowledge of making a fire out of the most scanty materials, prepared breakfast. Whilst we were thus engaged we were passed by numbers of Indians carrying goods and provisions. Young and old were hurrying rapidly forward, urged by some impulse which we were unable to comprehend, towards a destination which was to us unknown. They looked wild and restless, and when addressed were shy and reserved. In the evening before sunset we arrived at some farm buildings, and I slung my hammock to the rafters of a deserted, half-ruined shed. Augustin obtained from an adjoining hut some tortillas, frijoles* and eggs, the three chief elements of Indian domestic existence, and with these, together with a good supply of sacate for the mules, we made ourselves at home in the Cordilleras.

In accordance with a custom that I usually adopted whenever it was possible, I established friendly relations with an Indian family in the neighbourhood in order to obtain some knowledge of their language or dialect. I had a list of words in Spanish to which I obtained the local equivalents. In this manner I made a small vocabulary of the dialects spoken by the Indians amongst the Altos near Guatemala, by the Quichés at Santa Cruz and San Tomas, by the Kachiquels near Las Godinas, and by the tribe near Patinamit. This custom was not only useful in helping me to understand the various links or differences in the tribes that we met, but it was also a means of

---

* Small black beans.

bringing about a small degree of friendliness, and
of overcoming that very decided unsociability which
forms such an integral part of the Indian nature.

At sunrise we were in our saddles, and soon found
ourselves to be riding over a difficult and rugged
country. The hills were steep, and the mule tracks,
in many places, almost impassable. In the afternoon we crossed a high mountain ridge. and
then descended towards the Indian hamlet of San
Lorenzo, and pushed on as fast as possible, in order
to reach Gueguetenango before the night. On our
arrival, we rode up to the convent gate, where I
was welcomed by Padre Juan Batista de Terran.
He was in a highly disturbed and irritated state of
mind. His convent had been battered and almost
destroyed by the artillery of the Indian rebels, commanded by Cruz, and his church was filled with
soldiers who had been quartered there, and were
eating and drinking, gambling, and leading wild
and irreverent lives within the shrines.

On the following day I called upon the Corregidor
and obtained a passport for Augustin, and then sent
him and the baggage mule back to Guatemala. He
had faithfully performed his duties as guide and
attendant, and had been careful in looking after the
wants of the mules, often taking great trouble in
finding for them a proper supply of forage wherever
we were quartered in the night. But he had not
expected to meet with such rough tracks as we had
passed over amongst the sierras and down the barrancas, and was glad to be able to return by more
secure and better known roads.

The inhabitants of Gueguetenango, at the time of

our arrival, were in an excited and disorganised condition. They had not recovered from the alarm
caused by the recent events of the rebellion. The
Plaza was crowded with wild looking Indians, and
throughout the town there was an unusual movement of armed men. My chief preoccupation was
the search of a trustworthy guide, which was a
matter for considerable difficulty. Finally I succeeded
in securing the services of an Indian belonging to a
local tribe of the Mams. He bore the name of
Carlos, and spoke Spanish sufficiently well to enable
me to keep up a tolerably intelligible conversation
with him.

I now thought it advisable to make some changes
with regard to the manner of travelling. Hitherto
I had managed very well with Augustin and one
spare mule. The mule carried in the saddle bags,
provisions for several days, together with a change
of clothing in case of wet weather, but experience
had shown me that it would be better to reduce
the weights to what could easily be carried by an
Indian in his pack, and who, at the same time,
could act as guide. I should thus avoid the risk of
being detained by any accident happening to the
cargo mule. My own good mule carried nothing
but its rider, and a great coat and hammock, rolled
up in military fashion, and strapped over the pommel
of the saddle.

Everything being satisfactorily arranged, Carlos
appeared at the convent steps at daybreak with his
pack duly placed over his shoulders, and carried by
the head band. Into this were put two days' provisions, and part of the change of clothing. My

mule carried the halter wound round her neck. A
small supply of fodder was added to the Indian's
load, and thus we started. Carlos took the lead by
breaking into a quick, rapid pace, or steady Indian
run. The mule followed at her best speed, and
before the sun had risen above the summits of the
Cordilleras, we were well forward on our way towards Jacaltenango and the Mexican frontier.

————

Gueguetenango, the chief city of the Department, was a place
of importance before the conquest. It was the capital of the
Mams, a warlike tribe, whose caciques and principal families
were of the same race as the Quichés. They were conquered
and reduced to submission by the Spaniards in 1525. There are
certain circumstances respecting that campaign and the methods
of defence adopted by the Mams, which should receive particular
attention in connection with the theories and Indian traditions,
respecting the migrations of the mysterious tribe who have been
named the Toltecs, and who appear to have been the predecessors of the Aztecs. There are, in the accounts of the campaign several details which are valuable, as leading to the conclusion that the Mams, Quichés and Kachiquels, whose leaders
were all of the same race, pursued systems of defensive warfare,
which had analogies with the habits of the tribes who raised
the fortified hill works in Ohio.

When it was decided by Alvarado to attack the Mams, a force
suitable for the purpose was organized. It consisted of a main
body of Mexican Indian allies who were supported by a small
force of Spanish cavalry and infantry ; there were three hundred
Indians carrying spades and hatchets acting as pioneers, and
many others who were employed in the work of transport. After
an engagement with the Mams, who were defeated, the attacking
forces advanced to * Gueguetenango. Upon their arrival at that
place the Spanish General was informed that the Mams had retreated to their fortress of Socoleo. The position of this

———

* Juarros, Baily's Translation, p. 457.

entrenched camp was so strong, that it was not possible to capture it by direct assault, and the Spaniards in the end reduced the Indians to surrender by famine.

The historian Fuentes who is stated to have personally examined this fortress about the year 1695, reported (according to Juarros) that the approach "was by only one entrance and that was so narrow as scarcely to permit a horseman to pass it; from the entrance, there ran on the right hand a parapet, raised on the berm of the fosse, extending along nearly the whole of that side; several vestiges of the counter-scarp and curtain of the walls still remain, besides parts of other works, the use of which cannot now be easily discovered; in a court-yard there stood some large columns, upon the capitals of which were placed quantities of pine wood, that being set on fire, gave light at night to the surrounding neighbourhood. The citadel or lofty cavalier of this great fortification was in the form of a square, graduated pyramid, rising twelve or fourteen yards from the base to the platform on the top, which was sufficient to admit of ten soldiers standing on each side; the next step would accommodate a greater number, and the dimensions proportionably increased to the last or twenty-eighth step. The steps were intersected in unequal portions by parapets and curtains, rendering the ascent to the top so extremely difficult, that Fuentes says, he attempted several times to reach the platform, but was unable to perform the task, until his Indian interpreter acted as his guide and conducted him to the summit. The ruins of several buildings were then in existence; they appeared to have been intended as quarters for the soldiers; were extremely well arranged, and distributed with due regard to proportion. Between each three or four of these buildings there was a square court-yard paved with slabs made of stiff clay, lime, and sand; every part of the fortress was constructed of hewn stone, in pieces of great size, as one which had been displaced, measured three yards in length, by one in breadth."......" As the place was circumvallated by a deep ravine, there was no way by which the walls could be approached."

From the above description of Socoleo it is made clear that its construction and position were in accordance with the principles and objects which governed the selection of the strongholds at Patinamit and Utatlan. The pyramidal structure called the citadel must have closely resembled the Resguardo which guarded the entrance into the Quiché fortress.

It is of importance to note that the account given by Fuentes of Socoleo, establishes to a great extent, the accuracy of certain portions of the manuscripts composed by the young Quiché caciques which relate to the traditions of the migrations of the Quichés from Mexico, and the manner in which they divided into separate governments the countries which they had conquered, under the names of Quiché, Kachiquel, Mam and Zutugil. With regard to the three first-named divisions the methods adopted to secure their domination, were so identical, that there can be no doubt that the statements recorded in the manuscripts, so far as they relate to the historical accounts of the Quichés after their arrival in Central America, may be assumed to be trustworthy records of the Indian traditions.

According to the dispatches of the Spanish conqueror Alvarado, he found that the Quichés inhabited the town of Quezaltenango, and it was after the decisive battle fought near that place, that they retreated to their entrenchments at Utatlan; thus adopting the same tactics as were afterwards followed by the Mams, who fought their chief battle near Gueguetenango and then after their defeat fled to Socoleo. This custom of the Quichés appears to be similar to that of the Mound Builders in Ohio, who established their fortified camps in positions which were naturally nearly impregnable or most difficult to approach, and it is such as would be considered advisable by the chiefs of tribes who hold their territories by conquest, and would therefore endeavour to maintain their power by having large entrenched encampments, within which they would be secured from danger in the event of being unable to meet their enemies on the plains.

CHAPTER XII.

On our way to Jacaltenango we had to cross the
Sierra Madre, a range of mountains which traverses
the centre of Guatemala. The mule track led us
over some steep and rugged ascents, and through
a long and deep barranca filled with a cold damp mist.
During the greater part of the day we were enveloped in clouds which covered the summits of the
hills. We finally reached the hamlet of Todos Santos, and obtained shelter at an Indian rancho.

Towards night-fall we heard the distant bell of
the chapel ringing for evening prayer.* The Indians

---

* In Guatemala this prayer is called La Oracion.

This custom is familiar to those who have travelled upon the
Italian coasts, or who have visited the western parts of Brittany
near Carnac and in the Morbihan, where the faith of the peasants
still remains strong.

The Indians living amongst the hills frequently assemble in

BARRANCA, CENTRAL AMERICA.

INDIAN HUTS.

stood in front of their huts, and looking in the direction of the sound of the bell, recited the Ave Maria. This is one of the religious customs taught by the Spanish friars that retains its influence upon the inhabitants of these remote highlands.

Darkness rapidly succeeds daylight in tropical latitudes, and upon my return to the rancho I observed that the hut was lighted by a method mentioned by the early historians of the conquest as having been in universal use amongst the Mexican Indians. In the centre of the room was a rude wooden stand, upon which was placed crosswise, a lighted piece of resinous pinewood. The flame gave a sufficient light for all practical purposes. After turning into my hammock, I watched by the fitful glare of the firebrand, the domestic habits of the Indians. The first thing done, was to put the child to bed, and this was managed in the following manner :—The mother wrapped the child tightly in swaddling clothes, until it looked like a mummy. The head was left exposed. It was then fastened upon a flat board about three feet high and eighteen inches wide. This board was put upright against an angle of the wall. The child remained throughout the night perfectly quiet. The bed upon which the

---

considerable numbers, and, kneeling on the ground, worship outside the doors of their churches ; and there is a singular resemblance in the manner of their devotion to what is to be seen at the " Pardons " of the Bretons, where the peasants come from long distances, light their candles, and kneel before the church door, the line of the worshippers often extending beyond the precincts of the churchyard.

father and mother slept, was a low wide frame resting on four legs, and raised a few inches above the ground. Everything was of the rudest simplicity. The smoke from the fire rose directly upwards and escaped through the roof.

In the morning, while Carlos was making a cup of chocolate, the Indian came to my side and said that he wished to ask me a question about the people who lived beneath the earth (abaxo). He had been told, that men like ourselves were living and moving about below us, and he could not understand how this was possible. I endeavoured to explain to him that the world was round, and that on the other side of the earth beneath, things were much the same as at Todos Santos. My attempts to teach the laws of gravitation were, however, not successful, and he went away in a state of bewilderment, probably under the impression that the people below were upside down.

After leaving the hamlet, we passed by the little church whose bell we had heard upon the previous night. The door was closed, and I noticed that it was charred by burning and blackened by smoke. I was told that this remote church was frequently closed during the time that the priest was away in other parts of the district, and when the Indians came here, they stuck lighted candles upon the door as nearly as possible in the direction of the image to which they wished to make their offerings. The church door was consequently deeply marked by the flames. Here, as also before the closed doors of other chapels in the mountains, the Indians have the custom of raising a temporary altar outside,

before which they place offerings, and sit patiently
in silence for many hours. They then fill a brazier
with chips of resinous wood, and light their candles
and the brazier and go away to their huts, leaving
the incense burning. This is possibly a survival of
the ancient usage of burning copal incense before
their idols.

During the forenoon we went over several steep
ranges of hills, and down very abrupt descents until
we arrived at the village of St. Martin, when we
stopped at a deserted shed, and Carlos proposed
that he should get ready the breakfast. It was
always a pleasure to watch an Indian lighting a fire.
His materials are usually a few dry sticks, some
leaves, a flint, a steel, and a roll of prepared cotton,
which, when slightly burnt, easily catches fire from
the sparks of the flint. There was often, however,
a difficulty in getting the fuel to burst into a flame,
and the steady persistent patience of Indians in
doing this is extraordinary. It was a great comfort
in riding amongst the sierras, to have always the
power of making a fire. It was of still greater
importance to carry your own bed.

Each morning when starting upon a journey over
an unknown country, with much uncertainty as to
where quarters would be found for the night, there
was a sense of satisfaction in seeing placed upon the
pommel of the saddle the hammock in which you
intended to sleep. It gave freedom from all anxiety
with regard to the future. There was no cause to
feel any doubts respecting the beds at a Spanish
posada, or the rough interior of an Indian hut, and
there was always the prospect of obtaining, after

the fatigues of the day, a good night's rest.   In thus
travelling and having at hand sufficient provisions
and fuel to guard against being by any accident in
want amongst these mountainous regions, there
was a feeling of independence which was very exhilarating.   This kind of gipsy, Bohemian life was
singularly attractive, and the small element of risk
from the possibility of meeting hostile Indians was
too slight to have any influence upon the mind.
There was a certain degree of solitude in thus
riding without a companion, as the guide ran several
hundred yards ahead, but this was not much felt, for
there was a never ending change of scene, and every
hour brought something new and unexpected.

In the evening as we descended the slopes of the
valleys, we met numbers of Indians carrying
heavy loads on their backs.   I had noticed when
riding amongst the higher parts of these hills that
crosses were placed upon all remarkable positions,
and at the corners where paths branched off
towards the hamlets.   When passing these crosses
the men invariably took off their broad straw hats,
and showed by their manner great respect.

I was surprised at observing in the valleys that
the Indians suffered much from goitre.   This un-
sightly growth seemed chiefly to affect the women.
It was the same in size and appearance as that
which exists amongst the inhabitants of several of
the secluded valleys in Switzerland.

At intervals during the afternoon we heard the
distant sound of the beating of a drum calling the
attention of the Indians for some purpose which
we did not then understand.   When we drew near

to Jacaltenango we became aware that something was occurring which caused considerable excitement amongst the people. We passed an open space at the entrance of the pueblo, upon which had been built, temporarily, a "Santo" house. It was a small round hut, within which was an image, which had been removed from the church and placed there, in order that it should receive special honour and devotion. Before this shrine a dance was taking place. It represented incidents of the wars between the Spanish Christians and the Moors during the period when the latter were finally driven out of Spain. A little beyond the "Santo" house was the church where an Indian festival was in progress, and an orchestra was busily engaged within, performing a musical service. I stopped for a few minutes to look at the strange and fantastical scene, and the groups of swarthy, wild looking Indians, and then rode on to the convent, where we were welcomed by Padre Juan Chrysostemos Robles. My guide Carlos went away to join in the festivities of his tribe.

In the morning an Indian passed rapidly through the village beating a small drum, and later in the day, a large crowd of Indians assembled in the square in front of the church. It thus became known that an important meeting was to be held in order to bring about a settlement of some difficulty or disagreement between two hamlets, with respect to the buying and selling of lands. About three hundred of the men, chiefly interested, gathered together. The speaking began in tones so harsh that it was almost inconceivable that human language could have developed into such rough and grating sounds.

These Mams were men of strong and muscular frames, compact and well made, but they were all short in stature. Their general appearance was wild and they had a restless manner. They came from the adjacent hills, and it was noticeable with them as with other Indians I had seen in the mountains, that they were darker than those living on the plains. The meeting lasted for about an hour, and as soon as the business was ended they immediately left Jacaltenango and returned to their homes. I was told that the matter in dispute had been settled to the satisfaction of all present, and that there was no longer any fear of local disturbances.

Meanwhile the numerous orchestral services within the church were still proceeding. It was a curious scene. The chief instrument was a large wooden marimba made on the principle of short and long sounding boards, the upper notes of which were played by the leading performers, whilst three other men kept up a continuous accompaniment on the bass. It was evidently an improvement upon the African marimba which had probably been introduced into America by the negro slaves. There were also violins and several rudely constructed guitars. The musical ceremonies were performed before the altars, the Indian congregation maintaining a complete silence. Not the least strange part of the function was the fact that Padre Robles was an unconcerned spectator, although it was his church that was occupied by the Indians and his

" Santos " that were being carried about and worshipped, and to whom offerings were made.

Although the music was noisy and monotonous,
the players seemed to have a correct knowledge
of harmony. The Padre explained how this happened. He said that this comparative knowledge
of music was obtained in consequence of the teaching of the friars before the dissolution of the
monasteries. These friars devoted much of their
time to the education of a certain number of Indian
lads in orchestral music, in order to train them to
take part in the church services, and he supposed
that the instruction then given was kept up in some
way which he did not understand, and that young
Indians were taught in their villages for this work.
He thought that the preparations for the church
festivals and for the dances were also arranged in a
similar manner.

In the afternoon we went to the entrance of one of
the valleys, as the Padre wished to show me the position of an Indian *"adoratorio"** situated on the side
of a steep mountain. He said he had not seen it, but
had been told by his Indians what occurred there.
An idol, held in much reverence by the Mams had
its shrine inside, and the Alcaldes' charged with the
duties of the religious rites and other ceremonies
relating to Indian sacerdotalism, visited it at certain
seasons of the year and offered sacrifices to it. The
idol had also days for the performance of penances,

---

*A name given by Spanish priests to the ancient temples and
shrines of the Indians.

and there was one special day when there was a solemn feast, and turkeys were killed and eaten with peculiar observances, and the blood of the turkeys was sprinkled and offered in a manner unknown to him.

After passing through the place where the "Santo" house was erected, and before which dances and other ceremonies were still going on, we returned to the convent.

Soon after sunset an event occurred which proved that a disturbance had taken place in the interior of the earth. We were sitting inside the precincts when we were alarmed by, what was to me, a quite unknown rumbling sound amongst the adjacent mountains. At first I thought that it was caused by distant thunder reverberating amongst the valleys, but it was soon evident that the sounds were of an entirely different character.

The Padre, who was listening attentively to the noise, said, after a few moments' pause, that it was a "Temblor" or trembling of the earth below, and that it was quite different from a "Terra Moto" or earthquake, as it never caused any harm, although it was considered to be a warning. According to my map, the nearest crater was the Volcan de Tacara, fourteen leagues away in a south-easterly direction. The deep sounds rolled like thunder beneath the massive ranges of the Sierra Madre.

When living amongst these mountains, and hearing these intimations of great volcanic movements below the surface of the ground, it can be understood how it came to pass that the superstitious and fanatical Indians living in these regions believed that the earth beneath them was peopled by evil demons capable of doing injury, who required to be propitiated, and that when seeing the expression of their anger in the fire, smoke and ashes issuing from the craters, thought it necessary to appease them by offering them their daughters. It is probable that the sacrifices known to have taken place to the volcanoes near Atitlan and Quezaltenango were also customary throughout the long range of volcanoes in this part of Central America.

When talking about the present customs of the Indians living in these sierras, the Padre said that the ancient rule of young men serving for a certain time the parents of the girl they wished to marry had ceased, and that now it was usual for an Indian to make up his mind on the subject, and then to begin his courtship by giving presents of maize, fowls, or clothing to the parents.* Finally he proposes to take the girl in marriage, and if they consent, he pays for her according to his means, generally about two dollars, but sometimes as much as eight dollars.

Upon the morning of our departure from Jacaltenango, whilst I was engaged in superintending the saddling of the mule and the various prepara-

---

* Las Casas, who was Bishop of the adjacent diocese of Chiapas in the sixteenth century, mentions that it was the custom there amongst the lower classes to give a year's service to the parents.—" Pero la gente comun tenía de costumbre de servir in sus labores un año al padre de la que por mujer queria, de la manera que Jacob sirvio à Laban por sus hijas Rachel y Lya." This was also the custom in Yucatan.

tions for the day's journey, which from the neglected
state of the road was expected to be long and
fatiguing, I observed Padre Robles walking rapidly
backwards and forwards in front of the convent,
evidently in a state of much anxiety and alarm.

Presently, when Carlos had moved to another part
of the courtyard, the Padre hurried to my side and
said, in a very decided tone, " Señor you must go
back at once to Guatemala." I said, " What
is the meaning of this ! What has happened ? "
He replied, " I must not tell you, but I know that
if you do not go back to Guatemala you will be
robbed and perhaps killed," and, he added with a
look of much distress, " they will steal your beautiful
mule." I told him that it was quite impossible
that I should return to Guatemala, and that I
intended to go forward. " But," I said, "if you
know anything about which I ought to be informed,
you should tell me what it is that you fear."

After some hesitation, he took me aside close
to the convent wall and said, " It is this, Señor :
last night my housekeeper overheard two Indians
talking together in a low tone. One of them was
your guide, the other was a man whom she did not
know, and she listened to what they were saying.
They were sitting in a corner of the courtyard, just
beneath her window, and she could hear what they
said. She heard them arrange a plan to rob you
and to take away your mule. Their plan was this :
At about an hour's journey from this pueblo, you
have to pass a long hedgerow of aloes; when you arrive
at the aloes, an Indian will jump out from behind
them into the road. Your guide will then come to

you and say, that the man is his brother who wishes to go to Comitan, and he will ask if he may be permitted to accompany you. After you have gone on for some distance, the Indians intend to come behind you and take a favourable opportunity to attack and rob you, and, whatever happens you will certainly lose your mule."

After walking together within the quadrangle for a few minutes to discuss the subject, I said, that I had no reason to doubt the fidelity of Carlos. He had been recommended to me by the priest at Gueguetenango as a trustworthy guide, and was considered to be a good and honest man. He had proved himself, so far, to be faithful, and was willing and careful; consequently I should still continue to place confidence in him. With respect to the conversation that had taken place, I thought that the housekeeper must have made some mistake, and had been unreasonably alarmed. In any case, however, I said it was necessary for me to proceed across the frontier. The Padre looked very unhappy, so I told him that he must not be anxious about my fate, and that I would take care to send him information about my movements. I hoped that he would soon hear of my safe arrival in Mexico. He then gave me a letter of introduction to his brother Captain Robles, who commanded the small force stationed on the frontier at Lenton.

By this time Carlos had filled his pack, fitted the head band over his forehead, and was waiting to start; so I said good-bye to the kind Padre, and as I turned round in the saddle to get a last glimpse of Jacaltenango, the most beautifully situated village that I had seen in Guatemala, I observed him watching us from the top of the convent steps.

I had ridden about a league or more and had quite forgotten all about the housekeeper and her forecast of events, when I noticed that we were approaching a long row of tall aloes bordering the left side of the path, and soon afterwards an Indian— a most villainous and evil-looking scoundrel—jumped from his place of concealment amongst the aloes and stood before me on the road. At the same moment Carlos ran back close to the mule's head and told me that this man was his brother who wished to go to Comitan and asked permission to join us.

The scene was like the realisation of a dream. For a few moments I was in doubt as to the best course to pursue, but having been forewarned I was forearmed, and knowing that the Indians could not have the slightest idea that I was aware of their plans, I decided to go on without showing them that I had any suspicions. I said to Carlos "you tell me that this man is your brother and perhaps you are stating the truth, but he is a stranger to me and I do not like his appearance." However I gave him permission to join us. Carlos thanked me, and the other Indian, who did not understand Spanish, gave a guttural sound of satisfaction, and then both men ran forward and kept their places well in front, at about a hundred yards distance.

In the forenoon we passed St. Marcos and halted at St. Andres, in a district remarkable for the luxuriant growth of fruit trees and plantains. We then descended a long hill at the foot of which we halted for breakfast.

As the mule had shown signs of distress, I took off the saddle and noticed that there was a broad low swelling upon her back. A muleteer happened to be passing by on his way to Jacaltenango, and I asked him to examine the swelling and give me his opinion about it. He told me that the mule was ill from a " pica de luna " or moonstroke, and that upon some previous night I must have tethered her out in the open air exposed to the light of the full moon, whilst her back was still warm after the saddle had been removed. I said that I remembered this having been done. The muleteer said that the injurious effects of the moon was well known, and that the mule ought not to have been exposed to it so soon after I had dismounted. He thought that the swelling would not prevent my riding her, provided that the pressure was taken off by resting the saddle upon pads placed upon each side of the swelling, and he arranged some rolls of padding for the purpose.

In the afternoon we were going through a desolate and uninhabited part of the country, when I observed that my guide and his brother were lagging on the way. Finally they dropped behind, and began to run together a few yards in the rear. The time had now come when it was necessary to take a decisive action. I had to be careful not to let Carlos suppose that there were any doubts in my mind about his fidelity, for I knew nothing of the road, and it was important that I should appear to have entire confidence in his guidance.

I stopped the mule, and called Carlos up to my side, and said, " Carlos, you must not run behind me. You are the guide, and must keep in front to enable me to follow you, and not miss the track, and," I added in a more marked manner, "remember that you are to keep well ahead. Let there not be any mistake in this matter, and your brother is to be with you." Carlos immediately obeyed my orders. There was no danger to be apprehended so long as this precaution was taken, for I always carried with me a small loaded revolver to defend myself in case of attack, an event which I thought to be improbable.

When we arrived at Lenton, we were given rooms within the quarters of the garrison. Captain Robles, the commandant, showed me every attention, and at supper I joined the officers' mess. In the morning it was found that although every possible care was taken to raise the saddle above the swelling, the mule could not bear any pressure. Consequently I asked Captain Robles if he could provide me with a horse. After some difficulty an animal was obtained, which although of very rough appearance, I thought would answer the purpose of carrying me the two days' journey to Comitan. An Indian lad, called a mozo, was hired to bring the horse back, and lead my disabled mule. By the time that all these arrangements were completed it was getting late in the morning. More than three hours daylight were lost, and it was important with regard to my Indians to reach our next stopping place before sunset.

For eight leagues the road led through a dreary desert without any signs of habitation, and then we reached a pond called San José where we halted for an hour. It was quite dark when we reached a hut

near Sinigiglia within the Mexican frontier, and
where I decided to stop. An Indian and his wife
were inside, but they not only refused to open the
door and give us shelter, but to all applications for
food or water, replied in the words so usually employed by all Indians when asked for anything, "No
hay." "There is nothing." The only thing to be
done was to make the best of the circumstances, so
a supper was made from our store of provisions, and
with the saddle for a pillow, and the hammock
stretched upon the ground, I passed the night.

On the following day the sun was sinking below
the horizon when we entered the town of
Comitan, and I was not sorry to find myself within
the walls of a comfortable posada, called the Hotel
de la Libertad, where I was given a room looking
into the court. I was not, however, destined to
pass the night without disturbance.

After having been asleep for several hours I was
startled by hearing a peculiar noise. It was a gentle
and continuous tapping, accompanied by the word
Señor spoken in a low, soft voice. It was quite dark
so I lighted the candle and asked who was there, and
I heard "Señor it is your mozo from Lenton, and I
have brought your saddle, and wish to speak to
you." I opened the door and told the lad to explain
the reason for coming to me in the middle of the
night. He came in looking very frightened and said
that he was afraid of my Indians for he thought they
were bad men. He had heard them say that it was
their intention to go back with him, and he feared
that when they were in the deserted part of the
country they would steal the horse ; so he came to

ask my permission to leave at once. The Indians were asleep but he was afraid that they would soon awake and prevent him from getting away alone. He said also that the mule was safe in the stable, and that he had brought with him the saddle, sheepskin and halter which he placed upon the floor in a corner of the room. I thought that the fears of the lad were perhaps well-founded, and gave him directions to leave at once and get on as fast as possible. As he still looked anxious, I assured him that measures should be taken to prevent the Indians from following him for several hours. The mozo thanked me and disappeared into the dark court-yard, and I never heard of him or the horse again. It is to be hoped that he arrived at his village in safety.

Shortly before sunrise I was awoke by a loud tapping at the door. This time it was the landlord who came to tell me that my Indians were making a great noise and were very excited. They were calling out that the mozo had gone away during the night with my horse, and they wished to see me immediately and be paid and discharged. I told the landlord what had happened and that the mozo had left by my orders, and then requested him not to permit the Indians to leave the inn, and to tell them that I would not see them before the middle of the day. "I understand you," said the landlord, "and will do all that is necessary."

In the afternoon at the time when I estimated that if the mozo had made a proper use of his start he would be at least forty miles away, the Indians were discharged, and an hour afterwards I was informed that they had been seen on the road running fast towards the frontier.

It was now necessary to take steps to cure the mule and get a guide. Don Manuel Castillo, to whom I had a letter of introduction, was away at his hacienda, but his friend Don Mariana Godillo in the kindest manner undertook to arrange everything for me. Upon an examination of the mule it was considered advisable that she should have a few days' rest to allow the swelling to subside, and in the meanwhile, the experience of local muleteers was made available in applying the most approved remedies.

During this time the town of Comitan was in a state of unusual excitement in consequence of the arrival of numerous bands of Indians to take part in the festival of San Caralampio, to whom was dedicated one of the churches. In front of that church numerous Indians were assembled. In some respects the scene was like that which took place at Jacaltenango, but the proceedings were more of the character of a fair than of a religious ceremony. The plaza was covered with booths, and a local Indian traffic was being busily transacted. Indian musicians with drums, fifes, and fiddles were engaged in making an incessant noise. The interior of the church was always crowded, and continuous services were performed at the shrines. The women wore white hoods which were drawn tightly across the lower part of their faces. The men usually wore black yergas.*

---

*Long capes made of sackcloth.

Upon the fourth morning of my stay in the town, as I could not see any signs of improvement in the state of the mule, and it was necessary not to lose any more time, I held a small meeting of experts in the stable. It was thought that some weeks must elapse before she would be fit to travel, and Señor Godillo proposed to give me one of his best mules in exchange for her, and also insisted upon giving me twenty dollars, as he considered my mule to be well worth that additional value. In the end this arrangement was carried out, and thus with infinite regret I parted with my intelligent and surefooted companion.

It was reported at Comitan that the border provinces toward Palenque had become settled and had ceased to be in a lawless condition. This state of things was undoubtedly due to the remarkable influence of the President Juarez over the Indian tribes, and it was probable that the cause of this influence was attributable to the fact that, like Carrera, the first President of the Republic of Guatemala, he was by birth an Indian.

Juarez was known to be an Indian of a good unmixed stock. He was born in Oaxaca, the province bordering Chiapas on the west. Of his early youth but little is known, but as a young man he took a prominent part in the political movements which preceded the declaration of Independence. He was elected a Deputy to the Congress, and in 1858 became President, and was given very extensive authority. In considering the characteristics and capacity of the Indians in Central America, it can never be forgotten that, during a period of great revolutionary agitation, two unknown Indians should, in a most extraordinary manner, have risen to the surface, and controlled the destinies of the new Republics.

Under such conditions, requiring much administrative ability, it might have reasonably been expected that men of a white race, either Spaniards or belonging to the large population of half-castes of partly Spanish descent, would, in consequence of their superior qualifications, or their education, or military training, have taken the lead in these revolutions. As a matter of racial capacity, it is strange that ordinary Indians with absolutely no help from their surrounding circumstances, should have attained the highest power.*

---

*When I passed through Mexico, the execution of the Emperor Maximilian and the unhappy fate of the Empress Carlotta, were subjects of discussion. It has often been a matter of surprise, that Juarez should have thought it necessary that the sentence of the court-martial should be carried out. The French troops, upon whom the stability of the empire depended, had been withdrawn, and the success of the National party was assured. An act of forbearance upon this occasion would have met with approval, and have been acknowledged as a wise exercise of superior authority. It was however otherwise determined, and the Emperor was shot outside the walls of Querétaro.

In the American official book upon Mexican affairs, there is a memorandum of the conversation between Mr. Seward, the Foreign Secretary, and Señor Matias Romero, the Mexican Minister, at Washington. Mr. Seward stated, that England, France and Austria, had desired the United States to use their good offices for Maximilian, and further observed, that " Mr. Seward does not fear any contingency possible in virtue whereof any European power may attempt to invade or interfere in future in Mexico, or in any other Republican nation on this continent. For this reason he does not think that Mexico need fear any attempt at reprisals on the part of any European powers, as a consequence of any extreme decision which the Mexican Government may take; but at the same time, Mr. Seward also believes that a feeling universally favourable, conciliatory and friendly towards the Republic of Mexico and the other American Republics, would probably be the result of the act of clemency and magnanimity, which the United States have thought proper to recommend."

Clemency is not a quality that naturally exists in the mind of a North or Central American Indian.

CHAPTER XIII.

It was a fine February morning when we left Comitan. An Indian named Lopez was hired to guide me as far as Ocosingo, three days' journey distant. No trustworthy man could be found who was acquainted with the country beyond that place. With regard to the subject of safety and fidelity, it was arranged that Lopez should receive half his wages in advance and the remainder upon his return. The money was deposited with my friend who engaged him. Lopez was also to bring back a letter from me to the effect that he had performed his duty, and that I was satisfied with his conduct. These measures of precaution were considered to be advisable.

After a long day's ride we reached a place where we decided to pass the night. It was upon an open plain where we saw some muleteers encamped.

As there were no trees upon which to hang the hammock, it was necessary to sleep on the ground. There was a heavy mist and everything was very damp. We noticed that the muleteers had taken off the halters from their mules and tied them together and placed the long rope thus made in a circle, within which they were sleeping. Lopez said that I must follow the same plan, which he explained to be a method employed to prevent serpents from crawling near them, the rough fibrous nature of the halter being so disagreeable to them that they would not pass over it. Consequently I was encircled in this manner and with a saddle for a pillow, endeavoured to get rest, but the thick mist was the cause of much discomfort. Lopez passed the time on guard, watching the mule.

The next day as early as possible we continued our journey. After passing a few huts called Jotána, we entered upon a wide expanse of undulating land well studded with trees. Here we met some Mexicans travelling on their way from their hacienda or farm They were men, women, boys and girls, all bright and gay, riding horses and mules, galloping over the smooth grass land and enjoying the sunny weather. I took the opportunity of occasionally joining the laughing cheerful group, and I was sorry when we had to part company and follow different paths.

In the afternoon we reached a steep, sharp ascent. The track was difficult to trace, and in several places was almost impassable. Large masses of stone had fallen over it. There were also numerous deep, slippery ruts, through which the mule plunged with difficulty. It was sunset when, after having made our way over several leagues of this rough ground, we came to an open space, where it was thought expedient to stop. We found two trees, between which the hammock was secured. The mule was tethered within reach, and Lopez went to an adjacent wood and got some twigs and leaves to enable us to make a fire. This was a work of difficulty requiring great patience; no one but an Indian would have succeeded. The first supply of fuel, after half an hour's useless endeavour, could not be ignited, and Lopez made a second expedition to find drier materials. Finally, when I thought that it was useless to continue the attempt, an accidental spark suddenly set fire to a dry leaf and we were soon sitting round a blazing mass of flame, and preparing a supper of tortillas and chocolate.

The air was too chilly and damp to permit of our expecting much rest, and the night was chiefly occupied in attending to the fire, and in listening to Lopez's account of his superstitions and religious beliefs, and those generally held by his tribe. There was something in Lopez's character which showed that he was possessed of a kind of devotional enthusiasm, which made his stories of Indian faiths, past and present, singularly interesting, because it was evident that he spoke with earnestness and as a man convinced. Thus the night passed away, and in the morning as soon the earliest signs of dawn appeared in the sky, and long before the sun had risen over the hills, we continued our journey northwards through Chiapas.

In the forenoon we reached the hamlet of San Carlos. I observed that Lopez went to the rising ground near at hand, and stood for several moments facing the sun, with the palms of his hands joined together and raised to the level of his face. He seemed to be muttering a request. When he returned I asked him what he had been doing. He said that the Indians of his tribe always thanked the sun in the morning for coming and giving light, and thus enabling men to work. In the evening they again thanked the sun for what had been done, and asked it to return again. They also offered prayers to the moon for the same reason, because it gave light and helped men to live. The stars they did not worship.

In answer to questions that I put to him, he said that the Indians always prayed or made offerings with reference to the world in which they lived, and for objects relating to themselves and their wants, and never took into consideration anything regarding a future life. He thought it was impossible to know if a man was to live again, or whether he was to be given some other shape or kind of existence. I told Lopez about the " adoratorio " in the Sierra Madre above Jacaltenango. He declared that the Indians near Comitan also had a stone image in a cave amongst the hills. He went there once a year to light a candle, " la sua candela," before it, but it was usual amongst the men of his tribe to go there more frequently. The image was about two feet six inches in height, and had its arms folded. It was one of the ancient idols worshipped before the conquest.

From San Carlos there was a ride of six leagues over a less difficult road, and as we approached

Ocosingo we passed through some fine scenery. The path followed the line of the summit of the hills, and commanded extensive views of both valleys. At Ocosingo, I called upon Don Remigio Salorzano, to whom I carried a note of introduction. Don Remigio told me that the ancient Indian ruins were over a league from the pueblo, but that there was very little to be seen there.

The temples were almost destroyed, and the materials had been taken away for building purposes. There were, however, fragments of stones covered with hieroglyphic characters still remaining thoro. I went with him to look at some idols that had been brought from the ruins. One of these at once arrested my attention. It was made of hard sandstone, and was about three feet high. The head was broken off, and had been taken away to prevent the Indians from worshipping it. I at first thought that the idol must have been made subsequent to the Spanish occupation of this part of Mexico, for by the costume it seemed to be intended to represent a Spanish cavalier. In front of the waist belt there was a small head surmounting a rudely shaped cross.

It appeared as if the native sculptor had wished to make the image of a knight holding before him a head, such as is not infrequently seen in early sacred pictures.* But although this was the vague impression made upon the mind by an examination of the

---

*It recalled to my memory an old Spanish picture belonging to Dr. Pusey, which always held the principal place upon the walls of his library in Christ Church, Oxford.

front of the statue, it was evident upon looking at the reverse side that the date of its sculpture was of a much earlier period, for it was covered with an upright line of hieroglyphics of the same character as those carved upon the idols at Copan. I examined with care the details of the figure, and made sketches of the front and back, as I thought that it would be

Indian statue.   Ocosingo.

useful to preserve a slight memorial of this idol which may eventually share the fate of many others and be destroyed.

Two larger idols were placed against the wall of the church. These were also headless. Don Remigio showed me several long stones that were used

for the door steps at the entrance of some of the
largest of the huts occupied by Ladinos and which
had been taken from the ruins. One of these, made
of limestone, was covered with deeply carved hieroglyphics still quite clear and distinct. In front of
one of the dwellings there was a flat stone measuring about three feet square. On the surface of this
stone were two figures. A woman in an imploring
attitude was presenting a cup to a man, who was
standing up and bending forward to receive the
offering. The wall of an adjoining house was partly
built with stones also taken from the temples. They
had a perfectly smooth surface and were each about
two feet long, one foot wide and two inches thick.
Similar stones were scattered about the pueblo, and
many were used as stepping stones across the stream
that flowed eastwards to join the waters of the
river Usamacinta.

The church, from its size and manner of construction, had been evidently of considerable importance.
It was then in ruins and the roof had fallen. As there
were no funds available for its restoration it was
deserted.

The Gefe Politico, who held the appointment in
this town and district of Civil Governor, spoke to
me about an expedition that was under consideration, for constructing a road or mule path to connect this part of Mexico with the English port of
Belize in Honduras. He thought that if such a road
was practicable it would become the principal line
for trade, and the ranges of mountains near Tumbalá
would be avoided. This was to be the primary purpose
of the expedition, but there were other objects which

influenced the minds of the inhabitants of Ocosingo.
It was thought that the surveyors might make
strange discoveries in the mysterious and unknown
region occupied by the Lacandon Indians. Possibly
amongst the forests in the sierras, temples and
hidden treasures might be found; or perhaps a
city where the ancient ceremonies and sacrifices
were still performed.

The Gefe said that a small band of explorers had
lately penetrated a few leagues into the forest, and
had seen several circular shaped huts, but the
Indians who lived in them had fled. They found
maize and tomatoes growing upon the open spaces,
but they saw no horses, dogs or other animals. He
pointed out to me the hills amongst which the wild
Lacandones lived. It was afterwards suggested that
I might take the post of leader of the proposed
expedition.

If I had been quite free, with sufficient time at
my disposal, I should have been much inclined to
assist to the best of my power in the formation of a
preliminary surveying party. I thought that a practicable route would be found to connect Ocosingo
with the existing road leading from Guatemala to
Flores, on the lake of Peten, and thence to Honduras,
and that, in this manner, the distance to Belize
would be much shortened. The first portion of the
survey would have to be conducted through a
region which is unknown, and possibly many interesting facts would be ascertained, and perhaps an
ancient ruined temple might be discovered.

Whilst staying at Ocosingo I collected a small
vocabulary of the words of the local dialect. These

were nearly the same as those spoken near Comitan,
and I was surprised to find that Lopez could not
carry on a conversation with these men. I asked
him how this happened and he said that the languages (lenguas) were quite different, and that he
could not speak with the Ocosingos. It seems probable that, in the course of time, the construction of
the phrases commonly used, or the manner of the
application of the words must have become changed.
Although it is only three days' journey between the
two tribes, it is evident that there cannot have
been much communication between them for several
centuries.

As Lopez did not know the country beyond
Ocosingo, it was settled that he should return to
Comitan. I was sorry to part with him. He had
carried the luggage and provisions, and although a
part of the journey must have been extremely fatiguing to him he never complained. He also showed
the utmost zeal in obtaining forage for the mule,
and was willing and attentive. Don Remigio hired
for me a guide named Bito, who spoke Spanish
and knew the paths as far as Chilon, about eleven
leagues distant. Bito brought with him a horse,
and thus we were able to travel at a fair speed.
After riding through several leagues of pine forests
we reached Bachajon in the afternoon.

Bachajon was a strictly Indian village, for the
natives objected to any white people or Ladinos
settling amongst them. In the Plaza we found
numbers of Indians congregated together. They
differed greatly from those that I had hitherto seen
both in appearance and dialect. The men wore a

white cloth folded round the head, and white frocks and trousers. The women wore a white frock cut open and square over the shoulders, and below this a blue skirt reaching nearly to the feet. Their thick black hair was tied back with a strip of bright red cotton. Many of the younger women were handsome, but their figures were spoilt and bent by the custom of carrying large water jars on the hip. The men were of a larger stature than the natives on the Pacific side of the Cordilleras, and their skin was of a dark copper colour. Their faces were broad, but the cheek bones were not so high as is usual with the North American Indians. Their hair was long, black and very thick, and their eyes were dark, large, round and restless. With all of them the nostrils were very wide.

The church was in ruins, the roof had entirely disappeared, and only the porch and outer walls remained standing. I remained for several hours in the Plaza, and my attention was directed to a remarkable observance. The Indians, when returning from their fields upon the completion of their day's work, invariably, before going to their huts, went to the front of the ruined porch. There they knelt down and prayed for some minutes. I was deeply interested in observing the practice of this custom. There was something that appealed strongly to the imagination in witnessing the simple and earnest devotion of these wild, ignorant and uncivilised people. It was impossible to conjecture what was present in their minds, as one by one they, in their solitary manner, knelt devoutly before these ruined walls. Possibly they worshipped in their memory the images that, many years before, had been enshrined within.

In the evening, as we approached Chilon, we met hundreds of Indians, men and women, all of whom came forward by the side of my mule, and inclined their heads saying " Tá " (Padre.) Bito told me that they supposed that I was a priest, and that they expected me to follow the custom of the priests and put my hand upon their foreheads. As I did not wish to sail under false colours, I made an objection to this proceeding, but Bito said that if I did not do it the Indians would feel distressed, and would not understand why they were treated in an unkind manner. He also begged me to do what they wished, or otherwise some trouble might arise, as many of the men appeared to be in a half-drunken condition.

At Chilon I was welcomed by the Justicia, to whom I had a letter from Don Manuel Cansino. The town was in a state of much excitement. It was the commencement of the Carnival, an event which caused a considerable degree of anxiety and apprehension in the minds of the officials. Processions of Indians, dressed in appropriate costumes, were marching through the town, and groups of wild looking men were dancing to the sounds of rudely shaped fifes and hollow wooden drums. In the morning these Indians, in accordance with their annual custom, performed a dance before the door of each house. These dancers were supposed to be dressed like the conquerors. They wore red, slashed doublets, and loose white trousers. They carried spears or lances with coloured pennons. The scene was bright, gay and picturesque.

During the day I discharged Bito, and obtained
a guide to accompany me to Yajalon. We arrived
there about sunset and the Presbitero Fernando
Macal received me with much kindness and attention.   At Yajalon the Indians had assembled in
great numbers and the Carnival was at its height.
Here as at Chilon, the performances chiefly consisted of processions and dances. There were also
horse races in front of the cabildo, and one of the
most curious scenes was the representation of the
Spaniards entering a captured city on horseback.
The Indians were Tzendales of the same race as
those at Bachajon and were very wild looking men.
An important part of the festival consisted in eating
as great a quantity of food as possible, and drinking
copious draughts of strong spirits.   In the evening
there was much drunkenness.

The Carnival lasted for three days, and during
that time I had to remain in Yajalon, as no Indian
could be found who would willingly leave this
scene of revelry and excitement. On the second
day the President called upon me at the convent,
and informed me that, in his opinion, it would be
highly dangerous for a white man who was a stranger, to venture out into the open country before the
Indians had recovered from the effects of the carnival, as, in consequence of their known hatred to all
white people, it was impossible to say what might
happen when they were in an excited condition. In
anticipation of local troubles he had organised a
small police force which was employed in patrolling
the pueblo day and night, for the purpose of preventing any quarrels of castes. He had also a

company of seventy soldiers prepared to act in the event of any serious outbreak. As far as I could judge, the Indians, when in a drunken state, were quiet and inoffensive, but the President was evidently very anxious about their conduct.

As I had no share in the responsibility for maintaining good order, the strange life and the sounds of drums and fifes and marimbas afforded me inexhaustible pleasure and amusement. The pretty dresses of the women also added much to the charm of the scene. Many of these Tzendal women were very handsome. Their heads were well set upon finely shaped throats and shoulders. Their costume consisted of a long white frock cut open round their neck, and embroidered with red and yellow squares, which had a pleasing effect of colour. But not only was the festival attractive from the quaint and novel character of the scene, but it was also most enjoyable weather. The skies were blue, the sun was bright, and the surrounding hills and valleys formed an agreeable contrast. There was perhaps a slight, underlying sense of danger and a doubt as to what would occur after sunset, and what might be the effect of the subsequent orgies upon the savage natures of these Indians. Possibly what began at daylight as a drama might end at night as a tragedy. The conduct of the timorous half-caste population or Ladinos was remarkable. They were conscious that they were hated by the Indians, and consequently they remained within their houses, and kept themselves out of sight.

The dances and processions are said to have been taught by the Spanish monks. It is evident that they usually have some connection with the events of the wars between the Spaniards and the Moors, for the Indians always speak of these representations under the general name of "los Moros." But they are also mixed up with other subjects which, not improbably, have some relation to events that happened before Cortes conquered Mexico.

There was a peculiarity in the Indian character which was noticeable in all their proceedings. This was the absence of all conversation amongst the numerous spectators. The games, races and processions, the beating of the wooden drums and the continuous sounds of the marimbas went on incessantly, but there was no other noise and no murmur of human voices. The gift of speech with these tribes seems almost unnecessary for the purposes of their lives, and the language of signs would possibly be sufficient for their requirements.

The Spaniards in the sixteenth century were astonished by the extraordinary debauchery of the Indians during their festivals. The events which occurred upon these occasions, especially in Yucatan, surprised the soldiers belonging to a nation remarkable for its sobriety. The Indians in Cuba, Hayti, and the islands of the Caribbean sea, and those inhabiting Florida, the valley of the Mississippi, and other parts of North America, had no knowledge of an intoxicating spirit. The origin of the excessive insobriety amongst the Mexican Indians is clearly traceable to the indigenous growth of the Maguey (*Agave Americana*). This aloe grows abundantly in the sterile regions of Central America, and supplies a fluid which, after undergoing certain preparations, is highly alcoholic.

At Yajalon, as at Bachajon and Ocosingo, the church was in ruins. There was nothing left of it except the bare walls, marks of the old altars and parts of the chancel. Long grass was growing over the ground of the nave. The convent was also in a ruinous condition and only one side of the quadrangle remained. The interior was overgrown with weeds and grass, and was used as a pasture for the horses belonging to the convent.

The Presbitero was eloquent upon the subject of the wrongs suffered by the Catholics in Mexico, and he particularly dwelt upon the harm that had been done to the people in consequence of the decrees which had nationalised the possessions of the church, suppressed the convents and abolished all religious fraternities. He thought that the withdrawal of the monks would have an injurious effect upon the condition of the Indians, and that they would gradually relapse into a state of ignorance and barbarism. Thus the system begun by Bishop Las Casas, and carried on afterwards by monks and priests would come to an end, and all their efforts to advance and benefit the aboriginal tribes be rendered useless and vain.

It is difficult at this distance of time to estimate correctly the value of the work done by Las Casas, and the consequences of the enactments in favour of the Indians, obtained by his appeals to the Spanish government. In this diocese of Chiapas his zeal led to the establishment of numerous churches and convents. Dominicans and brethren of other orders came over from Europe for the purpose of living amongst these Indians, converting them, educating them and forming centres of local civilization. To a certain extent the ceremonies of the church, and especially the worship of images, seemed to obtain a powerful hold upon the devotional nature of many of the tribes, and the monks obtained great influence over them.

Thus far the work begun by Las Casas unquestionably did much good in this and the adjoining provinces. The exhortations of the principal authorities of the Church in the sixteenth and seventeenth centuries, were also beneficial in moderating the hardships inflicted upon the natives by the Spanish landowners. But in advocating the cause of the Indians, Las Casas, in the fervour of his zeal, created evils the effect of which he could not have foreseen. It was in consequence of the measures adopted through the representations of this ardent reformer that negro slavery was introduced into America. It was also chiefly owing to his efforts that consecutive ordinances was decreed, which, although issued with the intention of putting a stop to the harsh treatment of the Indians, made it almost impossible to carry on successfully the government of New Spain. Thus, by the abolition of forced labour, it was found that there was an immediate danger of the lands granted to the Spaniards becoming thrown out of cultivation and their owners ruined. In no part of New Spain was this danger more to be apprehended than in the neighbourhood of La Antigua Guatemala, and in the country through which I passed on my way to

Santa Cruz del Quiché. The lands there were fertile and the farms prosperous. The Indians performed labour upon them under fixed rules which, although strict and exacting, were not opposed to their previous habits. When these regulations were withdrawn the Indians ceased to work. Finally protests were made to the government, and it was pointed out that this usage of forced labour was not introduced by the Spaniards, but that it had previously been practically the base of the tribal administration.

There was another usage which was stopped by orders from Spain. This was the employment of natives as carriers of merchandise. The abolition of this system was found to be disadvantageous to the prosperity of the country, and it was submitted to the king that it had always been the custom amongst the Indians to transport all things by men working as porters, for before the arrival of the Spaniards there were no horses or other beasts of burden. The practice of personally carrying heavy loads still forms part of the habits of all the inferior classes of Indians in Central America.

The restrictions enforced upon the Spanish land-owners did not however much affect the prosperity of the church, particularly in the more remote districts, where the priests and friars devoted themselves to the spiritual welfare and education of the natives. At the convents, schools were established for boys and, in the chief towns, sisters belonging to nunneries in Spain, came across the Atlantic to teach the girls. The monks also endeavoured to arrange that the boys upon completing their studies, should teach other Indians and thus spread education amongst them. These exertions which, in their origin, seemed to promise well were not subsequently attended with success, and the authority of the brethren declined. Finally the declarations of Independence, the revolutions, and the establishment of republics, dealt a fatal blow to all educational work.

Amongst the various consequences of the nationalisation of ecclesiastical property, it had come to pass that in the country parishes, there were no funds available for maintaining the churches in repair, and they were all rapidly falling into ruins. The Presbitero was convinced, now that the influence of the priests upon the characters of the tribes was no longer felt, and the church services were not maintained, that the Indians, especially the Tzendales under his care, would return to the practice of their ancient idolatries.

Upon a subject so doubtful as the effect of the teaching of the priests upon the minds of the Indians it is difficult to form an opinion. In the sixteenth century the Roman Catholic religion appeared to be willingly accepted by the natives; but several of the priests that I had met and who discussed this question, were in doubt as to whether this readiness to conform with the ceremonies had not some vague connection with some previous religious customs. The influence of the friars also possibly had some relation to the system of Indian priesthood before the conquest; for, according to the statements of the Spaniards, there was a strange and inexplicable coincidence between certain regulations by which they were bound, and those of the Franciscans and Dominicans.

It was fortunate that during my detention at Yajalon I was the guest of a man so well informed and highly educated as the Presbitero Fernando Macal. It was an exceptional fate for him to be thus placed in that parish, with its numerous detached hamlets, to perform clerical duties amongst these intractable tribes. At the convent in the evening, the Presbitero usually discussed questions of theology, together with his opinions upon the aboriginal and mixed races in Chiapas. The President occasionally joined us, but his mind was preoccupied with anxiety about the maintenance of order. All the time, both day and night, the pueblo was disturbed by the continuous and monotonous sounds of native music.

On the fourth morning the Carnival was over and a dissipated, savage-looking Tzendal named Villafranca appeared at the convent wall, and volunteered to act as my guide to Tumbalá and Palenque. The necessary arrangements were made to secure the fulfilment of his duties. The mule was brought out of the quadrangle and we were soon ready to start. I was warned that the paths over the sierras were in a bad condition, and that many difficulties would have to be overcome in passing through the forests.

CHAPTER XIV.

An Indian steam bath.—Tumbalá.—Sierras and Forests.—San Pedro.—Desertion of guide.—Alguazils.—Construction of Indian huts.—Habits of Indians.—Cargadores.—Crossing a River.— Forests beyond San Pedro.—Powers of endurance of Indians. —Arrival at San Domingo del Palenque.

THE base of the sierra whose summit we had to reach before night, was about two leagues from Yajalon. After having ridden that distance I expected to see some indications of Tumbalá, but not being able to make out anything, I asked Villafranca where it was. He pointed upwards towards the sky, and said " En el núbe, (in the cloud) Señor." In effect it was just possible to see the church amongst the clouds which were sweeping over the highest ridge of the Cordilleras.

The greater part of the day was passed in making the ascent, which was a steep and continuous rise for over three leagues. In the afternoon, when we had attained to a considerable height, we left below us the bright and sunny daylight, and entered into the region of cloud-land. The weather became cold and gloomy, and as we approached Tumbalá it was scarcely possible to see our way for we were moving in a dark fog. Near the outskirts of the hamlet we passed close to a structure of an unusual shape, not unlike an oven. I was afterwards informed that it was used by Indians in time of sickness and was practically a steam bath. The methods of using it were similar to those adopted by many of the tribes in North America. The patient finds inside a supply of water to generate steam. Heated stones are passed in from outside and these he drops into the water. This system is said to be efficacious in the disorders to which men living amongst the Cordilleras are subject, and which are probably caused by exposure to sudden changes of temperature. It was strange to see amongst these remote sierras a practice which seemed to establish the fact that there were links connecting these Mexican Indians with the Dakotas in North America, the natives of Hawaii, and the Maoris in the distant islands of New Zealand.

When we arrived at the walls of the convent it was evident that there was a general state of commotion without and within. Some event had happened, the nature of which I was unable to ascertain. The precincts were crowded with numerous groups of Indians and Ladinos. The priest was living in a large shed. The quadrangle was apparently used as a farmyard and was filled with cattle, horses, mules, turkeys and fowls, all wandering about at their own free will, and causing an indescribable disturbance. The mists were so thick that it was quite impossible to make anything out clearly.

Inside the shed the state of affairs was equally confusing. Men, women and children were busily engaged in preparing to pass the night under the protection of the roof, and were choosing their sleeping places. As it was necessary to find room without delay, I told Villafranca to hang my hammock to the rafters as near to the fire as possible. We then went out and tethered the mule upon a level open space beyond, which we thought to be convenient for the purpose, but the clouds were so dense that we could not see what we were doing. After some further trouble, supplies of forage and water were obtained, and placed within the mule's reach. We then returned to the shed within which the priest was endeavouring to find suitable quarters for his numerous visitors.

Later in the evening we were joined by a young couple who had just been married, and wanted shelter. It happened that there was an Indian bedstead available and this together with two extemporized pillows was placed at their disposal. When it became night, we sat round the fire and cooked our suppers, and then sleeping mats were unrolled and spread upon the ground. The Cura placed his mat near the fire, beneath my hammock. Amongst the crowd were several young mothers who had their infants with them. These little creatures were duly attended to and their wants supplied. The mothers then proceeded to roll them up tightly in swaddling clothes until only their heads were visible. They were afterwards placed in a row against the wall, where they looked like diminutive Egyptian mummies, their large round eyes staring at us in a most unmeaning manner. When all these various arrangements were completed the doors were closed.

What happened during the night I do not know, but upon awaking in the morning I found that I

was alone and that the shed was empty. All the
numerous inmates of the previous night had de-
parted. I turned out of my hammock and joined the
Cura who was walking in front of his ruined convent. He said he would accompany me for a few
hundred yards to the outer edge of the sierra, to
look at the world around and beneath us.

The clouds had disappeared, the sun had risen
brightly above the eastern horizon, the sky was blue,
the air felt pure and exhilarating, and the view was
magnificent. Not only did we command range upon
range of these Cordilleras, but there were also extensive views of the valleys below us. Beyond,
looking northwards, were the savannahs and the
tropical lowlands near Palenque; and in the far
distance the sunlight was flashing upon the calm
waters of the Laguna de Terminos.

Near at hand were groups of wild-looking Indians
watching our movements. The Cura said he believed they belonged to the Maya race, and were
allied to the tribes that occupied Yucatan. In their
appearance they were like the Tzendales near
Bachajon. They were strongly built men, rather
low in stature, and very dark in colour; their eyes
had peculiarly rounded orbits, and their long black
hair was cut square over the forehead. They spoke
a language which sounded very rough and abrupt.
The Cura observed that the Indians dwelling
amongst the mountains were daily becoming neglected, and that they were left entirely free to follow
their own beliefs and customs. In consequence of
there being no regular stipend for the clergy, it had
become impossible to maintain a sufficient number

of priests to carry out the duties. He had to superin-
tend the parishes at Tumbalá, San Pedro, Palenque
and the districts around Las Playas, near the river
Usamacinta, and therefore he could not attend
personally to the numerous and scattered Indians
placed under his charge.

Upon our return to the convent, Villafranca came
to me and reported that the mule was ready and that
he had got his machete sharpened in order to
clear away any branches or brushwood that we
might find to be obstructing the track. He added
to his pack some part of the weights carried by the
mule, as it was necessary that she should be as free
as possible, to push her way through the woods, and
we reduced the quantities of food and other necessaries to the lowest amount practicable. A young
Mexican who was going to the sea-coast came with
us as far as the entrance to the forest. He then
told me that he should not attempt to go through
it with his clothes on, so he stopped and stripped
to the skin, and tied his clothes up in a bundle
which he fastened to the top of his head. He
was a white man of mixed descent and in his action
he showed some elements of the nature of his remote
Indian ancestry. He ran rapidly to the front,
plunged into the forest like a lithe athletic young
savage, and was soon out of sight.

As it was not possible to ride I dismounted, and
we began to descend the steep sides of the mountain.
It was very hard work. Villafranca led the way. I
followed close to him, holding the halter at its full
length, to prevent the mule as she slipped forward
from falling upon me. This manner of progression

was made difficult by the obstinate conduct of the mule. She would occasionally attempt to choose her own way and go the wrong side of a tree, and as no energy expended in trying to get her back was of any use, I had always to yield and to follow her round the trunk. Upon one occasion she got away into the forest and was nearly lost. The guide at once threw off his pack and went after her.

The instincts of an Indian were apparent in his proceedings. He carefully marked every step of his advance through the dense undergrowth by cutting down small branches of the trees and placing them on the line of his track. He also here and there, but always on the left hand side, cut notches in the trees or bent some twigs backwards. After a few minutes interval he returned triumphantly with the mule, and after this experience I took care not to allow the halter to leave my hands again.

The fatigues of the day were beyond description. I had been prepared to expect difficulties from the steepness of the ascents and descents and the growth of the underwood, but there were other obstacles which were previously unknown. Our track was constantly barred by creepers which crossed from tree to tree in festoons like thick ropes. They hung loosely in bends and bights in every conceivable shape, but usually they swept the ground in semicircles. Others were hanging in graceful loops three or four feet above the ground, so that the mule was unable to pass under them. There were also miry, swampy places in which the mule sometimes sank to an almost dangerous depth. But what I found to be the most serious trial was the

want of ventilation. There was absolutely no movement in the air or any sounds of life, and there was
very little daylight, for the rays of the sun above did
not penetrate to the ground.

The forest was dark and gloomy, and the atmosphere most oppressive. The want of a proper supply
of fresh air to breathe made the journey extremely
exhausting. After struggling for several hours
down the rugged slopes of the first mountain, we
reached a narrow valley and crossed a small stream.
We then had to climb up another sierra so steep
that it required all my available strength to reach
the summit. From this height there remained
another league to be traversed down a steep rocky
slope to a wide open savannah, upon which was
situated San Pedro. Towards sunset we arrived at
the village and found shelter under a shed, within
which was installed the official who ruled over the
district, and who was called the Maestro.

In the morning I discovered that during the night
my guide had deserted. Possibly some accident may
have happened to him, but in my opinion his conduct was a deliberate act of desertion. I reported
the case immediately to the Maestro, but Villafranca
could not be found and I never saw him again. It
was supposed that he found the work and fatigue of
the day greater than he had expected, and was not
willing to make his way on the morrow through the
equally dense forests between San Pedro and Palenque. If this surmise was correct his view of the
situation was quite intelligible, but as I did not
consider that an act of this kind should remain un-
punished, I arranged with the Maestro that a letter

from me should be dispatched to Yajalon where the man had been hired.

I wrote to the Presbitero Macal an account of the desertion and requested him to bring the case to the notice of the alcalde, in order that Villafranca should receive a punishment in accordance with the custom of the country, and that he should be deprived of his wages which had been left in the Presbitero's charge. I also requested that this money should be given to any of his deserving or distressed parishioners. In justice however to this Tzendal, it should be noted that he did not rob me. I found everything carefully piled up in a corner of the shed ; saddle, clothes, rug and the remains of the provisions sufficient for one day. The mule was safely tethered outside the door.

I was thus placed in a very insecure position and had to rely entirely upon my own resources. The hamlet was surrounded in all directions by sierras and forests, and I had not the slightest knowledge of the mountain passes. With regard to food I could manage very well as I was able to make a fire and was prepared to make the provisions last for more than one day if necessary, but in other respects I was entirely dependent upon the good will of the San Pedro Indians about whom very little was known, but who were considered to be untrustworthy.

The Maestro declared that he would do all that was in his power to assist me, and promised that he would get a guide who would go with me to Palenque. But he said that he could not find a man at once, and that it would be necessary that I should stop in

the convent until the following day. In some respects I was not sorry to be detained, for I was thus
enabled to have some spare time to see something of
the habits of life amongst the inhabitants of this
isolated village, so singularly placed in the heart of
these remote Cordilleras. I observed that the
Maestro maintained towards those who were placed
under his rule a dignified and reserved manner. He
was supported in his authority by two alcaldes, and
two alguazils who were Indians elected annually for
these posts. The alguazils wore suitable dresses
and performed regular police duties, walking at intervals about the village, carrying long wands of
office. It was also their custom to visit the Maestro
occasionally, attend to his wants, and render such
personal service as he required. In obedience to his
directions, they obtained for me supplies of maize
and water for the mule, and tortillas and beans for
myself, and thus I was able to cook a tolerable
breakfast.

During the day I wandered amongst the huts
within and near the hamlet in order to see
something of the natives who lived in them and
were said to follow the ancient customs and habits
of domestic life. Near the borders of the savannah some Indians were building a large hut
and I observed a method of construction which,
although absolutely the reverse of any system that
I had previously known, was most suitable for their
wants. In the first place the roof is built. This
when completed, looks like an open thatched shed
resting upon upright poles. The eaves are brought
down low, but sufficiently high to enable a man of

moderate height to pass under them without stooping. When the roof is considered firm and secure, the four walls inclosing the room are made. They are usually constructed of crossed laths and sticks, and thickly-plastered over with a kind of mud which has a good binding consistence.

The walls are raised until they reach within a short distance from the slope of the roof, a sufficient space being left for the escape of smoke. The size of the hut and the height of the walls are determined by the width and slope of roof. A few rough cross poles are placed across the top of the walls for the purpose of hanging up any household goods, and sometimes at one end some of these poles are placed close together so as to form a platform, where bags of maize and other farm produce are kept or dried. When the roof is wide and the overhanging eaves are low there is an agreeable and well shaded space outside the main hut, where the Indians rest during the day.*

As far as it was possible to judge from a passing observation the Indians at San Pedro seemed to be a contented race. They cultivated their milpas or corn fields sufficiently to get enough to supply them with maize bread and pozole, and at most of the

---

* The method of building their huts varies amongst different tribes, but the general principles are much the same. I have passed many hours of the day and night within them, and noticed their practical convenience in tropical climates; and although, according to civilised ideas of comfort, there is much that is wanting, yet for the purposes of the simple and solitary lives of these shy and inoffensive Indians, it would be difficult to contrive any shelter more suitable for their requirements.

huts there were fowls and a few pigs. The women laboured in some form of household work, and much of their time was occupied in grinding the maize to make tortillas. At this village, as in others chiefly inhabited by Indians, there was an absence of any human sounds. In the interior of the huts, as also outside them, all the occupations of life were performed in silence. In the evening, when the men returned home from their work, there was the same manner of moving about without noise. There appeared to be also an absence of all interest in what was happening around them, which gave an element of sadness to the scene. Their lives seem to be passed in a state of quiet melancholy and listlessness.

This condition of the Indians is practically the same throughout this part of Central America. The problem of existence is worked out in its lowest terms. It cannot however be said that they live in want and poverty, because they have no wants. They exist, and are apparently content to exist, in the state in which they find themselves placed. The bare ground, a thatched roof, bedstead, a few mats, some firewood, and a small store of maize suffice for the necessities of their lives. Their submissive natures assent to these conditions and they seem to accept their fate with passive resignation.

Upon my return to the shed in the evening, I found that it was enlivened by the arrival of a busy, loud-voiced Spaniard named Don Pepe Ortiz. He informed me that he was travelling from Oaxaca towards the coast of the Gulf of Campeachy with a cargo of tobacco. He had with him a band of

INDIAN WOMAN GRINDING CHOCOLATE, CENTRAL AMERICA.

cargadores to carry the bales. He also employed for his own personal use a man of great strength to carry him in places where he could not ride a mule. The direction of his journey over the sierras was for some distance the same as my own, and he proposed that we should, without delay, make arrangements for crossing a river which occasionally was difficult to pass over. I had not heard that there was a stream of any importance in our way, and I asked Don Pepe to do what was expedient. Accordingly he sent on an Indian to order several canoes to be in readiness for us on the following morning.

At sunrise my new guide José arrived and we all started together. After riding about a league we reached the bank of a river, called the San Pedro, which we found to be a deep stream about three hundred yards wide. The passage was not made without difficulties, chiefly caused by the conduct of the mules, when they reached the opposite bank, which was very steep. The canoes were in attendance, and I selected one which seemed to be convenient for the moderate weights to be carried. The mule was fastened by the halter to the stern of the canoe, and swam across with ease, but she obstinately refused to go on shore at the proper landing place, and consequently, after several unavailing attempts, I allowed her to go free and choose for herself. She swam down with the current for about a hundred yards, and then with much good judgment she selected her own spot and scrambled safely up the bank.

After having successfully accomplished my crossing, I watched the movements of Don Pepe and his men in their canoes. It was a picturesque scene, but it was within two hours of midday before we were all established on the northern side of the river. We then commenced the dreaded ascent about which many warnings had been given to me. It was a steep climb for five long leagues and it was nearly sunset when we reached the summit. We stopped for the night in a small shed which sheltered us from the dew.

Don Pepe's Indians arrived after us and insisted upon lighting a large fire just outside the hut, with the object they said of keeping away tigers, and kept it burning like a bonfire as long as it was dark. At daylight José and myself and mule began the descent of the opposite slope of the sierra. I had been told that we should find this part of the journey very arduous, but it exceeded in difficulty anything that I had imagined.

The track, or opening through the trees had almost disappeared, and we had to make our own way between detached masses of sharp, angular rocks. Frequently it was necessary to scramble over them or to slide down them, and it occasionally seemed to me that we were going at random down the side of the mountain. But what made our progress more than usually difficult was the fact that, in several places, decaying trunks of large trees had fallen across our path, and as it was not practicable to get the mule over them, we were obliged to diverge into the forest to pass round them. When it was thus necessary to quit our line of direction, José would instantly draw his machete and mark our movements by cutting down branches, so as to secure the means of retreat to our starting point, in case we failed to find the path again. I was quite aware of the importance of this action. It was astonishing to find how in a few seconds in a dense forest and amongst thick growth of underwood and creepers all knowledge of direction seems to be lost.

The length of this precipitous descent was a little more than five miles, and we took four hours to accomplish the distance. During that time I never saw a glimpse of the sky, although I knew that, above the trees, the sun was shining brilliantly.

In the forenoon we reached the banks of the Nopá, which ran at the base of the sierra, and halted there to rest. We then passed over the river, and pushed or cut our way through two leagues of dense forest and thick brushwood. There were also several small streams with low but steep and slippery banks that had to be crossed. Finally we reached and forded the river Michol. The worst was then over, and we emerged from the forest and saw before us a savannah where we decided to encamp. I obtained a slight shelter under the sloping roof of a little open hut, which had been left there by some passing Indians. Thus ended a most fatiguing day.

Don Pepe and his Indians arrived after sunset and encamped near us. The methods adopted by these Indians when preparing to pass the night upon an open savannah were instructive. In the first instance they placed upon the ground a quantity of broad dry leaves to protect them from the damp grass. They then dispersed, and in a few minutes

the adjacent forest resounded with the noise of the
blows made by their machetes. They returned
bearing loads of firewood and also several strong
forked branches. These they sharpened at one end
and fixed into the earth near the camping place
to form supports to carry the bales of tobacco. In
this manner the cargo was raised about three feet,
and thus they carried out the invariable rule of
Indians who never leave anything upon the ground
at night. They then lighted a large fire.

There were characteristics with respect to these
Oaxaca Indians, which I had already observed on
the previous day, but which more particularly came
under my notice upon this occasion. They had gone
through a long day's work of most severe labour,
and yet upon settling down for the night's rest they
neither ate any food or drank any water. My
guides, who were not, like these men, trained
to carry great weights for considerable distances,
were also able to live upon very small quantities of
food and never seemed to be tired at the end of the
day's journey.

It was the custom of each Indian before leaving
his home to provide himself with a small quantity of
a substance called pozole, which was prepared for
him by his wife. This was usually made in the
following manner. A sufficient quantity of maize was
partly boiled, until the grain could be easily removed
from the husks. These softened grains were then
ground upon the metatl or grindstone until a thick
paste was made. This was either put into a little
bag or rolled up in a green leaf. This paste was
the principal part of the food that was carried, but

sometimes the wives gave their husbands a supply of tortillas. To make these, the grains of maize, after being slightly boiled, are put upon the metatl, and rolled out into a very thin pancake; this is taken off the stone and put upon a large leaf and made into a round shape. It is then placed upon a pan and held for a few minutes over the fire, until it is properly baked, when it becomes a tortilla. With a few of these and his scant store of pozole an Indian always considers himself to be amply provisioned until he returns to his village or secluded country hut.

My guides took their principal meal about noon. A portion of the paste was taken out of the leaf and placed upon the palm of the left hand, a small quantity of water was then mixed with it until it became slightly fluid and then it was eaten. In the evening they usually took more pozole and a tortilla, after which they would drink some water mixed with enough of the pozole to make it become the colour and consistency of thin milk. In this manner they avoided drinking pure cold water. This was the daily food of my Indians, upon which they could go long journeys carrying considerable weights, and they never appeared to be tired.*

The cargadores are trained from boyhood to carry heavy burdens over great distances. Don Pepe, expected them to travel eight leagues a day. But

---

* I had previously observed when travelling in the Cyrenaica in the regions around Cyrene, that the Bedouins could perform a long day's hard work and subsist upon a few handfuls of grains of wheat moistened with water.

when carrying lighter loads they will sometimes travel for several consecutive days at the rate of nearly forty English miles a day. When the cargo-bearers were moving in single file with their burdens, they looked like the Tamemes bearing tribute to Montezuma as represented in the ancient pictures. It is probable that these men were enduring labours similar to those that had been performed by their ancestors for centuries before the arrival of the Spaniards.

In the morning the Indians proceeded on their journey towards the coast. We followed a path leading in another direction, through open and wooded lowlands. Finally after a ride of four leagues we reached the savannah upon which is situated the village of San Domingo del Palenque.

Never have I known a moment of more keen pleasure and satisfaction, than that when José pointed out to me this beautiful spot. I had become fatigued by the hardships of the previous days, and the buoyancy of mind that was felt in getting at last into a region of life and sunshine cannot be adequately expressed.

We stopped to ask where Doctor Coller lived, and were shown the position of a low, thatched cottage, at the door of which stood the only European living in the village.* I was received by him with friendly

---

* Dr. Coller was surprised to see me. It was supposed that I was the first Englishman who had come to Palenque from the coasts of the Pacific, Mr. Stephens, my predecessor being an American. I am however under the impression that his companion, Mr. Catherwood, was an Englishman.

welcome. My hammock was placed under the shade
of the projecting thatch. The mule was set free to
wander at will amongst the plains, and I was
advised to take twenty-four hours complete rest. On
the following forenoon I made arrangements for proceeding to the ruins, and a few Indians were sent
there to open the path, and to clear the inner courts
of the palace from weeds and brushwood.

San Domingo del Palenque is placed upon a rising
grassy slope studded with fine trees. The church was
in ruins and roofless. The population consisted
chiefly of Ladinos. The Indians lived in secluded
places near the out-skirts, where they cultivated
their milpas or cornfields. There was a charm about
this sunny fertile savannah and the simple habits of
life of its inhabitants, which must be attractive to
men of sensitive temperaments. The land is fertile,
corn is abundant, and cattle, horses and mules
wander over the green pastures in freedom.

It was an unusual series of circumstances that had
caused Dr. Coller to settle for life in this remote
part of the world. He told me that he was a native
of Switzerland and was born at Zurich. He was
educated in that city but completed his studies at
Berlin. Much of his early life was passed in different
countries. About ten years before my arrival, he felt
a wish to see Palenque and found his way to this
region from the shores of the Gulf of Mexico. Upon
reaching the village he was fascinated by its beautiful situation, its repose and its proximity to the
ancient ruins in which he felt the strongest interest.
He found that the life at San Domingo had an
attraction for him which he did not wish to resist,

and he decided to make this place his home, and married a native who possessed, in her own right, some land in the neighbourhood.*

Dr. Coller was a man of varied and extensive information and an excellent linguist. He had devoted much time, not only to the investigation of the Indian antiquities, but also to the study of the geology and botany of the district, and I was much pleased when he proposed to accompany me to Palenque. It was of the greatest advantage thus to have the benefit of his accurate knowledge of the positions of the mounds and temples.

---

* Dr. Coller's hut at San Domingo del Palenque was not a Castle of Lirias, but probably the lines quoted by Gil Blas were often in his mind. Indeed there are many others who, if they saw that hamlet as I saw it in the month of March, would concur with him in saying :

      " Inveni portum.   Spes et Fortuna valete.
      Sat me lusistis: ludite nunc alios."

CHAPTER XV.

It was a bright tropical morning when we mounted
our horses and followed the narrow path leading to
Palenque. After riding for a league through woods,
savannahs, and cornfields, we reached and crossed
the river Michol.

As we approached the ruins, the forest was so
thick that we were not able to see anything beyond
the track which had been cleared for us by our men.
At a distance of about three Spanish leagues from
San Domingo, we came to the borders of a small
running stream. Dr. Coller stopped and said that
at this point we should dismount, as we had arrived
at our destination. We then went up a steep slope,
on the summit of which I could see dimly, the pillars
and ruined roof of the "Palace."

Our Indians met us at the entrance. They had
already cleared the brushwood which had overgrown
the quadrangles, and had removed all that interfered

with any exploring work that they thought we might wish to carry out. The luxuriance of the vegetation was surprising. In one of the open courts we observed a large plant which we found to be a species of arum. The leaves were of an extraordinary size, and averaged four feet six inches long by three feet six inches wide ; the stalks were over seven feet high.

The greater part of the day was occupied in making a survey of the ground plans of the building, as far as it was possible to trace them amongst the accumulations of fallen ruins. Upon the completion of this work, and after having made an examination of the series of small chambers below the corridors, it became evident that the building was erected with the intention of establishing a monastery, similar to those which were described by the historians of the conquest of Mexico as being dedicated to the use of the priests who worshipped and performed ceremonies at the shrines of the god Quetzalcoatl, and who, in addition to those duties, were given the charge of educating the children of the chiefs. They also trained those youths who were intended to become priests.

It is to be regretted that this great structure was called by its first discoverers "The Palace," and that its purpose was rendered perplexing by theories connected with the dwellings of Kings or Caciques.

According to the investigations of Mr. Stephens, its extreme dimensions were two hundred and twenty-eight feet long, by one hundred and eighty feet wide. The height of the rectangular mound upon which it is placed has been variously estimated. It appears to have been about twenty feet high.

Upon the summit of this platform was built with stone and mortar, the various foundations upon which the buildings and galleries of the monastery were erected. The base upon the east front was about ten feet high. The height of the building may be estimated to have been nearly twenty-four feet. Thus it may be concluded that the whole height from the ground to the roof must have been approximately fifty-four feet. The architectural proportions seem to have been well designed.

The interior gave me the impression of being Moorish in its style, especially with respect to the open inner courts, the arrangement of the corridors and the lavish employment of stucco ornamentation, brilliantly coloured. A closer investigation into architectural details left the subject in doubt, but there still remained upon the mind the feeling that in some unintelligible manner, the construction had been directed either by foreigners or by Indians who were partly descended from men of foreign origin. The forms of ancient mosques and of the inner courts and quadrangles of Arabian or Moorish and Spanish public buildings were indistinctly recalled to the memory. It was however to be observed, upon an examination of the methods adopted at Palenque in supporting the weight of the roofs, that the arches (if it is permissible for that term to be applied to straight converging slopes covered with flat coping stones,) are absolutely exceptional and unlike any other arch that is known. I was reminded, to a certain extent, of the ruins of Alatri, near Mycenæ on the plains of Argos, and of an Etruscan tomb near Perugia, but the system employed by the American architects, in placing the cap or terminal cross stones was essentially different.

In the exploration of the ruins our attention was chiefly directed to certain doubtful points, particularly with regard to the chambers which are beneath the corridors, and are entered from the level of the courts. There have been several conjectures respecting the purposes of these cells. I think that it is probable that they were used as dormitories. In some of the chambers there was a low, wide stone table, placed against the wall at the end. These benches were large flat smooth slabs of limestone supported on four stone legs. In height, shape and dimensions they were like the wooden bedsteads used by the Indians at the present time.

There is a square tower in one of the inner courts which must be considered as the most singular structure in Palenque. In position and manner of construction it is abnormal in character. It was probably intended for some special object, after the monastery had been completed. When Captain Del Rio saw this tower, in 1787, he estimated its height to be sixteen yards. In 1870 there were heaps of rubble and fallen stones piled against the base, which made it difficult for me to make exact measurements, but an approximate estimate gave the sides of the square near the base as twenty-three feet, and the height about forty-five feet. The peculiarity about the construction is the fact that it consists of a tower within a tower. The inner structure contains a steep and narrow staircase. Light is obtained through large openings in the sides of the outer tower, and then through

smaller openings in the walls of the interior one.
The steps appear to have led up to the top. The
walls are formed of rough slabs of limestone
which had been thickly coated over with cement,
portions of which still remained. It was raised to a
height which commanded views of the adjacent
temples.

Upon my return to the eastern front, I found
that the Indians had slung the hammocks in the
outer corridor overlooking the forest. A few minutes
before sunset we heard the strange and beautiful
notes of a solitary bird singing amongst the ruins.
The song resembled in its tone that of a thrush.
Dr. Coller said that the bird was a kind of nightingale, and that it was only known to live within and
around the Palenque temples. The bird sang in a
slow, deliberate manner, each of the notes having a
short interval of time between them. The song was
maintained during the twilight, and ceased as soon
as it became dark and the night had begun. It
was an evening hymn to the setting sun. The hoarse
screams and movements of troops of monkeys then
disturbed the precincts. These harsh noises gradually stopped, and as the night advanced the forest
became silent. The moon was up and we knew that it
was shining brightly above the trees, but we could only
see occasionally its faint glimmer. I had expected
to hear the croaking of frogs or the sounds of cicadas,
the usual accompaniment to a tropical evening, but
although there was a running stream of water at the
foot of the mound, these familiar sounds were absent.

The brushwood covering the ground was made
brilliant by numerous fireflies. The light which shone

from these beetles far exceeded anything of that
nature that I had seen in other regions, and I took
the opportunity of ascertaining the strength of the
illuminating power. I sent one of the men into the
wood to catch the largest firefly that he could find,
and then, after having made the corridor dark by
extinguishing our candles, the insect was held about
two inches from a blank page of my note book,
Dr. Coller watched the experiment. We found that
the light was steady and shed a soft clear phos-
phorescent glow over the paper. The luminous power
was sufficient to enable us to read or write with ease
over a surface two inches square. After writing a
few notes upon what had been done during the day
we added :—

> " Written by the light of a firefly in the Palace, in
> the ruins of Palenque, the night of Wednesday,
> March 10th, 1870, the candle (firefly) held by
> Dr. Albert Coller. The light about equal to that
> of a small wax candle and very pure. The light
> rather greenish."
>
> " Dr. A. J. COLLER."

Before turning into my hammock I visited the
horses tethered at the base of the mound near the
stream. They were much worried by flies, mosquitos,
and small ticks called garrapátas, which find their
way under the skin and cause great irritation. In
the corridor, thirty feet above them, we were not
troubled with any of these pests, but there were
numerous bats. The Indians said that, sometimes,
horses were seriously injured by bats biting them
above their hoofs.

In the morning, upon the earliest indications of

dawn, the solitary nightingale again began its song, and the clear staccato, and singularly musical note was again heard amongst the ruins until sunrise, when it ceased. Thus this bird sang its song of praise as the herald of the day.

At sunrise Dr. Coller returned to San Domingo, leaving me alone at Palenque to carry out the investigation of the mounds and temples, a work which he thought would be laborious and oppressive. My guides were however well acquainted with the ruins, and I consequently knew that I should be spared all unnecessary exertion. But until I began the exploration I had no idea of the difficulties that had to be encountered. The men were employed in cutting a path through the brushwood and it was impracticable to do more than follow a certain line of direction and obtain ideas of distances by counting the number of paces or by noting intervals of time. I soon ascertained that with the means at my disposal it was hopeless to expect to do more than obtain a general knowledge of the extent and form of the chief structures, and the positions of the mounds. It was a serious disappointment to find that it was impossible to make a thorough examination without the aid of a large number of Indians to cut down the trees and clear the ground. This would have been a work involving much time and expenditure and was entirely beyond my power. The forest was sombre, for the light that penetrated through the trees, was insufficient. It was however possible to obtain a fair knowledge of the extent of the space covered by the mounds, and their distances from the monastery. The ground plan of the inclosure could also be approximately understood.

The first and, with respect to its altar, the most
important building that I saw, was that known by
the name of the Temple of the Cross.   Before as-
cending the sides of the mound upon which it stands,
I examined the formation of an ancient causeway
which covered, for some distance, the stream near
its base.   I traced it for about one hundred and fifty
yards.   A small portion was sufficiently preserved
to enable the system of construction to be ascertained.   It appears to have been intended for the
purpose of confining the rivulet that ran beneath
it, and thus to secure a dry roadway, or crossing,
during the rainy season.   It was stated by the
Indians, that there still existed, in the forest, the
remains of a stone bridge.   As far as I could understand their description, it appeared that in shape it
was not unlike the ancient Chinese bridges, and rose
to the centre by steep gradients.

After finishing the measurements of the causeway
we began to ascend the mound.   About halfway up
the slope, the men stopped and pointed to a place
where, lying with its face on the ground, was the
stone of the cross.   As this tablet had been the subject of much investigation, and is undoubtedly, with
respect to its meaning, the most remarkable monu-
ment at Palenque, I was anxious to examine it with
the utmost care.   I directed the Indians to turn it
over and thoroughly clean it from moss and dirt, so
as to enable me to make a sketch of it.   I found
that, in consequence of the action of the earth upon
the face of the stone, parts of the sculpture were
difficult to trace, but the central figures were quite
distinct.   I was able to make a satisfactory outline,

chiefly confining my attention to the cross, the bird surmounting it, and the dress of the man, having in his hands what seemed to be a child, which he was presenting as a votive offering.

The bird, with its long double tail feathers, was probably the representation of the Quetzal, the sacred bird of the Quichés, and thus it may be assumed that the temple in which this tablet formed the centre of the altar piece, was dedicated to the worship of the god Quetzalcoatl. But, judging by the peculiarities of the dress worn by the principal worshipper, I formed the opinion that he was not, as has previously been supposed, a priest offering sacrifice. The worshippers and the offerings have, I believe, other significations.*

The temple, placed upon the top of the mound, must have been—when it was externally perfect—a graceful and well proportioned shrine ; but when I saw it, the outer walls were so enveloped in brushwood and enclosed by trees, that it was not practicable to do more than obtain a conception of its proportions. After having measured the length, breadth and height, and made a ground plan, I examined the interior. A corridor ran along the front ; within was the chamber which had contained the inscribed stone slabs which formed the back of the altar, in the centre of which had been the figure of the cross. This, and the right and left hand tablets, had been

---

* In the final chapters, xix–xx, will be found the conclusions that I have formed with regard to the temple and tablet of the cross.

all closely joined together so as to form one subject,* the meaning of which was probably explained by the hieroglyphic characters. The right hand tablet, which had been removed, I had already seen at the museum in Washington.

After leaving this sanctuary, we descended the southern slope until we reached the base, and then began to ascend the adjoining mound, on whose summit was another temple. Thus we proceeded until we reached a singular little structure which has been considered to be exceptional, from the fact that the figure upon the altar had been placed upon a base supported by what are supposed to have been two tigers. I could only trace the remains of the feet, as everything within and without the temple was in ruins. Following the direction of the quadrangular precincts, we finally crossed over an unusually lofty mound, and then arrived at the back or western face of the monastery.

We had completed a slight survey of the mounds and temples on the sides of the inclosure, having passed successively over them and examined the altars, as far as their more or less ruined state permitted. These all varied in their dimensions, but they were evidently built for analagous purposes as shrines for the worship of the Indian gods.§   There

---

* See frontispiece.

§The areas occupied by the temples differed considerably in their extent. The largest of them which I measured was that of the Temple of the Cross.

Its interior dimensions were forty-three feet seven inches long by twenty-five feet four inches deep ; the outer walls were three

was, however, one important exception which requires to be noticed.

At the south-west angle of the monastery—and connected with it in such a manner that it seems to have been an adjunct to the main building—are the ruins of a structure which has been considered to have been a temple, but which, I think, served for a different purpose. It stands upon a mound about forty-five feet high. Its frontage was found to be longer than that of any of the other temples. In the interior there was no altar, but the upright slabs of stone placed upon the inner wall were covered with hieroglyphs. When the Indians, who accompanied Mr. Stephens, saw these groups of characters they declared that the building was an escuela or schoolhouse. Other opinions were also given, but the subject has not received any investigation. I think it is probable that the opinion of the Indians was correct, and that it was here that the boys were taught the meaning of the hieroglyphic symbols, and were thus able to read and interpret the signs placed upon the idols and altars.

In the afternoon we re-entered the monastery. We had been for nearly seven hours occupied in crossing over the mounds and clearing a path through the forest, and yet at no time did I estimate that we were more than five hundred yards from our starting point. At the end of this part of

---

feet thick. Therefore the ground space covered by the building was nearly fifty feet in frontage and a little more than thirty-one feet in depth. Its exterior height was about twenty feet. The measurements of the temple on the adjoining pyramid were less.

the day's work, I found that I was able to establish
some deductions respecting the positions and heights
of the raised platforms and the character of the
stone edifices.

It may be concluded that Palenque consists of a
group of mounds having buildings upon them exclusively devoted to the purposes of religion. In the
year 1840, five of the mounds had temples upon
their summits which were in a fair state of preservation. The survey of Captain Antonio Del Rio
was made in the year 1787, and, as he was an
officer of the Artillery, his Report, with respect to
the general plan, and the bearings and distances of
the mounds then remaining, may be accepted as being
correct. He states that he visited the ruins called
Casas de Piedras (stone houses) on the 5th of May,
and finding that nothing could be distinctly made
out in consequence of the forest, he engaged a large
number of Indians from Tumbalá, who felled the
trees and afterwards cleared the ground by fire, thus
opening up a sufficient space to enable him to observe
the true positions of the mounds and buildings. He
found that they were all contained within a rectangular area, four hundred and fifty yards long
and three hundred yards wide. In the centre was
the mound upon which stood the largest structure.
This was surrounded by other edifices, "namely:
five to the northward, four to the southward, one to
the south-west, and three to the eastward."

Thus it appears that in 1787 there were thirteen
mounds with buildings upon their summits, besides
the large platform earthwork upon which was placed
the "Palace." In 1806, nearly twenty years after-

wards, the Spanish Government ordered another survey to be made. The expedition was placed under the orders of Captain Dupaix, who had served as an officer in the Dragoons. He reported that, at that time, eleven temples were still standing. Thirty-four years later, Mr. Stephens could only discover five temples not utterly ruined. It is strange that in these short intervals of time, such changes should have happened amongst monuments of this nature. With regard to this subject, it is of consequence to notice the statements given by the local authorities who made the original discoveries which led to the survey of Del Rio. The explorations were conducted, under the orders of the Spanish authorities at Guatemala, by one of the principal inhabitants of the village of San Domingo, named Calderon, aided by the Government architect, Bernasconi. In their Report, which was made only three years before that of Del Rio, they declared that there were evidences of the ruins of numerous houses occupying a large space of land to the west of the temples. Nothing was known by my Indians upon this subject. It should, however, be observed, with respect to undiscovered ruins, that any rumours relating to what may, or may not, exist in the heart of a tropical forest, must necessarily be doubtful, for where nothing can be seen, except what may happen to be found in the direction of the path, much must be unknown.

On the slopes of the ground in front of one of the temples I saw a large and rudely carved statue, which in consequence of its form and manner of sculpture is of much importance. There is reason to believe that it was intended to represent Quetzalcoatl, an Indian god, a mythical or real personage, who, for many reasons connected with Palenque, requires to have an especial consideration given to him. It is a distinctive characteristic of this statue, that the features are essentially different from those of the Indians whose figures are to be seen upon the altars of the temples and within the courts and corridors of the monastery. These have receding foreheads and sharply defined prominent faces, quite unlike the present races in Central America, but in a marked degree resembling the tribes of the North American Indians, who had the custom of flattening the heads of their children.

The statue by my measurement, was a few inches more than eight feet in height, exclusive of the lower part of the stone, which tapered off in such a manner as to show that it had been originally placed upright and fixed in the ground. The feet stood on a base upon which was carved the hieroglyph which probably denoted the name. The forehead was low and straight. The face was completely different in type and expression, from that of any known race of Indians. The head was surmounted by a kind of high tiara. The left hand held in front of the figure a small head, in the same position as in the little figure at Ocosingo.

As, after completing the circuit of the mounds, there were still a few hours at my disposal before leaving Palenque so as to reach the village before night-fall, I decided to devote the time to the investigation of certain problems regarding the age and construction of the buildings. But in the first place, attention should be directed to the manner in which the open courts within the monastery are disposed, and access is obtained to the rooms beneath the corridors. Commencing from the east front, there are two ranges of corridors which are separated throughout their whole length by a strong wall,

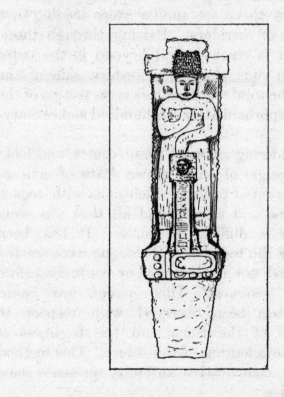

which receives the thrust of the two inner slopes supporting the roof. There is only one entrance or means of communication between them in the existing northern portion of the ruins. The interior width of each of these galleries is about seven feet four inches. After passing across them, the principal court is reached and the floor of the open space is seen ten feet below. A wide flight of large and well hewn stone steps leads down to the bottom, which appears to have been paved with several layers of cement. This court is twenty-eight paces wide. The rooms are entered through doorways in the sides of the inclosing walls. Opposite to the first flight of steps there are similar steps leading to a second series of corridors. Passing through these, another court is reached, and beyond is the outer gallery which runs along the western side of the building. The total width of this cross section of the monastery is approximately one hundred and seventy-six feet.

When wandering amongst these courts, and looking at the vestiges of an unknown state of civilisation, I endeavoured to form conclusions with regard to the purpose and antiquity of all that was seen. The problem is difficult to solve. It has been surmised that the temples of Palenque were erected during a period not exceeding four centuries before the Spanish conquest. This opinion was based upon what has been observed with respect to the condition of the ruins, and the freshness of portions of the colouring of the stucco. This method of estimating comparative antiquity presents some local difficulties.

The square tower was originally faced with thick cement, and then covered with washes of colour, in the same manner as the walls of the Teocallis in the Quiché city of Utatlan upon which the faded colours are still visible. If the existing outer coating was the only one that had been given it would

be reasonable to infer that the age of the tower was
not great. But it happens that in those places where
portions of the stucco have fallen, there have been
numerous applications of colour, and therefore
admitting that the latest may look bright and fresh,
it is not possible to estimate the periods that may
have elapsed between the dates of successive layers.
Although I was at first inclined to think that the
building could not be ancient, yet a more careful
examination left the subject indeterminate. Any
conclusions which may have been thought probable
on account of the state of the walls and roofs
are equally uncertain. With regard to this matter
it is necessary to take into consideration certain
existing conditions.

Immediately behind the ruins are the slopes of the
sierras which I traversed on the way from Tumbalá. They are covered with loose fragments of the
limestones of which they are formed. These were
the building materials used by the architects of the
temples. Their small size and flat surface were
suitable for the purpose, when combined with
mortar, the mixing of which the Indians well
understood. The walls of the monastery were made
with layers of these flat stones bound together with
quantities of this mortar. The outer faces were carefully arranged to receive a thick casing of cement,
which was so hard and sound, that it is evident
the builders must have had an accurate knowledge
of the best proportions of the substances required
for its composition. The cement had a smooth surface and in several places it was still perfect. The
colours laid upon it are red, blue, yellow and white.

They appear to have been made more or less vivid
and varied in accordance with what was thought
necessary to obtain good contrasts. The stucco
figures and scrolls were skilfully designed, and were
coloured in a manner which was harmonious and
effective. The sound state of the cement where it is
sheltered from the action of the rain is extraordinary.
It is strange that in this tropical climate where, for
half the year there are continuous and heavy rain-
falls, the variations from the damp, close atmosphere
in the summer to the dry season of winter should
not have had a more destructive influence upon
buildings, mainly composed of rubble and mortar.

In one instance, that of the tower, the astonishing growth of tropical vegetation has had the effect of
preventing its fall. Thick creepers have wound themselves like strong ropes around the walls and bound
them firmly together. The walls at the corners of the
entrances to the courts were remarkably uninjured.
The cement was intact, and this even in positions
where it might have been expected that, in a long
course of time, in consequence of being partly
exposed and partly sheltered, it would have broken
away and fallen.

It would be justifiable to conclude from these
evidences of stability that the buildings are comparatively modern. But there is a difficulty with
regard to this assumption which has to be considered.
In the year 1525, when Cortes on his march from
Mexico to Honduras passed with his expeditionary
forces within a few leagues of this place, the temples
had been already abandoned. Consequently not
less than four centuries must have now elapsed since

Palenque was deserted. If then, within the tropics, buildings made of such perishable materials have remained for that long period in a fair state of preservation, it may be inferred that there are some local circumstances which have caused an exceptional power of resistance to the disintegrating action of the climate. The forest may have afforded some protection, and therefore the age of the monastery may be greater than might be estimated from the condition of the ruins.

There are, however, other facts which are opposed to any theories of great antiquity. The Indians had cleared, for my inspection, the stone steps leading from the western side of the principal court. Upon these were carved groups of hieroglyphs which were in an almost perfect state. The edges of the steps were unworn. It was therefore made evident that in an open court, completely exposed to the weather and the influence of the tropical rains, inscriptions graven upon the surface of these flat stone slabs had remained uninjured.

After looking at the sculptures, and the coloured stucco figures which adorned the piers and inner walls, I endeavoured to establish some standard of comparison by which I might be able to form well-founded conjectures regarding their age. I thought of various ruins in Egypt and Asia Minor, then of those belonging to later periods in Italy and Great Britain, but there were such essential differences in the materials used, and the influences of the atmosphere, that it was not possible to establish any assured conclusions. Opinions formed upon the results of an examination of the temples on the mounds would be equally unsatisfactory, for some of them, especially in their interiors, were in a comparatively good condition, others were in ruins. But, there are proofs of a moderate antiquity. The lintels that once supported the walls over the doorways and other openings have completely disappeared. In only one instance, which came under my notice, were there any signs of the thick, hard beams of zapote wood which had been employed for that purpose. A broad lintel in the monastery had left its impress upon the under surface of the wall which had weighed downwards upon it. The marks of the fibre and the shape of the lintel were clearly defined upon the mortar. Dr. Coller found amongst the ruins a piece of this wood. It was exceedingly heavy and close-grained, and was of the nature of what is known, in the East Indies, by the name of iron wood. The zapote trees grow chiefly in the forests in the valley of the Usamacinta and towards the lake of Peten.

When the evening drew near, I called my Indians together and entered the forest on the way back to the village. As I rode slowly forward I felt that these mysterious ruins contained a secret which has yet to be unravelled. The priests of a powerful race, having strange and unknown forms of religion, had been for centuries worshipping at these shrines. Within the sanctuaries were graven upon tablets of stone those records which, when interpreted, may throw some light upon what is now obscure.*

---

*A clear and instructive memoir by Professor Charles Rau, upon the subject of the interpretation of the Palenque hieroglyphs, is to be found in one of the Smithsonian Contributions to Knowledge, published in 1879.

Investigations have also been made in England, France and Germany. I believe it has been ascertained that a dot means one, a bar five, a bar with two dots seven, and two bars represent ten. It has also been discovered that the hieroglyphs are to be read from left to right, and from the top downwards. If this is correct it is a discovery of considerable importance. Upon an examination of the illustration in the frontispiece of the Palenque altar tablet it will be observed, from the position of the leading groups of figures on the left slab, that the heads are probably intended to represent the chiefs of the Toltec tribe.

The numerous explorations that have latterly taken place throughout Mexico, Guatemala and Yucatan have practically determined the positions and extent of all the ancient Indian ruins that still exist in those lands. Therefore it is not expected that any more discoveries of importance will be made. It is however possible that one or more small temples or structures may be found hidden among the forests in the line of direction between Ocosingo and Flores.

In the United States much attention is being given to the study of the Mexican and Maya manuscripts.

It is to be hoped that methods of interpretation will be established upon a sound basis, and that the characters written upon the codices, and the hieroglyphs graven upon the idols and stone tablets will be ultimately deciphered.

CHAPTER XVI.

AT San Domingo Dr. Coller showed me a chart
which he had drawn of the country around for a
distance of twelve miles, exclusive of the neighbourhood of Palenque where the forest prevented him
from making a survey. Upon this chart he had
placed the positions of eleven mounds that he had
discovered. They were situated near the left bank
of the Usamacinta. On the slopes of these mounds
were loose slabs of worked limestone which he
thought must have formed part of houses built on
their summits. Some excavations had been made
and it was proved that the mounds were not burial
places.

I met in the village the proprietor of a small
hacienda near Balancan. He told me that in one
of his fields there was a large mound forty feet high,
which must have had a building upon it, for on the
top there were large blocks of squared stone. He

wished to know what the mound contained and had therefore dug through it, but he found nothing but a curved grindstone precisely similar in shape and size to those now used by the women in the neighbourhood. In the adjoining land he had found near the surface numerous terra-cotta idols, but he had not seen any human bones. It is a coincidence perhaps of some importance, with reference to the origin of the race once occupying Palenque, that a grindstone was also the only thing found within the mound opened by the orders of Carrera on the plains of Mixco, in that part of Central America which, before the conquest, had been occupied by the Quichés.

San Domingo is occasionally visited by groups of the wild Indians called Lacandones who live isolated amongst the adjacent forests. Dr. Coller told me that during his ten years' residence, he had seen several of these men enter the village for the purpose of exchanging beans, tobacco and wax for spirits and other goods. They were always dressed in long white cotton frocks which reached nearly to their feet, and they wore their hair loose and very long. They seemed to be of a shy and inoffensive disposition. It is probable that they are of the same tribe as the Indians who live scattered amongst the Cordilleras near Comitan, a few of whom occasionally come down to that town from the forests bringing for barter bags of cocoa beans.

The journey from Palenque to the coast of the Gulf of Mexico had to be made by rivers and lagoons. The embarkation place was at Catasaja, where canoes were to be obtained. After riding eight leagues through forests and savannahs we reached " Las

Playas," where I was welcomed by the Licenciado Vadillo. Catasaja was a flourishing village, prettily situated on the upper waters of a branch of the Usamacinta. It was in an unusually busy state. Preparations were in progress for holding a fair, and celebrating the annual festival of the church. Great numbers of Indians and Ladinos were expected to arrive from the surrounding country, and sheds were being built as shelters for them. In the morning, at an early hour, I found that Señor Vadillo had made all necessary arrangements for my journey, and had secured for me a good canoe manned by trustworthy Indians. With his assistance I was able to sell my mule. The saddle and hammock were retained as I should want them in Yucatan.

In the forenoon the men reported that the boat was ready. After paddling swiftly down the stream for several leagues we entered a channel whose muddy banks were covered with alligators. The river also swarmed with them. Upon several occasions I thought that the canoe was in danger of being capsized by the waves made by the alligators, in consequence, as we approached them, of their habit of slipping off the bank into the river, and I told the Indians to be careful. They said that the canoe was perfectly safe, but that if, by any accident, we should be rolled over there was nothing to be feared, as the alligators never attacked people in the water. I was doubtful about this theory, although it may be correct. It is well known that natives in other parts of the world have been seized by alligators when incautiously going too near them when they were watching for their prey on the banks.   But I do not know if there is any evidence to show that they would seize men in the same manner if they were actually floating in the water.*

---

* Some years after my return to England I had a long conversation upon the subject of alligators with Mr. Bates, who was then our Secretary of the Royal Geographical Society, and whose knowledge upon all matters concerning the habits of animals in tropical lands was very extensive.   In his book "The Naturalist on the Amazons," he mentions a case that happened at a place called Carcara.

An Indian, one of the crew belonging to a trading canoe, whilst in a half drunken state went down to bathe in the lake and stumbled. A pair of gaping jaws seized him round the waist and dragged him under water; after a short lapse of time the brute came up to breathe and was seen with one leg of the man sticking out from his jaws.

Other instances of this kind have been mentioned by naturalists, but I do not remember any cases of men being seized when actually swimming in the water.   Possibly my Indians may have known from hearsay or experience the truth of what they stated.

It has been said that alligators, owing to the formation of their throats, cannot swallow their prey in the water, but are obliged to go to the banks for that purpose.

It was not, however, upon the subject of the danger to men from approaching these reptiles that the conversation chiefly turned.

We discussed the question of their food supply.   Mr. Bates said that they lived upon fish.   I observed, with reference to that part of the river where I had seen them congregated in such amazing numbers, that it was impossible that the supply of food from fish alone could be sufficient, and also that in consequence of the filthy state of the water no fish could live in it.

Mr. Bates after some consideration said that their food must be fish, but he added, that it was probable that they could live in an almost torpid condition for long periods.

Mr. Bates felt assured that fish formed the food of alligators. It was not possible to feel quite satisfied with this solution of the problem, especially under circumstances where alligators

Lower down the river we came to a place where the stream was sluggish. The banks were flat and covered with dense vegetation. Here we saw an extraordinary scene. The water was thick, green, and putrid with animal matter. The surface was covered with the inflated bodies of dead alligators.

Large carrion birds were feeding upon them in the most revolting manner. Their claws were firmly fixed upon the hard skin of the reptiles, and they drove their beaks, like pickaxes, deep down into their entrails and gorged themselves with the decaying flesh. The stench was horrible, and together with the oppressive heat, the foul state of the air and the enormous mosquitoes, made this part of the journey very disgusting.

At sunset we arrived at a place called Jonuta, near the junction of the river Palisada with the

---

abound in stagnant lagoons in which fish must necessarily be scarce.

In the unfrequented parts of the estuaries of rivers flowing into the Caribbean sea, it can be understood that at certain seasons of the year the supply of fish may be great, and we have the authority of that careful observer Mr. Bartram, for the statement that upon those occasions the numbers of alligators crowding the rivers in Florida were astonishing.

In 1853 the " Vestal " happened to be cruising off Cuba, and I was sent in charge of the boats to look for fresh water in Guantanomo harbour, at a spot which was reputed to have been a favourite haunt of pirates in the seventeenth century.

After some search we discovered a small stream, but the entrance was defended by such crowds of alligators that we had great difficulty in passing through them. If, as was possible, they were waiting for the arrival of fish from the upper waters, it may be inferred that a comparatively small supply of food suffices for their sustenance.

river Usamacinta, and the canoe was hauled up on
the bank. We could not have been far from the
spot where Cortes crossed over on his march to Honduras, one of the most extraordinary military expeditions, through an absolutely unknown country and
amongst unknown men, that has ever been successfully accomplished. This part of the march through
the forest and across the numerous streams of the
estuary of the Usamacinta was especially difficult
and laborious, and at one time, the forces were driven
to great straits for want of provisions. The events
that occurred here are described by Bernal Diaz, who
accompanied the troops, and by Cortes in his des-
patch to the Emperor Charles V. One of these
events was so remarkable that it at once arrests the
attention.

The Spaniards and their Indian allies had been
for several days suffering from famine, and the state
of affairs in the camp was becoming serious. It was
then discovered that several acts of cannibalism had
taken place. "It appeared," states Bernal Diaz,
"that certain Caciques from Mexico had captured two
or three of the Indians belonging to the villages that
we had passed through, and had brought them
hidden amongst their baggage, and on account of
the hunger on the road they killed them and roasted
them in ovens which were made under the ground
with stones, as was their custom in Mexico, and they
devoured them, and in the same way they had also
secreted the two guides that we had with us who
had run away, and they ate them. When Cortes
knew what had happened he ordered the Mexican
Caciques to be called together and spoke angrily to

them, and told them that if such things occurred
again he would punish them. The Franciscan friar,
who accompanied us, also preached to them many
holy and good sayings and after he had concluded
his sermon Cortes, as a matter of justice, ordered a
Mexican Indian to be burnt on account of the
murder of the Indians that they had eaten."

Cortes in reporting this punishment to the
Emperor says,—"I ordered him to be burnt, giving
the said Señor to understand the reason for this act
of justice. That it was because he had killed an
Indian and eaten him; which act was forbidden by
your Majesty and that I, in your Royal name, had
notified and ordered that it should not be done, and
that therefore for having killed and eaten him I
ordered him to be burnt." *

Another strange event that took place whilst the
troops were in this region, was the tragic fate of
Guatimozin, who had succeeded Montezuma as
Emperor of Mexico. It is difficult to understand
what could have been the object that Cortes had in
view when he ordered this monarch to be executed.
He may have thought it expedient to destroy, as far
as possible, the whole race of caciques thoughout
New Spain and thus minimise the risk of any
organized rebellion. These chiefs ruled with absolute power over the natives, and it is possible that
the Spanish authorities deemed it advisable to get
rid of them. Hundreds of them were burnt alive

---

* "Cartas de Hernan Cortes," collected by Don Pascual de
Gayangos, p. 407.

at the stake upon the slightest pretexts. After one of the local insurrections the officer who suppressed it reported that he had burnt forty of the rebellious caciques. In a similar manner the leaders in Cuba and Haiti were also destroyed.

In the case of Guatimozin, Cortes considered that he and his cousin, the King of Tlacupa, had been proved guilty of conspiring with other Indians to kill the Spaniards; and he accordingly ordered them to be put to death. The sentence was immediately carried out, and the two Mexican monarchs were hanged upon a tree within sight of the army as it continued its march through the forest.

The positions where these events occurred can only be approximately determined. The wooden bridges which were constructed for the passage of the troops have disappeared. All local records of this famous march have passed away. The villages or pueblos mentioned by the conquerors no longer exist, and their names are forgotten. It is only by the most attentive study that even a presumptive knowledge of the route can be obtained. From the accounts given in the official despatches and the statements of Bernal Diaz, and also from the fact that Cortes steered a straight course by compass, it may be concluded that the forces must have passed near Jonuta and about twenty-eight miles from the ruins of Palenque.

With respect to the acts of cannibalism it should be observed, in justice to other tribes, that the caciques who devoured the bodies were Mexicans, and there are reasons for believing that before the arrival of the Aztecs cannibalism was unknown in

Central America. The method of cooking by baking
in ovens which, after the holes had been dug out of
the ground, were surrounded and covered by heated
stones, are the same as those that were customary
with the Maoris in New Zealand, who, after their
fights, feasted upon their captured enemies in that
manner.

Upon the evening of the day upon which we left
Jonuta, we reached Palisada and brought to an end
our wearisome canoe voyage down the Usamacinta.
At Palisada the logwood, which is obtained in the
forests bordering upon the upper parts of the rivers,
is gathered together and shipped upon small schooners
which carry their cargoes of palo tinto (red wood)
to the town of Laguna on the island of Carmen,
whence the wood is sent to Europe and other parts
of the world.

In one of these little fore-and-aft rigged schooners
I embarked and proceeded on my way down the
river. In the afternoon we stopped in a place where
we could get some shade until sunset. I found a
shelter within a hut near the bank. Throughout
the night the atmosphere was very oppressive. We
slowly made our way by the help of a small boat,
manned by our Indian crew, which took us in tow.
All of us suffered greatly from the attacks of myriads
of mosquitoes. On the following day we arrived at
an open sheet of water, called the inner lagoon,
where it was perfectly calm and we had to endure
on the open and exposed deck, the full strength of
the tropical sun. In the evening a strong head wind
called " el Norte " sprang up, together with heavy
squalls and showers of rain which continued all that

night and the whole of the next day. As we
could not make any headway we anchored. The
sun was very powerful and it was not possible to escape from its influence. The Indians
appeared to be much affected by the weather
and were in a worn and prostrate condition. I had
to endure, equally with them, the alternate exposure
to extreme heat and cold driving rain. During the
night the wind moderated, and towards the morning
we weighed our anchor and proceeded to the entrance
of the outer lagoon and waited for daylight. As the
sun rose, the wind suddenly shifted, and we sailed
rapidly across the bay to the anchorage off the town,
arriving there early in the forenoon.

Thus terminated the voyage " par los rios" (by the
rivers). The exposure to the sun by day, the attacks
of mosquitoes by night, and the sickly condition of
the banks of the rivers and lagoons, had combined
to make that part of the journey across the continent
extremely exhausting.

The long narrow island of Carmen is placed like a
natural breakwater, sheltering the bay from the open
sea of the Gulf of Campeachy. The earliest notice
of it occurs in the Reports of the Spanish expedition
under Grijalva in 1518. Bernal Diaz, who was one
of those who took part in it, mentions a fact that
throws some light upon the religious customs of the
Indians. He observes that the fleet after having
visited the coasts of Yucatan arrived at this island
and remained for several days at anchor in the bay.
Many of the officers and men landed, he being
amongst the number. After traversing the island it
was ascertained that it was not inhabited, but some

small temples (adoratorios) were seen. These were made of stone and mortar, and contained many idols made of clay and of wood, some were like figures of gods, others like women, and many seemed to represent serpents. At the present time there are no remains visible of these adoratorios. The fact, however, of their having been erected upon this island is instructive. It tends to prove that temples were placed in positions where there were no inhabitants, and thus, to some extent, supports the theory that certain holy places were set apart for religious purposes, and were not necessarily attached to centres of population.

During the stay of Grijalva's fleet, a greyhound, belonging to one of the ships, strayed on shore and was lost. The following year, upon the arrival of a second expedition, when the ships anchored, the dog was seen on the beach watching them. Bernal Diaz relates how the dog knew his own ship, and fawned upon the crew when they landed, showing the utmost happiness and affection. How the dog had obtained food and water through such a long period was not known.

Soon after my arrival I was informed that a small schooner called the Rosita was about to sail for Campeachy and that her skipper would take a few passengers. I accordingly made arrangements with him and went on board. I found that the only accommodation was the open hold under the main hatch. Here on the top of the cargo, made smooth and level for the purpose, were placed mats. We embarked two ladies and some Spanish officials and left La Laguna at daylight. The wind was against us and we had to make a long tack towards the Yucatan coast, near Champoton. During the night the wind became more favourable and in the forenoon we sighted the white walls of Campeachy. The cathedral and mediæval fortifications looked very picturesque from the sea as we approached the coast. The Rosita did not draw much water, so we were able to anchor within half a mile of the landing place. I was glad to find in the town a tolerable inn called the Paloma, and a worthy, attentive landlord named Ruiz. The constant exposure and the hardships endured latterly had seriously affected my constitution, and I felt weak and ill. It was a comfort to get shelter and quiet, and the shade and rest which was obtained by having a large room opening upon an inner court. Here I remained for several days suffering from very severe headaches and without feeling that I was, in any perceptible degree, regaining my strength.

On the morning of the fifth day I heard a gentle tap at the door, and my landlady asked if she could come in. She looked at me with much sympathy and said, "Señor, may I speak to you?" I replied, "Certainly." She then said, "Señor, you have upon you the lagoon fever, from which strangers seldom recover, and I have come to ask you where you keep your money and where your friends live, so that I may be able to carry out your wishes." I said, "My kind donna, perhaps I may get better if I change the air. Do you know how I can get away?" The landlady looked pleased and said that she knew that a certain Señor Escalanta was about to start for a village called Tzibalché, and that perhaps he

would share with me the expenses of a conveyance.
This arrangement was made, and in the forenoon a
covered cart, with three mules harnessed abreast,
was drawn up at the door of the inn. I took my
place upon a mattress, and before midday we were
several leagues away breathing the pure and bracing
air of the open country. The change acted like magic.
The fever seemed almost immediately to leave me,
but there remained a persistent headache.

We stopped at a village to get dinner, and
met an intelligent man who was employed as con-
structor of a new road that was being made on this
part of the coast. It had happened, that in the
course of his work, he had made several cuttings and
excavations, and discovered many things of much
antiquarian importance.   He told us of a large
pyramidal altar or Kue which was situated in the
neighbourhood, and as I particularly wished to see
it, Señor Escalanta consented to halt whilst an
examination of it was made.

We found the altar to be one of that type of
structures upon the summit of which the Mexican
priests were accustomed to perform human sacrifices.
This Yucatecan Kue was more than fifty feet high
and was entirely faced with large, squared, well
hewn blocks of hard limestone. It was very steep.
I estimated the angle of the slope to be about 70°.
There were two ledges, respectively one third and
two thirds up the pyramid and on the top was the
platform, which was in a ruinous condition.

There were a number of small stone chambers
built on the sides. The existence of these singular
little cells had caused the people in the adjacent

hamlets to form the opinion that the Kue had been inhabited by dwarfs. We examined these chambers very carefully, and although it was not possible to come to any satisfactory conclusion with regard to their purpose, it was clear that they could not have been intended for habitation. It seemed probable that they were either places for idols or that they were used as vaults for burial. They were built with much skill, and the squaring of the masonry was perfect. The inner wall of these cells was formed by the stone casing of the pyramid. Several small idols were found here. We were chiefly interested in examining the method of construction followed by the Indian architects. This was made apparent by the fact that portions of the outer casing had been demolished. It appeared that the inner portion was a solid mass of stones and mortar which, when completed, was covered with thick slabs of masonry, smooth and well jointed. On the west face there were the remains of a large chamber, but as that part of the pyramid was in a ruinous condition, its dimensions could not be measured.

It is strange that so little is known concerning the ancient rites and ceremonies performed by the priests upon these high altars. Immediately after the conquest these Indian customs ceased, and all the signs of their religion and religious usages disappeared like a dream. When Grijalva's expedition reached the Bay of Campeachy, they saw a large Kue which must have been similar to that we were examining. Bernal Diaz in his history relates that they landed to get a supply of water for the ships near a spot where there was a village. The natives came down

to the beach in a friendly manner, and asked them if
they arrived from the spot where the sun rose. They
then proposed that they should go with them to
their pueblo, and took them to a large building made
of stone and mortar. Whilst the Spaniards were
looking about them and observing the habits of the
people, "Ten Indians dressed in long white cloaks
came out of another adoratorio. Their long thick
hair was clotted with blood and so twisted, that it
could not have been combed or spread without cutting it off. These men were sacerdotes of the idols,
and in New Spain they called themselves Pápas.
Again I say that in New Spain they called themselves Pápas, and thus I shall name them hence-
forwards. These Pápas brought to us perfumes
like a kind of resin which they call copal, and with
earthen braziers filled with fire they commenced to
incense us." Diaz thought that the stone buildings
were altars, and he saw numerous idols, and "it
appeared to us," he says, "that at this time they
had been sacrificing to the idols certain Indians to
give them the victory over us."

On their further voyage near another part of the
Mexican coast, where is now situated the town of Vera
Cruz, the fleet arrived at the Island of Sacrificios, a
name that was given to that land in consequence of
what was observed to take place there. The island
was explored by the Spaniards, and they discovered
two Kues made of lime and stone, and ascended by
steps. "In these altars," observes Diaz, "were idols
of evil figures which were their gods, and here they
had sacrificed on the previous night five Indians.
Their breasts were opened and their arms and thighs

were cut off and the walls were covered with blood."
It happened that the Chaplain-General of the Fleet
wrote an itinerary of this voyage, and he also visited
these temples. He mentioned the extraordinary fact
of having noticed within one of the shrines "some
bordered stuff made of silk, similar to what was
worn by the Moors and which were called by them
" Almaizales." * At another temple, situated near
the coast, four Indian priests were seen, who had
lately been performing sacrifices. In this instance
they had sacrificed two young boys. Their breasts
had been opened and their hearts had been taken
out and placed before the idol as an offering. The
Spaniards were surprised when they observed that
these priests were dressed like Dominicans and
wore long cloaks and capes. This, together with
their manner of using incense, seemed in some inexplicable degree to resemble the observances of their
own monastic fraternities.

In the various accounts that have been given by
the conquerors concerning the Indians, there is
nothing mentioned about the burial customs, and
even at the present time the subject is obscure. I
was therefore interested in listening to the contractor's remarks about some discoveries made by his
workmen when excavating along the line of road.
They found the ruins of several houses. Each of

---

* " Almaizal, a sort of veil or head attire used by the Moorish
women, made of thin silk, striped of several colours, and shagged
at the ends, which hangs down on the back." Baretti's Dictionary,
1807.

them contained beneath the centre of the principal
room a vaulted tomb, in which it was supposed that
the proprietor had been buried when he died. They
also found, when tracing the direction of the work,
several small Kues of pyramidal shapes, around the
sides of which were numerous small stone cells. The
contractor told me that he had measured and surveyed these carefully. He had come to the conclusion that they were burial places.

These discoveries were important, and corroborated
in every essential particular the statements of several
Indian caciques dwelling beyond Uxmal, in the
sixteenth century. They informed the Spanish missionaries that it had been customary, with the
common people in Yucatan, to bury their dead either
inside their houses or at the back of them. In certain cases they afterwards abandoned these dwellings
and moved elsewhere. The bodies of caciques and
chiefs were burnt, and the ashes were placed in urns.
Small pyramids or temples were sometimes raised
over them.[*]

I was sorry when it became necessary to proceed
on our journey. The road contractor was an official
who took a comprehensive interest in whatever
related to the ancient inhabitants, and his practical
knowledge was invaluable.

It was late when we finished the survey of the
pyramid and its chambers; we consequently travelled

---

[*] See " Landa's Relacion de las Cosas de Yucatan," edited and
translated by L'Abbé Brasseur de Bourbourg.

throughout the night at our best speed. We passed through the pueblos of Tenabon and Hekelchakan and reached Señor Escalanta's house in Tzibalché at daylight. We were received by the ladies of the establishment with cold and tranquil apathy. Without saying a word, they turned out of their hammocks, and proceeded to carry out their respective household duties. It must be understood that the arrangements with all Ladino families are very simple. In the tierras calientes or hot regions every one sleeps in a hammock. The hammocks are slung to the cross poles in the principal, and often, only apartment. At night when the ladies wish to go to bed they turn in, to use a sailor's expression, all standing. The women of all ages, young or old, wear but one dress which is always a long cotton garment reaching from the shoulders to the feet. This is worn day and night. The languid indifference of men and women, towards each other and to all around them, is a marked characteristic of the whole of the Ladino race throughout Central America. Nothing seems to arouse their indolent natures, and although many of them are fairly educated, they do not appear to have those qualities which form the foundation of a good and energetic population. It cannot be considered that the enervating influences of a tropical climate are chiefly the cause of this inertness, for it exists in varying altitudes. It should, however, be acknowledged that this half-caste race retains much of the old-fashioned courtesy of their Spanish ancestors. The Ladinos have ceased to intermarry with the Indians, and there is now no sympathy between the two races.

The Indians have almost as great a dislike to them as they have to the Spaniards.

At Tzibalché I enlisted in my service an Indian, named Anastasio, and after some difficulty, hired a horse of doubtful merit. Anastasio declared that we could avoid the long round to Uxmal by the main roads, as he knew a short cut across the country which would shorten the journey. By that path, he said, the distance to the hacienda at Uxmal did not exceed nine or ten leagues. Accordingly we quitted the village at sunrise and soon afterwards entered the bush.

This part of Yucatan was covered with a thin light kind of brushwood which grew to a height of about twelve feet. Our path was cut through this bush which excluded all view to the right or left. Occasionally we passed through a few acres of open land where the Indians were cultivating some crops, but the soil was poor and stony. At noon we arrived at a farm; the proprietor was inclined to be hospitable and gave me food and shelter. I was suffering from a recurrence of what I had endured at Campeachy and could scarcely bear the fatigue of the journey, especially as the rays of the nearly vertical sun were very powerful.

During the afternoon, whilst resting in the shade, I listened to the loud, discordant, and grating sounds pronounced by the Indians around me. The language spoken was Maya, which has been ascertained to be the parent stock of most of the languages and dialects spoken in Guatemala, Yucatan and the bordering territories. I asked my host to give me a specimen of their dialect. He replied that he would tell me what had happened in the morning, and he leant forward and said :—" Ti lé kin béhilá, kuch yuayé humpel tzul ingles, bin tiar ten. Tumentin, katah uchi y etel tin káhol ta hatchutz apockzi chalé; katin kámá tin nayle, katin sah balu hante kati álá téné bin ku bétic Uxmal, tacthoh cásumac tuh lú mil." "This day came here an English Señor and spoke to me. Having questioned him and knowing him to be of a good heart, I received him in my house and gave him to eat. Then he told me that he was going to Uxmal, and thence to Merida and afterwards to his own land."

Towards the end of the day, when the sun was low, I ventured out of the hut, mounted my horse, and pushed forward rapidly towards Uxmal. After passing through several plantations of sugar-cane attached to small Indian farms, we reached some rising ground and I saw, about four miles distant towards the east, the great building, called the Casa del Gobernador, with its terraces and adjacent pyramids standing out high and distinct. The sun had disappeared below the horizon, and the sky was brilliant with the vivid colouring of a tropical sunset. The Casa del Gobernador was clear and well defined in the midst of this magnificent frame of evening splendour, looking scarcely less beautiful than a Greek temple on some lofty headland, when seen at twilight from Ægean seas.

It was getting dark when we slowly passed round the base of a Teocalli, and it was night when we halted at the hacienda. The proprietor and the agent were both absent, but the mayor-domo received me with much kindness. He gave me a large room next to one which he told me had been occupied by the Empress Charlotte when she visited Uxmal in 1866. The next morning, after giving Anastasio directions to join me at the Casa del Gobernador and to bring with him my hammock and provisions, I walked out to the ruins.

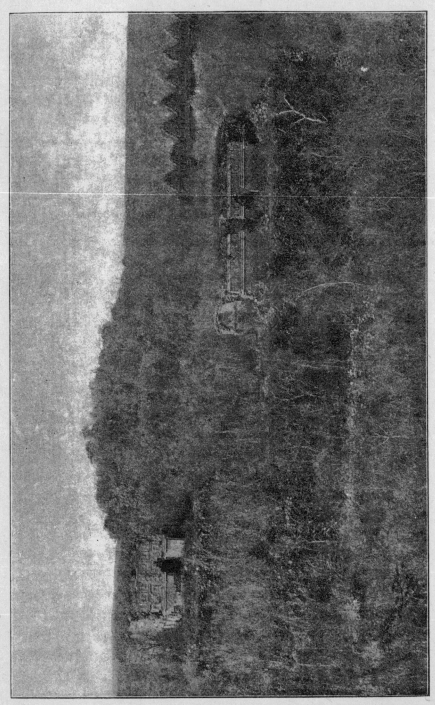

CHAPTER XVII.

IT is considered that the ruins of Uxmal are, in
extent and construction, the most important in
Yucatan, and therefore, excepting in certain particu-
lars, those at Palenque, the most remarkable in
Central America and Mexico.

The ground occupied by them is in length about
six hundred yards. The width is slightly more than five
hundred yards. Consequently the area within which
Uxmal is contained, may be approximately estimated
as being sixty acres.   It therefore exceeds by twenty
acres the space covered by the mounds of Palenque.
The buildings are irregularly placed.   The Casa del
Gobernador (House of the Governor) with its adjacent
pyramids form the principal group towards the south.
The Casa de las Monjas (House of the Nuns) is situated towards the north.   These are the two great

structures upon which the other temples and mounds seem chiefly to depend. There are two smaller edifices called respectively, the Casa de las Palomas (House of the Pigeons) and the Casa de las Tortugas (House of the Turtles). There is also a detached pyramid with a ruined temple upon its summit, which has been given the name of the House of the Old Woman. Looking at these ruins as a group, they appear to have consisted of quadrangular residences with pyramidal mounds attached to them, raised for the purpose of obtaining lofty sites for the altars of the Indian gods.

One of the most important of these is that known as the Pyramid of the Dwarf. I examined it with particular attention for the purpose of studying the character of a series of small stone vaults or cells placed round its base, which were similar in size and design to those that I had seen on the lower slopes of the Kue near the coast above Campeachy. Many of these cells were sufficiently perfect to enable their dimensions and shape to be verified. It seemed evident that they must have been made for sepulchral purposes. If this conclusion is correct it is probable that they were the burial places for the ashes of the caciques who ruled over this part of Yucatan.

Upon an investigation of the outer parts of the pyramid, it is to be observed that it was not only carefully constructed, but its plan must have been accurately drawn and the relative mathematical measurements calculated with reference to the space that was required for the temple. The magnitude of the base could not be determined, on account of

PYRAMID AND TEMPLE OF THE DWARF.

the quantities of fallen stones and other débris. In 1841, Mr. Stephens considered that it was two hundred and thirty-five feet long by one hundred and fifty-five feet wide. The perpendicular height to the platform was estimated to be eighty-eight feet.

The steps leading up to the summit are broad, and must have formed an imposing approach, but in consequence of the angle of the slope they are necessarily steep, and are placed so close together that there is barely sufficient width for the foot to rest. At the base of the pyramid there is an open court, which I observed to be similar in shape to one adjoining the base of an altar built by the Quichés at Utatlan, but it was larger in extent. The court leads to the entrance of the Casa de las Monjas.

This building may be considered to be the result of the greatest powers of sculpture and ornamentation that the Indians possessed, and judging from the condition of many of its chambers, it is probably one of the latest of their works. It is nearly quadrangular, and encloses an area of over six thousand square yards.

My first day at Uxmal was employed in making a rough survey of the land occupied by the ruins.

Upon my return to the hacienda, I found that an evening service, called "el Rosario," was being held in the chapel. A large number of Indians were assembled. These Yucatecos had attached to the fingers of the church images, many of their own small idols, made of metal. It was consequently impossible to know (as the priests in the Cordilleras

said of their Indian parishioners), whether they
were worshipping the saints, or following in secret
their ancient idolatries.

The next morning I established myself in the
" House of the Governor," and selected for our
occupation the largest of the outer series of apart-
ments, opening upon the eastern courts. The size
of these was necessarily regulated by the angle of
the converging slopes of the walls, for the builders
were limited in their plans in consequence of their
incomplete acquaintance with the formation of arches.
In one of the rooms there were some cross poles made
of zapote wood, to which Anastasio fastened my
hammock. The architectural proportions of the exterior are unusual. The length is about three hundred
and twenty-two feet, but the breadth is only thirty-
nine feet, and the low, narrow structure, is only
twenty-five feet high. The effect, however, of the long
and elaborately carved façade, is particularly pleasing
both to the eye and the mind. In all respects, the
Casa del Gobernador is rightly given the distinction
of being the grandest of the stone structures that
were built by Indians. The platform upon which
this great edifice stands, is forty feet above the level
of the ground. Sixteen feet below this is a large
open court, which is about one hundred and eighty
yards long, and over eighty-two yards wide, containing a level surface of nearly fifteen thousand
square yards—or more than three acres. There is
a third outer terrace, raised a few feet above the
plain.

The Casa de las Monjas is also placed upon three
terraces, but they are of smaller dimensions, and

CASA DEL GOBERNADOR.

AN ANGLE OF THE CASA DE LAS MONJAS.

the height of the base of the building above the natural ground, is not more than seventeen feet. The terraces were surrounded by strongly built walls. Wide stone steps gave access to each platform. When looking at these flat spaces, pyramids and temples, it is practicable to form reasonable conjectures regarding the nature of the religious ceremonies that may have taken place within, or before them.

Bishop Landa, in his work on Yucatan, which he wrote in that country soon after the conquest, gives an account of the feasts and sacrifices performed in the temples. His description was based upon information which he received from the descendants of caciques, who had governed a powerful tribe dwelling east of Uxmal. After mentioning the nature of the offerings made to the idols during certain festivals, he observes that, besides sacrificing animals, the priests would sometimes on occasions of tribulation or public necessity, command that human victims should be sacrificed. There is this statement given of what then happened.

" Every one took their part in offering contributions, in order that slaves should be bought, and some of the more devotional would offer their little children. Great care was taken of them that they should not run away or commit any fault, and whilst they were conducted from village to village with dancing, the priests fasted. Upon the arrival of the day, they all came into the patio (court) of the temple, and if the victim had to be sacrificed by wounds from arrows he was stripped naked, his body was anointed with blue, and a cap like a mitre was

placed on his head." He was then, after certain
dances made by the people in honour of the god,
killed by flights of arrows.

It will be remembered that a similar custom was
followed by the Pawnees in North America who,
upon certain occasions, chiefly in connection with
offering a propitiation to the Manito who had
power over the harvest, also killed the victim by a
flight of arrows.* The coincidence of this practice is
very strange.

Landa, after relating the manner in which these
Indians in Yucatan conducted the ceremony of inflicting death by arrows, proceeds to state what was
done if the priests, for some special reasons, directed
that the victim should be offered to the gods in
accordance with their more appalling rites. "If
it had been decided to take out the heart, he was
taken to the patio with much pomp, and was accompanied by many people, and after being daubed over
with blue, and his mitre placed on his head, he was
carried to the round step which was the place where
these sacrifices were made, and after the priest
(sacerdote) and his officials had anointed this stone
with blue colour, and had cast out the devil by puri-
fying the temple; the unfortunate man that was to
be sacrificed was then seized, thrown suddenly backwards upon the stone, and held there by the legs
and arms kept apart from the middle. Then came
the sacrificer with a stone razor, and struck with
much dexterity and cruelty, a gash between the ribs

* See chapter vii.

CASA DE LAS MONJAS, UXMAL.

AN ANGLE OF THE CASA DE LAS MONJAS.

of the left side below the teat; he then thrust in his hand and took hold of the heart like a furious tiger and snatched it out still palpitating, and put it upon a dish which he gave to the priest, who took it quickly and anointed the faces of the idols with the fresh blood." *

This statement of the sacrificial customs in Yucatan is in accordance with the Report made by Palacio ‡ concerning the sacrifices of the captives taken in war by the Pipiles, a tribe who were believed to be of Mexican origin and were then dwelling near the Pacific coast of Guatemala. It may also be surmised that the ceremonies performed by the priests of the Quichés upon the altars at Utatlan were of a similar nature. It thus seems evident that the barbarous practices that are supposed to have been introduced by the Aztecs into Mexico, during some period subsequent to the twelfth century, were becoming prevalent in Central America.

It is possible that the custom of offering human sacrifices, together with subsequent acts of cannibalism, may have become grafted upon the religious observances of an earlier and less cruel race. It is, however, to be noticed that the plan of the pyramid of the Dwarf with its altar, and the open court at the foot of the steps leading down from the temple, conform with the particular purposes of the ceremonies connected with the sacrifices to the idols.

---

* Landa "Relacion de las Cosas de Yucatan." p. 164.
‡ See chapter xi.

Bernal Diaz, when describing the manner in which the Spanish captives were sacrificed and eaten during the siege of Mexico, mentions facts which agree with the statements made by the caciques in Yucatan, concerning the events that occasionally happened in their sacred places.

"Sometimes," observes Landa, " the sacrifice took place on the stone upon the highest step of the temple, and then the body was thrown down the steps and rolled below. The officials then seized it and flayed off the skin excepting the feet and hands, and the priest, having taken off his garments until he was naked, covered himself with it, and danced with the others. This was considered to be a matter of much solemnity. It was the custom to bury those who were sacrificed in the court of the temple, or, if not, they were eaten by the chiefs and those who were able to obtain portions ; the hands, feet and head were for the priest and officials. Those who were thus sacrificed were held as saints (tenian por santos). If they were slaves captured in war their owner took the bones and kept them to show them in the dances as emblems of victory."

The aboriginal inhabitants of Yucatan were, like those dwelling in the neighbouring land of Guatemala, devoted to the worship of idols, and travelled great distances to take part in the ceremonies which were performed at the shrines of their principal gods. The Island of Cozumel was one of the sacred sites which was held in great veneration when the fleet of Grijalva arrived there in 1518. It was observed by the Spaniards that there and elsewhere, the pyramidal structures or altars were maintained in good order, and had regular priests attached to them for the purpose of executing the various duties connected with the superstitious usages. It was afterwards ascertained that several of the larger sacred temples in the interior had at that time been abandoned, although many of them looked as if they had not been long built. With respect to Uxmal, it was considered that the ruins were comparatively modern and belonged to a period but little anterior to the Spanish conquest.

The well preserved state of portions of the buildings is, at the present time, nearly four centuries after the arrival of the Spaniards, especially noticeable. I observed that the wooden lintel over the door of my room in the Casa del Gobernador was in perfect condition. The edges or corners were still sharp and unworn. It was also evident that, although the great weight of the masonry above must have exerted a heavy pressure upon the centre of the lintel, there were no signs of the slightest deflection. The strength of the wood seemed to be unimpaired. The preservation of many of the lintels over the doorways of the rooms in the Casa de las Monjas was, in several instances, equally sound. Many of the stone carvings on the exterior were also apparently uninjured by their exposure to the weather. But, before proceeding with this subject, it is expedient to take into consideration some of the characteristics of this building.

It is not known why it was called the Casa de las Monjas (House of the Nuns). Possibly the Spaniards may have been surprised by its similarity in plan with their own nunneries, but it is also not improbable that there may have been some tradition received from the Indians which caused the adoption of this name. It has been stated by Clavigero, and other historians, that there were certain especial customs attending the worship of the god Quetzalcoatl. Women served for terms of years

Entrance to the Casa de las Monjas.

within his temples. They were dedicated to the performance of religious service from an early age, lodged in a convent and instructed in religion. They were also educated and employed in a manner suitable to their station and sex. It was said that certain vows were made and various religious duties were performed.

The main entrance to the nunnery is through a gateway placed in the centre of the southern part of the quadrangle. Upon each side of this entrance there are four chambers, and it is to be noticed, as an evidence of the conventual character of the building, that these are the only rooms that have direct access to the outer world. All the others are within and look into the court. They had a blank wall at the back, which excluded all communication with the exterior. The principal front looks towards the pyramids adjoining the Casa del Gobernador. The architectural proportions of the archway are symmetrical. The height and span, like all other parts of these Indian structures, are practically determined by the angle of inclination of the converging sides. In this case the arch is about seventeen feet high and nearly eleven feet wide. After passing through it, a wide court is entered. It is surrounded on four sides by long ranges of low stone buildings. The base, or lower part of them, is built of plain square slabs of masonry. The upper parts are covered with fanciful designs, sculptured with great skill.

The whole of these buildings are exclusively arranged for the purpose of providing the greatest possible number of chambers or monastic cells. I did not count them, but it has been stated that there are altogether eighty-eight. It is perhaps important to note, with reference to this unusual number of rooms, that they are too numerous to admit of the theory that they were intended for the accommodation of the priests serving the adjacent temples, for according to the statements of Clavigero, the number of priests always corresponded with the

number of the Teocallis.   It is therefore presumable
that these cells had some other purpose.   The
priests may have been lodged in the Casa del
Gobernador.   That building contains twenty-four
chambers, the majority of which are of the same
size and plan as these in the Casa de las Monjas.   It
is useless to attempt to conjecture the precise purposes of these buildings, for there has been no exact
information obtained upon the subject, but everything points to the conclusion that the whole of the
structures at Uxmal were connected with the
worship of the gods, and had no relation to the
ordinary lives of the Indians.

It is probable that places like Uxmal and Palenque
with their temples and monasteries, were set apart
for religious purposes, and the Indians assembled
there from the adjacent country with the object of
being present at the ceremonies, in the same manner
as they are now accustomed to perform their pilgrimages when the patron saints of the churches have
their festivals.   When taking into consideration the
question of the period when it may be conjectured
that the temples at Uxmal were abandoned, it is
necessary to direct attention to the design or emblem
which is placed upon one of the walls of the interior
of the Casa de las Monjas.

Upon an examination of the accompanying illustration, it will be observed that the figure represented
is that of a huge serpent or rattlesnake.   A serpent
was also the emblem or Totem of one of the tribes of
the Mound Builders in Ohio, and there appear to be
singular resemblances between the reptile carved in
stone at Uxmal and that which is rudely made of

SERPENT EMBLEM, CASA DE LAS MONJAS.

earth and stones, and placed on high ground overlooking a valley in North America. Both reptiles
have peculiarly large mouths, opened wide, ready to
devour and swallow their prey or their enemies. It
is perhaps not unreasonable to infer that the tribe
who migrated from the north, conquered the
unwarlike natives of Yucatan, raised the great
pyramids, and built the temples in that region, were
subsequently conquered by a more powerful tribe of
the same race, also migrating from higher latitudes.
The former tribe were forced to desert their buildings,
and avoided slavery or extermination by escaping
into the interior. The serpent stands out in bold
relief. The whole of the façades of the nunnery are
elaborately sculptured, and the mechanical abilities
of the builders are well brought into notice.

As all investigations or theories respecting these
architects and their works, depend greatly upon the
conclusions that may be drawn from the evidence
regarding the period when Uxmal was built, I
directed my attention to certain points bearing upon
this subject. Conjectures upon the origin and civilisation of the Indians must be influenced by what
can be ascertained with respect to the probable dates
when these religious buildings were constructed.

It is to be seen in the Casa de las Monjas that
there was a lavish use of ornamentation in stone.
There is, throughout, a wealth of sculpture which is
astonishing when it is remembered that the sculptors,
as far as we know, had no proper implements to
work with. Stone chisels and obsidian scrapers
appear to be inadequate for the purpose.

It can be understood that if the Indian masons

and stone cutters had wished to show their ability, they might have adorned their buildings with barbarous figures or rude idols, such as were carved by the natives of Easter Island out of soft volcanic stone. But at Uxmal they revelled in their powers. The walls of the Nunnery and the Casa del Gobernador are covered with designs deeply cut and perfectly joined. Thus it is proved that the sculptors had not only much capacity as workmen, but they must have been able to chisel hard limestone with ease and facility of execution. In the interior of the Nunnery many of the designs are most artistic. Nothing can be more graceful than the block of buildings on the eastern side of the quadrangle. The lattice work, in its appearance and general effect, seems to have an indefinable accordance with the wood and stone carvings that are to be seen in the ancient quarters of Cairo, and the interior of the earliest Arabian mosques. Upon the opposite side of the quadrangle, the ornamentation upon the walls is of a different character and in some respects resembles the designs of Hindoo or Buddhist architecture. This confusion of styles is puzzling to the eye and embarrassing to the judgment.

At Palenque the long corridors, the courts, and the use of coloured stucco ornamentation appeared to have some vague relation to a mixed style of Moorish and Spanish architecture. If a corsair, with a crew of Moors and a cargo of Spanish captives, had been driven by the trade wind across the Atlantic, and the strangers, after landing upon the new continent, had married the daughters of the caciques; it would be intelligible that the descendants of the

INTERIOR OF THE CASA DE LAS MONJAS AND ITS ADJOINING PYRAMID AND TEMPLE, UXMAL.

mixed races might have constructed monasteries, temples and pyramids of this strange and complex design. Such was my impression when pacing the corridors at Palenque.

At Uxmal there were no coloured stuccoes and no corridors. The bold and fantastic style of the sculptures had a character more Eastern, and it might be permissible to imagine that wandering fakirs from Hindostan, or Buddhist pilgrims from Java, Burmah or Cambodia, had reached the Pacific coasts, and had implanted their incomplete acquaintance with the forms of Hindoo or Buddhist temples upon the barbaric ideas of the Indians, and that in this manner were produced the fanciful types of construction or symbolism that are present at Uxmal.

These are only conjectures, but it cannot be supposed that this knowledge of architecture and of sculpture arose as suddenly as it disappeared, and sprang into existence as the outcome of the natural capacity of the Indian mind. The problem is interesting and attractive. It is one that is exceedingly difficult to solve.

There are certain differences in the methods of construction of Palenque and Uxmal which have to be analyzed. The walls at Palenque are composed of compact masses of stones and mortar covered with thick layers of cement. At Uxmal no coatings of cement are used and the walls are faced with well-worked masonry. At Palenque there are great numbers of human figures either formed of thick stucco, or graven upon slabs of stone. At Uxmal there are no human figures, no delineations of

caciques, priests, or captive victims. The principle
of ornamentation is different.

Judging from the condition and appearance of the
buildings it is clear that Uxmal must be more modern
than Palenque, and this is particularly noticeable upon
an examination of the Casa del Gobernador and the
Casa de las Monjas. The influences of the tropical
climate (Uxmal is half a degree south of the twenty-
first parallel) are such as would be expected to act
injuriously upon exposed limestone sculptures, for
between May and November the rains are heavy
and continuous. But the façades of these structures
seem to have been very little affected by the
weather.

In forming opinions respecting the antiquity of
ruins, it is perhaps injudicious to give much weight
to considerations based upon appearance or state of
dilapidation, but in the instance of Uxmal there are
circumstances which make it impossible to admit that
it belongs to a period more than very few centuries
earlier than the arrival of the Spaniards. Thus the
preservation of the wooden lintels over the doorways
in the Casa de las Monjas must be taken into
consideration, when any attempts are made to estimate the age of that building. They have had to
bear considerable pressure, for there are heavy
masses of concrete and masonry to be supported.

With regard to this subject, it is necessary to
draw attention to the size and construction of one
of the principal rooms which I measured, and it will
be understood how the architects were limited or
restricted in their actions, and to what extent the
employment of wood was found to be requisite.

It was a narrow chamber twenty feet four inches long, twelve feet wide, and about twenty-three feet high. The height of the entrance was eight feet, the width six feet seven inches. The interior walls were perpendicular up to nine feet three inches from the ground, and then curved inwards until they approached within one foot of each other. They were capped by broad flat stone slabs. The curvature of the walls was correctly formed, and a considerable gain in space was thereby obtained. It was evident that the Indians were advancing towards a knowledge of the round arch and keystone. This form of rounding the inner roof was not however adopted in all the rooms of the nunnery. Many of them still retained the straight lines of converging walls, as at Palenque. The manner in which the advance in construction had been reached was simple and yet ingenious.

I measured a room in another part of the quadrangle which had different dimensions, and was more in accordance with the earlier system of building. It was twenty-two feet long and ten feet five inches wide. The height of the perpendicular portion of the walls was eight feet three inches, and the length of the upper slope to the cap-stone was eight feet nine inches. The total height of the room about sixteen feet. The doorway was a little over seven feet high and the width was five feet eight inches. The dimensions of the chambers round the quadrangle varied, but the instances I have given represent their average sizes. There were two lintels over each doorway, for the width of each piece of timber was not sufficient to

occupy the full depth of the wall. In the first-men-
tioned chamber they were each nine feet five inches
long, one foot wide and eight inches deep, and had
a bearing upon each wall of one foot five inches. In
this and other openings the inner lintel rested in its
place a little lower than the outer one. The object
of this singular method of placing these supports
was not apparent. The lintels were externally in
perfect condition, and were without any signs of
decay.

The main mass of the Uxmal walls is composed of
rubble limestones, made into a strong compact substance, by the plentiful use of good binding mortar.
Each facing stone was made into a triangular shape,
and the point or apex seems to have been pushed or
fitted into its place, and there firmly secured by
mortar. This method of applying the masonry was
adopted not only with the plain smooth blocks of
square stone used for facing the lower portions of
the buildings, but also with all the sculptured portions of the walls. The blocks fit closely together
in their places so accurately and with such careful
finish that the joints or edges can scarcely be distinguished. It is thus made evident that the stone-
masons who built Uxmal must have been men capable
of performing their work with skill. The architect
must have possessed a competent knowledge of the
preparation of a plan or design, and the masons, in
separately executing their part of the sculpture,
must have been able to follow the design with an
exactness that is almost mathematical.

There have been many theories respecting the
methods that may have been practised by the

QUADRANGLE, CASA DE LAS MONJAS.

Indians in executing their carvings upon stone, but
no knowledge has been obtained which throws sufficient light upon the subject.* No attention has
however been directed to the artisan qualities of
the workmen who shaped and fitted the lintels,
which however prove that the workers in wood were
as skilful as the masons. The lintels were made of
wood harder than mahogany. I examined many of
them with the utmost care, and could not detect the
slightest mark or dent. It is doubtful whether a
good carpenter's plane could have given them a
smoother surface. The zapote trees out of which

---

*The facing stones placed upon the walls of the ruins of Mitla,
in the Mexican province of Oajaca, are fitted, or bedded, into the
mortar and rubble in the same manner as at Uxmal.

At one of the evening conversaziones given by the Royal
Society at Burlington House, in the spring of 1892, I happened
to discuss the subject of Palenque and Uxmal with Mr. Woolner,
the sculptor. Some experiments had previously been carried out
in France which had proved that with stone chisels it was possible
to carve granite, limestones, and hard sandstones.

The investigations did not, however, make it clear how it could
have happened that the Indian sculptors were able to work with
such facility that they covered their buildings with deeply chis-
elled ornamentation. Mr. Woolner said that he thought it
probable that the Indians may have been acquainted with
some strong acids, and that they may have used these to soften
the stone and make it more workable.

We were looking at some photographs exhibited by Mr.
Maudslay, who had lately returned from Palenque, and the
question of the method of carving the outlines of the figures on
the stone slabs of the courts came under consideration. Mr.
Woolner thought that the subject was very difficult, but that it
was possible that the figures had been previously traced and then
worked with acid as he had already suggested.

they were formed, must have been fashioned into broad baulks of timber, and afterwards squared and divided into the required lengths. The face of the timber was levelled and smoothed, and the corners or angles were sharply defined. All this work had to be done, as far as is known, with stone implements.

Upon taking a final glance at these ruins it seems reasonable to form the conclusion that Uxmal was built exclusively for the purposes of religion. The pyramids and their teocallis or temples were devoted as shrines for the gods, and monasteries were attached to them. The human sacrifices and the ceremonies that were customary in time of war took place in the open courts attached to the high altars of the chief idols.

Upon the last day of my stay at Uxmal, the morning was fine and the sky was clear. In the forenoon I observed that there were dense volumes of light-coloured smoke covering the fields towards the east. As the day advanced the air became hot and oppressive, and the sky was obscured. Upon inquiring the cause of this smoke I was told that the Indians were burning their weeds and stalks in accordance with their custom at that time of the year.

In the afternoon, whilst I was engaged in sketching the southeast angle of the Casa del Gobernador, heavy drops of rain began suddenly to fall. As it was the dry season, this change of weather was unexpected. The rain drops soon ceased, but after an interval there were some slight showers which continued for about two hours. At the farmhouse I was told that such weather was unusual, and that the rain must have been caused by the smoke and heat rising from the fires. If this opinion was correct the change may have been caused by the heated air rising into a cooler region above, and thus producing an atmospherical disturbance.

This fact of rain being produced or caused by human agency supports the opinion that the efforts of the rain-makers amongst the North-American Indians were in accordance with some vague knowledge, and were not altogether absurd, and that the action of the Californian rain-maker, whose attempts to obtain rain were successful, was based upon an experience which was practical.

CHAPTER XVIII.

AT sunrise on the day of our departure from Uxmal, the Indians were hurrying along the paths on their way to the corn fields, and the women were engaged in carrying water from the wells. It was a busy scene of life and movement.

We proceeded to Múna and then journeyed onwards to the village of Abalá which we reached in the afternoon, having accomplished a distance of eight leagues. We obtained shelter in a public building called the cabildo, which was used as a travellers' rest house, where everyone, as in a Turkish or Syrian caravansary, selected whatever spot was available or unoccupied. Anastasio deposited the luggage in a corner and found a place where my hammock could be secured above the ground.

Upon examining my horse I found that it was quite unfit for work, and therefore I went at once to

the head man of the district, who was an Indian
holding the office of Judge, and was at the time
sitting in the Court-house. I asked him if he
would give directions that I should be supplied with
another horse or mule to carry me to Merida. The
Judge at first made some objections and said that
there were no horses, or that, if there were any,
they were in the fields and would have to be caught.
Finally, after a long discussion, the second or junior
Judge, who seemed inclined to help me, promised
that a horse should be ready at the cabildo on the
following day as soon as the sun appeared. Trusting in this arrangement, I discharged Anastasio and
sent him back with the old horse to Tzibalché.

In the morning the sun duly appeared but no
horse came, and as Anastasio had left at daybreak,
I found myself unattended, and surrounded by
strange groups of Indians passing through Abalá.
It was fortunate that, in accordance with a local
regulation, an Indian alguazil was in charge of the
cabildo, for this native official immediately informed
me that he would attend to my requirements. He
was useful in carrying out my wishes, and performed
his duties with care and zeal. After waiting for an
hour to see if any horse arrived, I went again to the
Court-house but found that the Judges were not
sitting, and that they were away for the day upon
other occupations. On my return to my quarters it
was evident that some event had occurred. I was
told that a band of muleteers on their way from
the interior had halted there, and intended to
proceed to Merida later in the day, after their mules
had been given rest and food. These men were

uncouth and noisy, but I thought it would be wise
to join them, if they made no objection. It happened
that they had with them a young horse that was
not laden. After overcoming some preliminary
difficulties, an agreement was made that I should
hire the horse, but that he was not to carry any
weight except that of the rider ; one of their mules
was to convey my luggage. As soon as all preparations were completed the leader of the muleteers told me that they would be ready to proceed
late in the afternoon and that he would call for me
at the cabildo. The men then dispersed.

Having the greater part of the day at my disposal,
I walked out beyond the village for the purpose of
being present at an Indian ceremony. It was the
commemoration of a death that had taken place in
the previous year. I was informed that in this part
of Yucatan it was the custom amongst the Indians
to have three services or meetings of this nature.
The first took place a week after the death ; the
second after an interval of a month, and the last on
the anniversary. This was the anniversary service
and was considered the most important. Very few
of the religious ceremonies of the Indians have been
permitted to be maintained, for they were so singularly connected with their worship of demons, that
it was found necessary to abolish everything that
recalled their ancient superstitions. These memorial
observances are, however, to a modified extent yet
performed.

Upon arriving at the hut I saw that it was
crowded with Indians. I was received in the usual
manner with apparent inattention, and was allowed

to take my place with the others. I noticed that my friend the junior Judge, who had promised to send me a horse, was one of the mourners. As he made no remark and I had made other plans the subject was not mentioned, and my attention was directed to what was going on around me. The Indians were engaged in making melancholy sounds of wailing. In the centre of the room was a table upon which was a large plain wooden cross. Before the cross were placed offerings of flowers, fruits and baked tortillas. I waited for some time to see what ceremonies were going to take place, but nothing happened. The wailing continued in a dreary and monotonous manner.

The scene reminded me in some respects of observances of a religious character that I had previously witnessed when travelling amongst the Cordilleras of Guatemala, and again at a village near Tzibalché, on the road to Uxmal. When the Spanish priests settled in their various parishes in these regions after the conquest, it was noticed by them that the Indians appeared to have a peculiar dread of death. This dread did not seem to be caused by any personal fear, but had its origin in connection with their belief in demons. They believed that death was an evil spirit that required to be propitiated, and whose influence over the sick or dying person was malignant. Thus it was usual to make offerings to this demon, who was supposed to be lying in wait somewhere near the hut. They imagined that he might be contented with what was given to him and not carry off his victim. When I was at Palenque, I was told that in some of the remote parts of the province, this

ancient observance still existed and that the Indians
placed offerings of food outside the door of the hut
in the hope that the demon would be appeased, and
pass by without stopping to enter within.* In
Yucatan a similar custom prevailed, but the method
of propitiation was slightly different. Various kinds
of food and jars of liquid were hung upon the walls
or thatch outside the hut to gratify the demon and
cause him to accept the offerings instead of human
life.

Amongst the ancient customs of the Indians none,
however, are more strange than those connected
with an almost unintelligible form of baptism.
The Franciscan missionaries who endeavoured to
convert the Indians at the time of the conquest,
observed with astonishment the veneration of the
natives for the Catholic rites of baptism and the
readiness of their converts to accept this part of
their teaching. In the course of their inquiries upon
the subject they discovered that a form of baptism
already existed, and was considered to be one of the
most important and essential of their ceremonies. ‡
Upon an examination of the accounts of the manner
in which the Indians performed their customary

---

*When I heard of this Indian practice my thoughts went
far away from the forests of Palenque. Memories of the Eton
playing fields were recalled and an old Eton Latin grammar, and
the familiar line, " Pallida mors equo pulsat pede pauperum
tabernas regumque turres." With Indians, as with others, the
fatal footstep cannot be turned aside.

‡For a description of this ceremony see Landa, chap. xxvi.
" Manner of baptism in Yucatan. How it was celebrated."

rites, it does not appear that there was much analogy with the ceremony that was insisted upon as a duty by the friars, except that the Indian baptism was a religious act performed by their priests, in which the children were touched with something that had been dipped in water.

The Indians, although disinclined to adopt the new faith, showed extraordinary ardour and devotion in this particular observance. It was found that they would frequently bring their children to be baptised again after they had already received baptism. Finally the conduct of the Indians in this matter became so unsatisfactory that special clauses upon the subject, were introduced into the laws established by the order of the Emperor Charles V. for the government of the Indians in Yucatan.

One of these clauses ran thus—

" Baptism is one of the sacraments which is not " to be repeated, and if this is done great offence is " committed against the Holy Ghost conferred upon " us by baptism when it is repeated.

" Many of the natives of this province say that " although already baptised, they repeat baptism " deceiving the ministers of the gospel, and further- " more they say that they baptise others and con- " sent that others should do so. For which reason I " order that henceforth no Indian man or woman " of this province who has once received legitimately " holy baptism shall return to be baptised or consent " to others doing it, or baptise on their own authority " any other person."

Since these orders were put in force many changes have taken place, and the Indians have become, in a manner reconciled to the new order of things. It is, however, stated that in remote parishes the priests are still frequently deceived, and that children are sometimes brought three or four times to be given baptism.

The circumstances under which the cross was placed upon the table in the hut near Abalá were peculiar. It was clear that the cross was looked upon as an idol, and that the offerings made to it were propitiations. In Yucatan there were instances known of several of the principal Indians keeping a cross in their house. This was not necessarily a Latin cross, for it was sometimes formed into a shape varying according to the imagination of the owners. The Indians are rapidly becoming so neglected with regard to all religious education, that it is not improbable that they will gradually return to many of their idolatrous practices.

In the beginning of this century the Spanish authorities in Mexico ordered an inquiry to be made regarding the condition of the Yucatan Indians, and directions were given to ascertain whether they still maintained any of the superstitious usages followed before the conquest. There was a Report made by the curate of Yaxcabá which was considered to be especially deserving of mention, because he had been in charge of a large parish and had lived for many years among his Indians, and was known to be well acquainted with their language and habits. One of the superstitions that he reported is remarkable from its having evident analogies with one of the methods adopted by the medicine men in curing

the sick amongst the Dakotas in North America. It
will be seen by his account of the custom of divining
through the medium of a crystal, that ignorant
human nature in Yucatan, as in many other parts of
the world, seeks to learn the future by similar
methods.

The curate, in his reply to one of the questions
put to him, stated as follows*:—"Amongst the
"common masses of the Indians there are many
"superstitions. In the first fifteen years that I held
"this curacy they told me much, but after making
"examples upon the delinquents by punishing them
"with floggings and penances in accordance with
"superior commands, it is now fully fifteen years that
"all is done in silence, and it is only from time to
"time that there is any sign.

"The most frequent divination is by means of a
"piece of crystal which they call *zaztun*. This is a
"clear and transparent stone, by which they say that
"occult things are seen and the causes of sickness.
"What I have been able to understand in this matter
"is that they have had some one who, by a compact
"with the demon, has divined by the means of the
"said *zaztun*: but the more ordinary way is that
"those that use it are certain cheating impostors who
"by this means gain credit amongst themselves and
"are consulted and are well treated so that they have
"idle lives, and with their artifices and cunning make
"the simple and ignorant believe that they have

---

* See "Historia de la Guerra de Castas de Yucatan," p. 77.
Merida, 1866.

" divined what they have secretly managed. I will
" take this example which is frequent : they make the
" sick man believe that by the means of the *zaztun*
" they have known that some malevolent person has
" bewitched him, and in order to discover the wizard
" or evil doer it is necessary to watch three nights and
" make preparation of ardent spirits or pitarilla,
" provisions and lighted candles ; during these three
" nights they enjoy themselves and eat and drink till
" they are satisfied. When the others are not
" observing or asleep they bury inside the house or
" near it a small figure of black wax having a thorn
" run into the part corresponding to that where the
" sick person feels the most pain. Finally when all
" are awake they commence to make their operations
" with the *zaztun* and go straight to the spot where
" they buried the little figure, they take it out within
" sight of everybody and make them believe that this
" was the witchcraft. They then apply for the cure
" any herbs that they can find and if sometimes by
" chance the sick person gets cured they gain much
" credit amongst the ignorant."

A most extraordinary account was given by the
curate of Yaxcabá, of a religious or superstitious
ceremony which at a certain season of the year was
performed by the Indians of his parish in the
beginning of this century. They erected near the
village a rudely constructed table upon which was
placed a turkey. When the ceremony commenced,
the Indian who acted as the priest poured into the
beak of the turkey a small quantity of pitarilla.
He then killed the bird and gave it to his assistants
at the table, who carried it away to season it and

prepare it for being eaten. Large tortillas were also prepared and when everything was ready the turkey and tortillas were placed upon the table together with several jars of pitarilla. "Then," stated the cura, "the sacerdote commences to "incense them with copal." . . . . "And then taking "some of the pitarilla upon a hissop he sprinkles "it towards the four winds invoking the four "*Pahahtunes* who are the gods and custodians of "the rains. Then approaching the table he raises "on high one of the jars, and offers it to the "mouths of the surrounding people, who are kneeling. "The function concludes by all eating and drinking "to their satisfaction."

Near a hamlet a few leagues from Uxmal, I observed a group of Indians performing ceremonies similar to those described by the curate of Yaxcabá, and I then formed the opinion that they were imitating what they had seen in the Spanish churches. It may, however, be possible that these native observances have some relation to practices that may have been customary amongst the natives before the conquest. Near Jacaltenango, amongst the hills of the Sierra Madre, ceremonies and sacrifices were still, at certain periods of the year, performed by the Mams ; turkeys were killed, and special and peculiar rites were customary. In Yucatan it was found necessary in the sixteenth century to enforce regulations, preventing the caciques from convening meetings of the natives which were held for the purpose of maintaining the ancient worship of their gods. These meetings usually took place in secret, and the services and superstitious propitiations were

taught or performed by men who were the descendants of the priests or caciques.

The tendency of the Indians to have religious
rites performed in their houses or in huts set
apart for the purpose, and their custom of having
these ceremonies conducted by one or more men
selected from among themselves to act as priests, or
" sacerdotes," is noticeable throughout Guatemala,
Yucatan and Chiapas.

Before leaving Abalá I visited a large and deep
cenote or well.   It was one of those natural caverns
the Indians of Yucatan were accustomed to use for
their supply of water, and which presumably mark the
sites of the ancient centres of population.   It was
chiefly fed by the waters penetrating through the
surrounding calcareous limestone formation.   As it
was late in the dry season of the year, the waters
were low and the natives were engaged in going up
and down the steps cut into and around the sides of
the cavern.   The work of filling their jars was
laborious, as the depth to which they had to descend
was nearly one hundred feet.

After examining this natural well, I returned to
the cabildo, where I found that everything was ready
and the muleteers were waiting for me.   We started
without delay.   At night we stopped at what
appeared to be a farmhouse.   The muleteers unloaded
the mules and found places to sleep in an outer
shed.   I unrolled my hammock and secured it to
the rafters outside the dwelling of the young pro-
prietress, and found protection from the dew under the
overhanging thatch.   From this exposed position I
watched for several hours the clear star-light,

regretting that this was the last time that I should lead this free and wandering life; for on the next day we were to be in Merida. At daybreak we continued our journey and arrived in the capital of Yucatan shortly before noon and halted in the market place.

My travelling companions then left me and I remained a solitary stranger amongst a crowd of busy Indians. I was told that there was no hotel, but that possibly I might get a room in an old disused convent which was being áltered for the purpose of receiving guests. I rode up to the gate and there saw a Spaniard who informed me that he had lately bought a portion of the ruins, and was re-arranging the interior sufficiently to enable him to keep an inn. He had a room at my disposal and assured me that he would be pleased if I would occupy it. This room had been a nun's cell, the door of which opened into the quadrangle.

I found that I was quartered within the Convent of the Conceptionistas, which after the suppression of the monastic orders had been abandoned. Thus, by a strange series of events, I had come from the ruined Indian "nunnery" at Uxmal to the ruined Spanish nunnery at Merida. The cells and the quadrangle of the Conceptionistas reminded me of the interior of the "Casa de las Monjas."

During my brief sojourn in Merida I was generally occupied during the day in observing the habits of the Indians who came into the town from the adjacent country. In the evenings, within the convent walls where, for many years, the nuns had led their quiet and secluded lives, I listened to the plans of my worthy and eager landlord for converting a building, constructed for the purposes of solitude and prayer, into a busy and prosperous inn. I frequently thought of the past of this land. The monastic institutions of an unknown race of Indians had flourished and had been destroyed, and were succeeded by the churches and convents established by an enthusiastic race of devoted missionaries who came across the Atlantic to spread their faith in the New World. Many changes had happened, the old order of things had passed away. The work of the Spanish priests for the education and conversion of the Indians, maintained for centuries with such zeal and self-sacrifice, was destined to become useless, and in their turn the monasteries of the Spaniards are doomed to fall into the same condition of ruin as the temples and religious structures of the Indians.

One evening the landlord (Miguel Yturran) told me that a brig had arrived and was at anchor off the port of Sisal, and was going to sail for Cuba on the afternoon of the next day. I accordingly arranged to leave on the following morning. A good level road led to the northern coast, the distance was about thirty-eight miles. We changed mules at a village called Junucuma, and reached Sisal before nine in the morning. We had left Merida at daybreak and travelled at an average speed exceeding twelve miles an hour. In the offing we saw the brig with her sails loosed, preparing for sea.

Upon getting on board I was told that she was the Aguinaga, belonging to the port of San Sebastian. She was manned by a crew of Basques. Shortly before weighing our anchor, I was leaning over the port side of the vessel looking at the long, low, line of coast stretching far away towards the east, when my attention was called to an animated conversation that was taking place between the Basques and a boat's-crew of Indians who had come alongside, bringing provisions and fruit. It was surprising to hear a conversation carried on between men of races so absolutely distinct, and I asked the skipper, who was standing near me, how this power of communicating ideas between his crew and these Yucatan Indians had been established.

He said that he did not know, but as a matter of fact, his men, speaking Basque, were able to make themselves understood by the Indians living on these coasts, especially in the regions around Tabasco beyond Carmen and the bay of Terminos.

In the afternoon we left Sisal and were employed in beating against a fresh N.E. wind, usually standing in towards the coast during the day and tacking out to sea at night. It was not until the sixth day that we weathered the parallel of Cape Catoche, the extreme eastern point of Yucatan, and it was with no slight satisfaction that, after having been nine tedious days at sea, I heard that Cuba was in sight. The confinement on board the brig had been extremely irksome, and had only been made tolerable by the novelty of being thrown amongst a race of men that I had never met before and whose language was unintelligible.

These Basques were excellent sailors, quick and handy at their work aloft or on deck, and although incessantly employed, were willing and obedient. My messmates in the cabin consisted of the

skipper, the boatswain and the mate, and a fellow
passenger who had been for the greater part of his
life a Honduras pilot.   There was also a second class
passenger who usually lived under the forecastle.
This man was a wanderer upon the earth ; an exile
from his own land who, in the course of his travels,
had seen much of men and manners.   He told me
that he was a Frenchman and had been drawn for
the conscription, but he managed to evade his duty
and had got away from France, consequently he was
not able to return to his home as he was liable to be
punished.   He had managed to subsist by following
various trades and he was about to try his fortune in
one of the islands.

Upon approaching Havannah we at last got a
fair wind and were able to find an obscure berth
amongst the merchant shipping without difficulty.*
After leaving the brig and her Basque crew I
proceeded across the Gulf to Florida.   Amongst the
various places that I visited was Tampa, situated at

---

*As the little Aguinaga was timidly seeking for an anchorage, I
remembered a far different scene in which I had taken part in
1853, seventeen years earlier.

The Vestal, a twenty-six gun frigate in which I was then serving, had captured three slavers off the north coast of Cuba.
One of them was a fast sailing vessel called the Venus. She had
become notorious for her success in evading our cruisers and
landing large cargoes of slaves.

When we arrived off the mouth of the port of Havannah we
formed our fleet of prizes into line and passed between the castles
in triumph : our movements being watched by thousands of the
Spanish inhabitants as we took up our anchorage in the centre
of the harbour.

the head of a bay, near the spot where Hernando de Soto landed in 1539 and began the conquest of that part of America.

About one hundred miles to the north of Tampa are numerous sand islets. Upon one of these was situated the old settlement of Cedar Keys. I was fortunate in meeting there a good seaman and enthusiastic antiquary named Clarke, who had made his home at that place. He was well acquainted with the various channels and bays of the coast, and in consequence of the interest that he felt in all that related to the customs of the Indian tribes, had gathered together a store of information that was exceedingly curious. He had also made discoveries respecting the haunts of the buccaneers, and knew of stories about hidden treasure. Fragments of old vessels that were supposed to have belonged to the pirates had been found, and clearings in the forest had been noticed, where it is supposed they formed their camps when the crews were landed. This part of the Florida coast with its tortuous channels and land-locked bays is precisely the position that buccaneers would have chosen for careening their vessels and for all purposes that required conceal-ment after their raids upon the Spaniards.

Upon one of the islands near the main-land there was an ancient kitchen midden or shell mound of unusual size. We found that it extended along the beach for eight hundred yards. It averaged eighty yards in width and was forty feet high. It was composed principally of large oyster shells, but there were also the shells of clam fish and numerous smaller shells. The mound through-

out its length presented on its face a series of
alternate layers of earth, about half-an-inch thick.
The thickness of these intervening deposits of shells
was greater than at Damariscotta in Maine, from
which fact it may be inferred that the tribes who
came here were more numerous, or that they were
capable of extraordinary powers of consuming
oysters. Upon cutting away portions of the outer
slope of the mound, we found many fish bones and
quantities of fragments of broken pottery.

Not far from the shell mound was an ancient
Indian burial place. Captain Clarke had made excavations into it, and amongst the accumulation of
bones he had found some flint arrow heads and a few
rude stone axes. I examined these and noticed that
they were similar to those that had been found in
several of the burial mounds of the Iroquois. As I
wished to see this mound for the purpose of ascertaining certain points respecting the methods of
burial adopted by the Florida Indians, Captain
Clarke proposed that we should make an examination of it.

The heap was irregular in shape and about four
hundred yards in circumference at the base. It
consisted entirely of quantities of human skulls and
bones. We examined it sufficiently to enable certain
facts to be made clear. From the manner in which
groups of skulls and thigh bones were placed and
separated, it was evident that the burials took place
at considerable intervals of time. This is in accordance with what is known of the funeral customs of
the Indians in Florida and the southern parts of the
Mississippi Valley at the time of the expedition of
De Soto

It was then ascertained that in each of the villages there was a large building in which were kept boxes containing human bones. Before the bones were collected in this manner, the bodies had been placed in the adjacent forest, exposed to the air but raised on a scaffolding sufficiently high to prevent them from being disturbed by wild animals. After a suitable time had elapsed the bones were separated and cleaned, and were then deposited in the charnel-house, where religious ceremonies were frequently performed. Upon certain occasions, when the boxes were getting full, the bones were taken away and conveyed to the tribal burial place.

Judging from the manner in which the bones were deposited in the mound, it is probable that they were brought in their separate cases, and that the contents of each case were carefully kept together and finally thrown out in separate heaps. The occasions when the bones were brought here, may have been those when the tribes made their migrations to the sea coast. The methods of cleaning and removing the bones of the Indians in Florida were similar to those of the Dakotas.

On the coast, a few miles north of Cedar Keys, there were other large shell mounds, and in Tampa Bay I was shown the position of a long and extensive range of similar heaps on its southern shores. It is evident that before the sixteenth century there must have been a numerous aboriginal race inhabiting these coasts. The scattered remnants of the tribes that remained in Florida at the conclusion of the last Indian war in this region, have been removed and placed upon lands beyond the Mississippi.

CHAPTER XIX.

Mounds and Earthworks in North and Central America.—
Migrations of the Toltecs and Aztecs.—The Quichés.—Aboriginal races.—Palenque.— Hieroglyphs.—Temples.— Desertion
of the Temples and stone buildings in Yucatan.—Conquest of
Yucatan by the Aztecs.—Antiquity of Palenque and Uxmal.—
Aztec custom of imprisoning captives in cages and sacrificing
them to the gods.—Civilisation of the Toltecs.—Note upon the
symbol or Totem of the Serpent.

In the following chapters I propose to bring together the various notes upon the Indians and their
temples and earthworks which were made when
traversing Central America, and to add to them the
conclusions which have been formed subsequently.

There are certain problems which particularly
require to be examined. With respect to the antiquity of the stone buildings and pyramids, it would
be difficult to attempt to do more than endeavour
to form reasonable deductions from the evidence
afforded by the state of those ruins, and the information given about them by the Indians at the time
of the conquest. The conquerors, after they had
settled in Yucatan and Guatemala, were accompanied
by Spanish missionaries of great ability. We possess
in the writings of Bishop Las Casas and Bishop
Landa works of the greatest value, for both those
prelates when they were engaged in their duties of

converting the natives, were acquainted with the
language of the tribes amongst whom they worked.

In the prosecution of researches into subjects
which relate to Central America, it is desirable as
a preliminary step to consider the comparative civilisation of the Indians, as far as that is brought into
evidence by what has been discovered with respect
to mounds and earthworks, not only in that region,
but also throughout the valley of the Mississippi. A
distinction must also be made between earthworks
which are unquestionably of great antiquity, and
those that possibly may have been raised since the
date of the arrival of European settlers. Therefore
the geometrically planned inclosures in Ohio should
be excluded from this inquiry. It is otherwise with
great ramparts such as those inclosing Fort Ancient
on the steep promontory in the valley of the Little
Miami, which are of special importance on account
of the parallelisms with the similar fortifications
made by the Quichés and Kachiquels in Guatemala.

There are exceptional circumstances connected
with the mounds in North America. It has to be
remembered that they were not always burial
places. When De Soto arrived with his fleet in
Florida, the chief cacique of the tribe dwelling
near the landing place, was living on the top
of a mound about fifty feet high. This mound
was pointed out to me when I was at Tampa. It
appeared to be made for the purpose of placing
huts upon its summit. The platform was sufficiently
large to give room for several dwellings. There are
also mounds near the western bank of the Mississippi, between Natchez and the mouth of the

Arkansas. One of them resembled that at Tampa, and had a wide level space on the summit.

When the earliest Spanish expedition passed through that part of the country, it was observed that the Indians frequently placed their houses upon artificial earthworks raised sufficiently high to be above the inundations. At Natchez the tribe, which, from their peculiar customs, have been called the sun-worshippers, raised mounds primarily for the residence of their chiefs, who differed from other Indians of that rank, in being invested with special attributes in connection with ceremonies performed before the rising sun. But there were customs with respect to them which require to be noticed. It was stated by Father le Petit, who was for many years a missionary amongst the Natchez, that when their principal chief died his hut was demolished and a new mound was raised, upon which was built the wooden cabin of his successor in that dignity. It can be understood that where a large tribe having this custom dwelt for a long time in one place, it might happen that a series of connected platform mounds, forming an inclosure, would probably have a rectangular shape.

Higher up the Mississippi, above the junction of the Ohio, are the Cahokia earthworks. There were also several mounds placed on high ground near the east bank of the river, not far from the borders of Illinois and Wisconsin. One of these, which was about forty feet high, was opened ten years before I went to St. Pauls. A vault was discovered beneath the level of the ground, which contained several skeletons sitting in a circle. The earth of which it

was composed was a kind of loam, not occurring in
the vicinity, and it was supposed that it must have
been brought from a considerable distance by Indians
who wished to show their respect for the burial
place of their chiefs, by bringing tributes of earth
taken from the ground near their encampments.
The high mounds placed around the edge of the
promontory, now called Dayton's Bluff, and which
are the most northern group in the valley of the
Mississippi, have been described in a preceding
chapter.

When I was in Chiapas, the Presbitero Macal
told me that he was present when two mounds were
examined in 1860, near San Cristobal. They were
each ten feet high and covered vaults made of large
flat slabs of stone. Within these tombs were two
skulls, but nothing else was found. There were no
weapons or fragments of pottery. In the vault
under the mound in Illinois there were several large
pieces of pottery, and on the surface, immediately
above the tomb, were ashes and other evidences of
fire.

But before proceeding farther with this subject, it
is necessary to bring under consideration the progress of archæological knowledge in North America,
since the date of my visit to the ancient mounds
and earthworks in Ohio. Great advances have been
made in the classification of the discoveries that
have taken place in the burial mounds that exist
throughout the United States. Deductions can
consequently be established with regard to the
civilisation of the Indians, and it has become possible
to establish, upon a scientific basis, their position

as a race.   A long series of investigations have been completed, and a summary of the results published, under the auspices of the Smithsonian Institution, by Professor Cyrus Thomas.*

"It seems desirable at the present time," he observes, "to make a statement explaining the plans " and describing the work of the mound exploring " division of the Bureau of Ethnology." . . . "The " questions relating to prehistoric America are to be " determined not alone by the study of its ancient " monuments, but by the study also of the languages, " customs, art, beliefs, and folk-lore of the aborigines. " Only by such a comprehensive study can the exact " relations of the ancient archæological remains to the " historic Indian tribes be made apparent.   Major J. " W. Powell, the Director of the Bureau, taking this " comprehensive and scientific view of the subject, " saw at the outset the necessity of deciding as soon " as possible the question 'Were the mound builders " Indians ?'"

The work was carried on for several years, and Professor Thomas states that " Over two thousand " mounds have been explored, including almost every " known type as to form. . . . Nothing trustworthy " has been discovered to justify the theory that the " mound builders belonged to a highly civilised race, " or that they were a people who had attained a higher " culture status than the Indians.   It is true that

---

* "Work in Mound Exploration of the Bureau of Ethnology, " by Cyrus Thomas, Washington, 1887.

" works and papers on American archæology are full
" of statements to the contrary, which are generally
' based on the theory that the mound builders
" belonged to a race of much higher culture than the
" Indians. Yet when the facts on which this opinion
" is based are examined with sober, scientific care, the
" splendid fabric which has been built upon them by
" that great workman, imagination, fades from sight."
" Professor Thomas also observes—" That the links
" discovered directly connecting the Indians and
" mound builders are so numerous and well estab-
" lished that there should be no longer any hesitancy
" in accepting the theory that the two are one and
" the same people."

The origin and nature of the American mounds,
and the customs of the Indians who raised them,
have also been investigated by Professor Lucien Carr.
He claims " that the mounds and inclosures of Ohio,
" like those in New York and the Gulf States, were
" the work of the red Indians of historic times, or
" of their immediate ancestors."*

With reference to this much debated question of
the formation of these inclosures, a re-survey of
several of them was made. The measurements of
Professor Thomas and his assistants appear to have
established the fact of the geometrical accuracy of
the octagonal, square and circular works near

---

* " The Mounds of the Mississippi Valley, Historically
Considered," by Lucien Carr, Assistant Curator of the Peabody
Museum of American Archæology and Ethnology, Cambridge,
Mass.

Newark.* In the introduction to the memoir upon the Ohio mounds, Professor Thomas observes that "The constantly recurring question 'Who constructed "these works?' has brought before the public a "number of widely different theories, though the "one which has been most generally accepted is "that they originated with a people long since "extinct or driven from the country, who had "attained a culture status much in advance of that "reached by the aborigines inhabiting the country "at the time of its discovery by Europeans. The "opinions advanced in this paper, in support of "which evidence will be presented, is that the "ancient works of the State are due to Indians of "several different tribes, and that some at least of "the typical works, were built by the ancestors of "the modern Cherokees." †

As a consequence of the examination of the Indian mounds throughout the United States, the majority of the modern American archæologists consider that the aboriginal inhabitants were never in a higher state of civilisation than they were when they first became known to Europeans. It is not however the questions of the burial mounds, and the importance of what has been found in them which have chiefly to be considered here. Attention should be prin-

---

* See Note, chapter iv. p. 69.

† In the sixteenth century, the Cherokees occupied the lands in that part of America where the States of North Carolina, Alabama and Georgia border upon the State of Tennessee.

cipally directed to the difficult problem respecting the great fortified ramparts of Fort Ancient.

The traditions of the Delawares,* which affirmed that the defensive earthworks of Ohio were built by the Tallegwi, have generally been accepted as being well-founded. They were stated to have been a powerful tribe who built fortifications and entrench-ments. Finally they abandoned their lands and went southwards, down the valley of the Mississippi and never returned. It may be conjectured, after observing the similar works and methods of selecting their defensive positions in Guatemala, that the Tallegwi were the same race who were afterwards known as Toltecs. The probability of this assump-tion being reasonable, becomes more evident when the group of platform and circular mounds on the plains near Mixco are observed to be similar to those raised on the plains of Cahokia near the banks of the Mississippi.

The question of the condition of intelligence amongst the North American Indians, has a direct bearing upon the problem of the origin of the civilisation of the Toltecs and Aztecs, and it is satisfactory to know that there are sound reasons for supposing that the Indians who constructed the fortified camps in Ohio were not more advanced in knowledge than the tribes who were dwelling in that region at the time of the discovery of America by Columbus.

Several years after the conquest of Mexico, the

---

*See chapter v., p. 94.

Spaniards sent expeditions into the southern parts
of Central America, and conquered the Quichés and
the surrounding country, in which were situated the
ramparts defending Utatlan and Patinamit. It was
subsequently considered desirable that investigations
should be made into the ancient systems by which
the aboriginal inhabitants had been governed by
their caciques, and orders were given to this effect
by the Emperor Charles the Fifth and by his
successor Philip the Second. In the reports of the
officers who conducted these inquiries, it was stated
that an extraordinarily rigid line of caste was maintained amongst the Quichés. There was an absolute
distinction between the ruling families descended
from the caciques, and the great mass of the races
who were under their control. It was also evident,
judging from the language of several appeals made
by Indian chiefs to obtain justice and to have their
rank and authority acknowledged, that they considered the working classes of Indians as their
absolute slaves.

" There was no instance," states the historian
Juarros, " of any person being appointed to a public
" office, high or low, who was not selected from the
" nobility ; for which reason, great anxiety was felt
" by them to keep the purity of their lineage unsullied.
" To preserve this rank untainted in blood, it was
" decreed by the law, that if any cacique or noble
" should marry a woman who was not of noble family,
" he should be degraded to the caste of mazegual or
" plebeian, assume the name of his wife, and be subject
" to all the duties and services imposed upon ple-
" beians." These services generally consisted of works

performed by forced labour. The lands belonging to
the ruling families were cultivated in this manner,
and, in fact, the Indians of the native and working
class were entirely at the disposal of their masters.
One of the Spanish bishops, whose diocese was in
Mexico, mentions that he had ascertained that
these mazeguales could be sold or killed by
their owners. There were marked differences in the
dress of the people. The mazeguales wore, as a rule,
nothing but the loin cloth, or sometimes, as is the
case now with the Lacandones, a long cotton
shirt, reaching nearly to the feet. It was a matter
of observation amongst the conquerors that the
inferior classes of Indians were submissive, but that
their rulers were intractable, harsh and warlike.

It is inexpedient to pursue this particular subject
to any great extent, for it is made clear by the
reports of the Spanish authorities that the relations
of the governing class of the Quichés to the other
Indians under their rule were those of a race of
conquerors to a race of slaves, and the victors
treated those whom they had conquered in a manner
in accordance with the habits of a savage and barbarous tribe of North American Indians. This much
may be admitted from the consideration of the
circumstances of the laws and customs of the
Quichés at the time of the arrival of the Spaniards.
But if a due estimation is also given to the evidence
afforded by the strange and otherwise inexplicable
similarities in the methods of choosing fortified
positions and raising ramparts with those in Ohio,
it becomes reasonable to infer that the Quiché
chiefs originally migrated from that part of North
America.

It is however necessary to note that, at whatever period their migration may have taken place, it cannot be granted or inferred that the Ohio tribes brought with them any knowledge of architecture, or of any form of civilisation, for had it been otherwise, they would have left behind them some vestiges of that civilisation or mechanical skill. It is especially remarkable that throughout the length and breadth of North America there is not the smallest fragment of any hewn stone building, or of any carved stone hieroglyphic characters. Thus the theory of migratory tribes of Indians bringing with them from the North into Mexico, a comparatively advanced knowledge of arts and sciences is opposed to all evidence. It is almost certain that the state of civilisation that at one time existed in the regions of Chiapas and Yucatan, was introduced into the country at some period subsequent to the arrival of the invading tribe, unless it can be established that the aboriginal races already possessed a competent intelligence, and an architectural capacity. A proposition of this character cannot be reasonably maintained, for it is known that in the fifteenth century the Indians in Cuba and Haiti, the Caribs on the coasts south of Yucatan, and the aborigines in the interior were savages, existing in a low state of human intelligence. This subject respecting the Indian migrations and the state of civilisation that was existing, or had existed, in Central America, can be more definitely considered after attention has been directed to the question of the antiquity and purpose of the buildings at Palenque and

Uxmal.   It is much to be regretted that Palenque was not known to the Spaniards when Cortes
marched within a few leagues of it in 1524.   Possibly,
at that time it had not been long abandoned, and
perhaps some of the caciques dwelling in that part
of the valley of the Usamacinta might have been
able to explain the meaning of the hieroglyphs.
Unfortunately the ruins were not discovered until
more than two centuries had elapsed, and nothing
could be ascertained from the Indians which gave
the slightest clue to their signification.   It has been
surmised—and there are good reasons for thinking
that the surmise may be correct—that the characters
relate to the migrations of the tribes.   But in
consequence of the incomplete knowledge of these
Indian hieroglyphs, it would be impossible to
attempt to form any satisfactory conjectures regarding their meaning.

There exists, however, graven on the tablet of the
cross, two figures which, if I am correct in my opinion
with regard to them, are of the greatest importance
in establishing certain facts with regard to the
builders of Palenque.   Upon referring to the illustration of the altar tablet that was placed within
the temple of the cross, it will be noticed that the
two standing figures offering sacrifice to the quetzal
or sacred bird of Quiché, are evidently intended to
represent persons actually living at the time that the
altar was designed, for there is nothing fantastic
in the costume that is worn by them.   If a careful
examination is made into the details of their dress
it will, I think, be concluded that these men were
the chief caciques of the Quichés.

" The nobles," observes Juarros, " wore a dress of
" white cotton dyed or stained with different colours,
" the use of which was prohibited to the other ranks.
" This vestment consisted of a shirt and white
" breeches, decorated with fringes; over these was
" drawn another pair of breeches, reaching to the
" knees and ornamented with a species of embroi-
" dery; the legs were bare; the feet protected by
" sandals, fastened over the instep and at the heel
" by thongs of leather; the sleeves of the shirt were
" looped above the elbow, with a blue or red band;
" the hair was worn long, and tressed behind with a
" cord of the colour used upon the sleeves, and
" terminating in a tassel, which was a distinction
" peculiar to the great captains; the waist was
" girded with a piece of cloth of various colours,
" fastened in a knot before; over the shoulders was
" thrown a white mantle, ornamented with figures
" of birds, lions and other decorations of cord and
" fringe. The ears and lower lip were pierced, to
" receive star-shaped pendants of gold or silver."
Upon an examination of the figures it will be
observed that, although their dress corresponds with
what is described as being worn by the Quiché
caciques, neither of them are wearing sandals.
But, on the altar of the temple placed on an
adjacent mound, the same figures are again offering
sacrifices, and the tallest of them is wearing sandals
precisely as described above. It was the custom
among the Quichés to associate with the principal
cacique another chief, to whom was intrusted the
control and management of the troops and the
conduct of all hostilities, and it is stated that some-

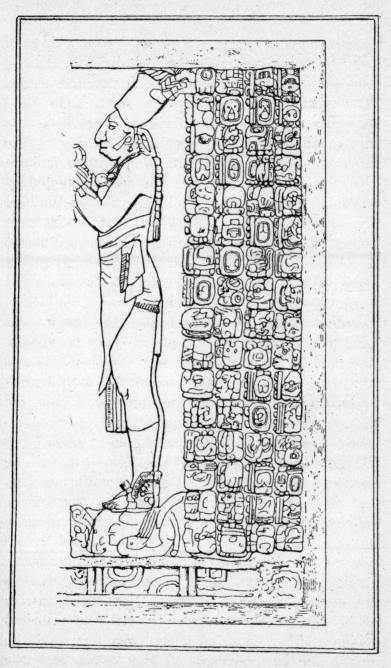

PART OF THE ALTAR-PIECE IN A TEMPLE AT PALENQUE.

times this chief was the eldest son of the cacique. As the second temple appears to have been dedicated to the god of war, it may be assumed that the shorter figure was intended to represent a war chief. He is dressed in accordance with that rank and wears a mantle and a heavy tassel. In this temple the chief is drawn as standing upon a kneeling captive, but in that dedicated to Quetzalcoatl he is placed upon a block of stone, upon which is a hieroglyph. To Quetzalcoatl the offering appears to have been in conformity with the attributes assigned to him, of religion and education. Possibly the child, held in the hands of the tallest cacique, was dedicated to serve in the temple after having been trained for the priesthood in the monastery.

It is satisfactory to be able to establish the conclusion that the figures are caciques of the Quichés, for it thereby become spossible to advance a few steps towards the solution of a problem which presents many difficulties with regard to the period of the construction of Palenque, and state of civilization of the builders. In a manuscript left in a Franciscan convent by one of the descendants of the Quichés, an account was given of the migrations of that tribe before they settled near Utatlan. It was stated that they reached that country after a long journey from Mexico, and adopted the name of Quiché in memory of one of their leaders; but before that time the people were called Toltecs.

Before endeavouring to establish conclusions with regard to Palenque, attention should be directed to the temples and other stone buildings in the

adjacent regions. With respect to the numerous
groups of ruins in Yucatan, we possess the testi-
mony of the Spanish priests who dwelt in their
parishes in that country at a period when many of
the governing class of Indians were of the same
generation as those who inhabited the land when
it was conquered. One of these missionaries was
Father Landa, who was not only zealous in the performance of his duties, but also studied the language
and civilisation of the race amongst whom he dwelt.
He was present in Tihoo soon after the capture of
that Indian settlement, which was afterwards chosen
for the site of the city of Merida.

He states that in that place there were several
stone edifices. He made a plan of the largest of
them from which it is evident that they were of
the same character as those at Uxmal. Tihoo was
occupied by the Spanish forces in 1541, and the
terraces, upon which were placed the principal buildings, were given to the Franciscans as a site for their
convent. The friars began their work in 1547. Thus
only six years had elapsed since the Indians had
left their town. Landa's descriptions of the state
and condition of the ancient ruins are therefore of
the greatest assistance in forming conclusions with
regard to them.

The principal edifice was placed upon the highest
of three terraces, each of which was surrounded or
faced by thick walls, and approached by steps.
There was a large interior quadrangle having ranges
of rooms or cells occupying the four sides. These
were similar to those in the " House of the Nuns "
at Uxmal. In the vicinity there were several pyra-

mids which had small temples on their summits. It was observed that all these structures appeared to have been disused for a considerable period. The Franciscans found that the Indian structures were covered with thick brushwood. This was cleared away. The buildings were destroyed and the materials supplied the stone required for their church and convent.*

The fact that the desertion of the temples had occurred before the arrival of the Spaniards is important. It explains many of the circumstances then existing in Yucatan which otherwise would be unintelligible. When the conquerors settled in that land they were surprised to find numerous stone buildings in various parts of the country, all of which were unoccupied. They were informed that they had not been abandoned in consequence of their conquest. They found that it was impracticable to obtain from the natives any explanation of the nature of the events which had happened and had caused this change. Thus the problem regarding the purposes of these extensive buildings, and the architectural skill of the constructors was as obscure to them at that time as it is now to the present inhabitants.

At Izamal, about thirty-five miles east of Tihoo, there were also numerous temples, and it was noticed by Landa that there were evidences of there having been a paved road between the two

---

*Merida now occupies the site of Tihoo. The stones, with which were built the pyramids and temples, were used in the construction of the new city.

places. A Franciscan convent was established at
Izamal, and a brief account of its temples was
written in 1663 by Father Lizana, in which he
states, with respect to the ruins in Yucatan, that
the deserted edifices appeared to have been of one
style of architecture, and that some of them were so
perfect that it might be said that twenty years had
not elapsed since they were built. These edifices
were however, he observes, not inhabited by the
Indians when the Spaniards arrived. The natives
lived scattered in huts amongst the woods, but they
used them as temples or sanctuaries, and occasionally
performed religious ceremonies and fasts there.*

The Franciscan missionaries were not able to obtain
from the natives an intelligible explanation of the
events that had occurred which had caused the temples to be abandoned. But they were informed that
an invasion had taken place about two hundred
years before their arrival, and many of the caciques
and ruling families had been driven out of the land.
The invaders did not occupy the sacred buildings,
and allowed them to fall into ruin, but they were
visited occasionally by those who still had faith in
the ancient gods and wished to offer sacrifices to
them. It was ascertained that the greater part of
Yucatan had become subject to the control of chiefs
belonging to the Aztec race, and that several of them
paid tribute to Montezuma.

The question of the antiquity of the temples of
Palenque, Uxmal and other structures of that

---

* Relation des choses de Yucatan, p. 351.

character must therefore, in a great degree, be
decided by the evidence upon which are based the
traditions of the migrations of the Toltecs who preceded the Aztecs, and were the first of the hordes
who conquered the aboriginal races of Central
America. The historians who have investigated
those traditions concur in considering that the
arrival of the Toltecs within Mexican territory
happened in the seventh century. After remaining
some time in the northern part of the country,
they migrated southwards to Cholula, Palenque
and Yucatan.* If the historic evidence is accepted
as being trustworthy, it follows that all the stone
edifices in these regions must have been erected
later than that date. The Aztecs arrived at the
close of the twelfth century. Therefore it may
be concluded that Palenque was built later than
the eighth century, and was deserted before
the fourteenth century. Uxmal is evidently more
modern than Palenque, and it may be assumed that
it was constructed after the tenth century, and

---

*According to Humboldt, the Toltecs arrived in Anáhuac
(Mexico) A.D. 648, and reached Tula in 670. The pyramids of
Téotihuacan, a few leagues north of the modern city of Mexico,
were built by them. They afterwards raised the great pyramid
of Cholula, and on its platform built a temple for the worship
of Quetzalcoatl. From Cholula, colonies of the Toltecs went to
Tabasco and Yucatan.

The Aztecs arrived in Mexico in 1190, and found there the
pyramids which they believed to have been the work of their
predecessors the Toltecs, who had obtained a knowledge of
hieroglyphics and of methods of computing time by calendars.
The Aztecs founded Tenochtitlan (the city of Mexico) in 1325.

abandoned not much earlier than a hundred years
before the Spaniards landed upon the shores of the
New World.

The Aztec chiefs introduced into Yucatan one of
their barbarous customs which was similar to what
was practised by them elsewhere. It was found by the
conquerors, that in Mexico they kept slaves and prisoners in cages, where these victims were fattened and
prepared for sacrifice.* After having been killed and
offered as propitiations to the gods their bodies were
eaten. In 1511, it happened that a Spanish vessel
was wrecked upon some shoals fifteen leagues south
of the island of Jamaica. The crew after having

------

*The custom of confining captives or slaves in wooden cages
for the purpose of being prepared for sacrifice, was supposed to
have been established by the Aztecs about a century after they
had settled in Mexico.

There is reason to believe that in consequence of their being
surrounded by enemies and engaged in constant wars, they considered it necessary to propitiate the war god in the most terrific
manner. Thus when the great Teocalli, erected for the worship
of Huitzil-pochli, was completed, many thousands of victims were
sacrificed as propitiatory offerings. When colonies of the Aztec
race were advancing in the direction of Tabasco and Yucatan,
similar sacrificial ceremonies were performed.

Bernal Diaz saw, in one of the Indian towns that had been
captured by the Spaniards, three large cages full of prisoners who
were waiting to be sacrificed. They were fastened by collars to
prevent their escape. They were taken out of the cages and
sent back to their own tribes. He elsewhere observes that the
Indians devoured human flesh after the victims had been sacrificed, in the same way as the Spaniards devoured oxen. It is
evident that great numbers of the aboriginal natives must have
been kept in slavery and, in time of war, were killed and eaten
by the Aztecs.

been thirteen days in an open boat, landed upon the north-eastern shores of Yucatan near Cape Catoche, and were made captives by the cacique of the district. Valdivia, who was in command, together with four of his men, were at once sacrificed and eaten, others were put in cages, but several of these men escaped. When the fleet under the command of Cortes anchored off Cozumel, in 1519, one of the captives, named Aguilar, went on board the flagship.

Bernal Diaz, who was with the expedition and saw this man when he arrived, relates that when Aguilar came before the presence of Cortes he cowered down according to the manner of Indian slaves. Aguilar stated that only he and another Spaniard named Gonzalo Guerrero, were then alive. Most of his companions had been sacrificed to the gods, but some had died, and two women who were with them had perished from misery and the severity of the labour of grinding maize. Guerrero had married an Indian woman and followed the native customs. He had been tattoed, his ears were pierced and his lips were turned down.* Aguilar had become acquainted with the Maya language, and was afterwards employed by Cortes as an interpreter. Guerrero remained in Yucatan with the Indians.

Upon a review of the facts ascertained by the conquerors in the sixteenth century in Mexico and Guatemala, and by the Franciscan and Dominican

---

* Bernal Diaz, chapter xxix, and Landa, p. 12.

missionaries in Yucatan and Chiapas, together with
the researches made since that time by archæologists
and explorers, it appears to be possible to form
certain conclusions. The architectural and mechanical knowledge, and the advance towards writing
characters, forming calendars and reckoning time by
astronomical observations must have been reached
within a period of less than four centuries. It is
therefore probable that the priests of the Toltecs
became acquainted with their arts and sciences
not long after they had left North America and
had migrated to the regions around Téotihuacan in
the direction of the shores of the Gulf of Mexico. In
what manner and under what circumstances their
knowledge was obtained, is a problem which requires
to be given a careful investigation.

In an Aztec or Toltec manuscript which forms part of the
collection of ancient Mexican codices placed in the library of the
Vatican, there is a representation of a cacique making an
offering to a rattlesnake.

The manner of propitiation resembles the methods of
sacrificing to this Manito which were followed by the Dakotas
(see p. 170). The head dress of the cacique which consists of
plumed feathers is similar to that worn by the chiefs of that
race, and is placed in the same position as the feathers of Rocky
Bear (illustration, chapter viii).

The rattlesnake appears to have been the Totem of the Toltecs
and is the chief emblem at Uxmal and Chichen Itza.

It is thought that a serpent is represented upon the central
stone of the tablet of the cross at Palenque and as the god
to whom the temple is dedicated was named Bird-Serpent
(Quetzal-Coatl), it is probable that the sculptors delineated the
symbol in a manner that was intelligible to the Quichés.

Upon an examination of the illustration of the centre tablet,

MEXICAN CACIQUE (?) MAKING AN OFFERING TO A RATTLESNAKE.

(FROM AN ANCIENT TOLTEC OR AZTEC MANUSCRIPT.)

which is an exact reproduction from a photograph of the
original stone (see frontispiece), these symbols may perhaps
be traced. I may here venture to express the opinion that the
Toltecs may have been the tribe that once dwelt in that part of
Ohio to the west of the river Scioto, where is still to be seen the
Totem of the serpent.

The illustration of the propitiation to the serpent is taken
from a part of the Mexican manuscript represented in Humboldt's "Vues des Cordilléres."

CHAPTER XX.

Conjectures respecting the descendants of the tribes who built the Temples.—Knowledge and education of the Caciques and Priests.—Traditions of the arrival of white strangers from the East.—Las Casas.—Quetzal-Coatl.—Crosses found in Yucatan. —Gomara.—Legend of the flight of Spaniards by sea towards the West after the conquest of Spain by the Saracens.— Fabulous island of Antilia.—Columbus on his outward voyage steers for Antilia.—Trade-winds.—Considerations upon the probabilities of vessels being driven across the Atlantic or Pacific Oceans towards America.

THE subject of the origin and migrations of the Toltecs has been given much attention. It has been a matter of conjecture whether any of the descendants of the people who built the temples of Palenque, and inscribed upon tablets of stone their hieroglyphic records, are at present living in Central America.

The chief difficulty in attempting to form a decision upon this question, is the uncertainty regarding the distinction to be made between the people belonging to the conquering Quichés and the aboriginal races whom they had reduced to slavery, and who constituted the greater part of the population. It is known that the caciques and other members of the governing families of Utatlan became gradually reduced to the utmost poverty. But there were other chiefs of tribes of Quiché origin who did not resist the Spaniards, and who volunteered to become their allies. Many of these were permitted to hold lands in the neighbourhood of Lake Atitlan, and lived in a prosperous condition until the early part of the eighteenth century, when they disappeared from notice. Possibly, in accordance with Quiché customs, they may have kept apart from those who were mazeguales, and intermarried amongst Indians of the same race as themselves.

The statements of the grandsons of the caciques of Utatlan, as recorded in their manuscripts, with regard to the dates of the arrival of their tribe, the building of the fortresses, and their system of dividing the country they had conquered into separate governments, are undoubtedly entitled to be considered as deserving of attention. They agree in a remarkable manner with what has been since ascertained. It may be inferred from the account of their migrations and the list of their kings or chief caciques, that they had been settled in Guatemala about three or four hundred years before Utatlan was conquered by Alvarado.

During the time that I was crossing the Cordilleras in the region which had been governed by the Quichés, I endeavoured to ascertain if there were any marked differences in the types or characters of the tribes then occupying the land. Near Patinamit I saw several groups of Kachiquels who were of the same race as the Quichés, and I noticed that in many respects they resembled the Dakotas, and in appearance were unlike the ordinary natives. I also observed in the district adjacent to Santa Cruz del Quiché that the Indians holding official positions in the villages were usually of a larger stature than the inferior men and, in their harsh and overbearing manner and features, recalled to mind the chiefs of the North American tribes. I found, however, that it was not possible to form definite conclusions based upon the facts that came within my personal observation. The Quichés are reserved in their intercourse with strangers. Whatever may be their comparative condition of wealth or poverty they all live in the same manner, and seem to be satisfied with the barest necessaries. Near Jacaltenango, when amongst the Mams, I met one of the richest and most influential of the Indians of that tribe. He was living like the meanest of the people, although he was the owner of a prosperous estate. This apparent equality in the habits of life is universal amongst the Indians.

In the sixteenth century, after the conquest, the caciques of the Quichés and Mams who had submitted to the Spaniards were accustomed to maintain a state ceremonial of considerable dignity; and at a later period the Indians who claimed to have held high rank and who were granted lands and privileges lived in a manner suitable to their condition. This comparative distinction has entirely disappeared. With respect to the migrations of the governing classes of the Quichés it is a matter of interest to observe that several of the Indian chiefs who accompanied the Spanish conquerors from Mexico, married the daughters of these Quichés, and said that they did so because they had discovered that they were of the same race as themselves.

In the consideration of subjects relating to the Indians it is necessary to discriminate between the observances of the aboriginal inhabitants and those of the races who were of foreign origin. Thus with respect to the superstitious and extremely devotional inclinations of the natives in Guatemala and Chiapas, it may be assumed that those instincts belong to the race who dwelt in those lands before they were conquered by the Toltecs and Aztecs; but the customs of sacrificing human beings to the gods together with other acts of barbarity were introduced from North America.

The Spaniards considered that the most evident proclivities of the masses of the natives were drunkenness and idolatry. The latter tendency prevailed to an excessive degree. Las Casas states that throughout New Spain the idols were so numerous that they could not be counted. During his journeys he found them in every place and of every kind, in their huts, in the villages, amongst the hills and in the sacred places. The numbers of them, he relates, were infinite. In the sixteenth century the Indians were gradually, but not without difficulty, brought under the control of the Spanish ecclesiastics. The idols were destroyed, and the superstitious practices, especially all those which were connected with the worship of demons, were suppressed.

The national instinct of idolatry still remains. There is in the nature of the aboriginal races a religious fervour which apparently forms an integral part of their character. They are also submissive and inoffensive, and it can be understood how any invading and warlike tribe would, without difficulty, conquer and control people having this mild disposition. It is not surprising that a fierce tribe of

North American Indians was able to reduce them
into a state of servile obedience. The Toltecs and,
afterwards, the Aztecs would undoubtedly have
introduced into Mexico the barbarous usages which
prevailed amongst the tribes dwelling in the valleys
of the Mississippi and Ohio, and these usages, when
grafted upon the vices which existed amongst the
natives, may have been the inciting cause of the
revolting condition of national demoralisation which
was so severely described by Bernal Diaz and other
Spanish historians.

The Dominican missionaries in Guatemala observed
that the Indians were passionately fond of dancing and singing. The joyousness which originally
existed in their nature or temperament has become
extinct. The usual tenour of their lives seems to be
accompanied by a quiet, subdued melancholy. It
is not improbable that, as a consequence of several
centuries of Spanish domination, the aboriginal races
have sunk into a dull and apathetic state. It is
however possible that other influences acted upon
the taciturn and wild natures of these tribes.*
The innate disposition of the natives to worship idols

---

*It was noticed soon after the Spanish conquest that the
Indians died rapidly from causes of a mental character. They
died because they did not wish to live. The conditions of
slavery they were forced to endure had such an effect upon
them that they gradually lost their strength. After submitting
for a time to the hardships imposed upon them they appeared
to become resigned to their fate. Life was a burden. They lost
heart and died from misery. This was particularly the case in
Cuba and Hispaniola.

in Guatemala was found to be equally existing with the Mayas in Yucatan, who also had the custom of making pilgrimages to the shrines. It is mentioned by Landa that the pilgrims stopped when passing near any of the deserted or ruined temples, and were accustomed to mutter prayers, and offer incense. This custom was in accordance with the acts of devotion which I saw practised by the Tzendal Indians in Chiapas before the ruined walls of the church at Bachajon.

There are circumstances connected with the domination of the Aztecs, and possibly also with that of their predecessors the Quiché-Toltecs, which require to be noticed. It is unquestionable that slavery would have been the fate of any tribe or race conquered by North American Indians. But the fact of slaves or captives being bought and sold for the purpose of being killed and offered to the gods is extraordinary. Great numbers of the natives were annually sacrificed, and astonishing acts of cannibalism were committed. Whatever may have been the hardships inflicted by the Spaniards upon the Mexican Indians, it is satisfactory to be assured that the discovery of America, and the conquests of Cortes put an end to the most horrible condition of things that has ever been known to have existed in any part of the world.

There are, however, other facts to be taken into consideration. It has been assumed that there was a condition of comparative civilisation amongst the ruling tribes, which seemed to be in such a progressive state as to lead to the conclusion that there were elements of knowledge which might have been so far

developed in the course of time as to have brought
these Indians into the ranks of · civilised nations.
With regard to this subject it should be observed
that when the Spaniards conquered Central America,
the progress that may have been partially made had
already ceased. The monasteries at Palenque and in
Yucatan had been abandoned. Even when they were
flourishing, the knowledge that was taught did not
extend to the people. It was confined to the priesthood, the caciques, and the few scholars who were
trained for the purpose of interpreting the signs and
characters by which information was spread abroad.
It was by one of these interpreters that Cortes was
made acquainted with the conspiracy that was being
organized against him by Guatimozin during the
march to Honduras. How or in what manner this
comparative intelligence arose suddenly in the land
is a problem of the greatest difficulty.

The possibility of a previous condition of civilisation having existed amongst the aboriginal tribes
cannot be considered as being within the limits
of reasonable conjecture, for there are no vestiges of
any stone buildings, sculptures, or of hieroglyphic
inscribed characters, used as a means of recording
events, except in those regions which are known to
have been occupied by the Toltecs or Aztecs. With
especial regard to the temples on the mounds at
Palenque, it is evident that these and their sculptures
and hieroglyphs were the results of a certain degree
of architectural knowledge obtained by the Quiché-
Toltecs after they had migrated into Mexico.

But admitting that this may have been the case,
it becomes extremely difficult to understand how

their mechanical skill could have sprung into existence within such a limited period of time. It was found that the Indian progress in their peculiar civilisation was very local. Bishop Landa, writing exclusively about Yucatan, states that all education was under the management of the priests attached to the monasteries. Similar systems appeared to have been followed in other regions which had been under the rule of the Toltecs.* The results of the investiga-

---

* The Indians in Yucatan, had a chief priest who had a general control over all matters relating to the priesthood. He nominated the priests to the villages, examined them in their sciences and ceremonies, provided them with books and sent them to attend in the service of the temples.

According to Landa " they taught the sons of other priests and the younger sons of the chiefs that were brought to them for this purpose when they were children, if it was observed that they were inclined towards this office. The sciences which they taught were the computations of the years, months, and days, the festivals and ceremonies, the administration of their sacraments, the days and times that were fatal, the manner of divinations and prophecies and coming events, the remedies for sickness and things concerning antiquities, and to read and write with their books, and characters with which they wrote and with figures which explained the writings."

In Yucatan, as in Mexico, the calendar was carefully constructed. The year consisted of three hundred and sixty-five days and six hours. Landa observes that the months were of two kinds. One was lunar and was regulated by the movements of the moon. The other method of computation was formed by dividing the year into eighteen divisions or months, each consisting of twenty days and there were five days and six hours over. Of these six hours one day was made every four years. For these three hundred and sixty-six days they had twenty letters or characters by which they were named. (Relacion de las cosas de Yucatan, pp. 42 ; 202).

tions into the subject of the extent and methods
which were adopted for the purpose of maintaining
knowledge amongst the Indians, confirm the opinion
that the literature and civilisation found to have
existed in Mexico and Yucatan was exclusively
caused by the teaching of the priests.

Explanations of the circumstances under which
the priests became acquainted with their sciences
were given to the Spaniards by the chief priests
attached to the temple of Quetzalcoatl at Cholula
and also by certain caciques in Yucatan.

Las Casas observes in his Apologética Historia, chapter cxxi,
that " the year of the Mexican people consisted of three hundred
and sixty-five days divided into eighteen months and five days.
Each month was twenty days, and the week was thirteen days of
which they had constituted a calendar, and for each day of the
week, of the month and of the year they had its idol with its own
name, and these names were of men, or of women which they
held or had held as gods ; and thus all the days were filled up
with these idols and names and figures in the same manner
as our breviaries and calendars have for each day its saint."

The illustration of the calendar stone is from a photograph
taken from the original stone in the city of Mexico. This great
astronomical record was discovered in the year 1790, buried
several feet below the surface, in the spot where stood the chief
pyramid and temple of the Aztecs. It is made from a large mass
of basalt, and the circular part has a circumference of more
than thirty-eight feet. It is probably one of the earliest
and one of the most elaborate of the sculptured works of the
Toltecs. It will be observed that the points have a singular
resemblance to those of the mariner's compass. The head
placed in the centre has been supposed to represent the Mexican
god of the sun. It is possible that it may have been intended to
represent Quetzalcoatl, the traditional teacher and originator of
the Mexican knowledge of astronomy.

MEXICAN CALENDAR STONE.

Las Casas relates that when he was making a journey within his diocese, he met one of his missionaries named Francisco Hernandez, who had been for some years living in Yucatan, and had become acquainted with the language. Thinking that this ecclesiastic would be useful for the work of converting the Indians to the faith, he made him his vicar and sent him into the interior to preach amongst the natives. After a lapse of several months he received a letter from the vicar stating that he had been told by one of the principal caciques, that it was known that, anciently, there had arrived in Yucatan twenty strangers. They were dressed in long robes, had sandals upon their feet, and taught religion. It was also mentioned that these men wore long beards,* and that they had a leader who was named Cucul-can (Quetzal-coatl).

Las Casas concludes by observing that " Certainly the land and kingdom of Yucatan gives us to understand most especial things, and of the greatest antiquity with regard to the grand, admirable and exquisite styles of ancient edifices, and writings of certain characters which are in no other place. Finally, these are secrets which God only knows. (Finalmente, secretos son estos que sólo Dios los sabe)." ‡

---

* The fact of men wearing beards would be considered extraordinary by the American Indians. Landa states that " Cuculcan raised several temples, established regulations for the maintenance of good order, and then left Yucatan and proceeded towards Mexico."

‡ Apologética Historia, chapter cxxiii.

But the most explicit statements with regard to Quetzalcoatl were those which were given by the chief priests of the temples raised to his memory at Cholula. They affirmed the tradition of the arrival of strangers of a white race and foreign origin coming by sea in vessels from the east. These strangers were said to have taught the Indians to build monasteries, and maintain seminaries for religious

---

* With respect to the ancient Indian structures it is expedient to give a brief consideration to those that were raised at Copan and Quirigua. The earliest account of the sculptures existing at Copan was given by Palacio in 1576. In his Report to the King of Spain he mentions that within the ruins was a stone cross three palms high, and beyond it " There was a statue more than four yards high, sculptured like a bishop in his pontifical robes with his mitre well worked and with rings in his hands."

After describing other large statues and the ruins overlooking the river, Palacio observes, " I enquired with all possible attention for any traditions from the ancient people as to what people lived here, and if anything was known of their ancestors, and whether there were any books concerning these antiquities . . . . . . They say that anciently there came there a great chief of the province of Yucatan who made these edifices, and after several years he went back to his country, and left them solitary and unpeopled. . . . . . It also appears that the style of the said edifices is like what was found in other places by the Spaniards who first discovered Yucatan and Tabasco, where figures of bishops were seen and armed men and crosses, and since such things have not been found in other regions it can be believed that those that made them were probably of one nation." (Report of the Licentiate Dr. Don Diego Garcia de Palacio to the King of Spain, 1576.)

It is recorded by Juarros that in the year 1700, Fuentes, who wrote the Chronicles of Guatemala, stated with respect to Copan, that the figures, " both male and female were of very excellent sculpture, which then retained the colours they had been enamelled with ; and what was not less remarkable, the whole

instruction. According to Clavigero, they taught certain natives the methods of arranging the divisions of time and the use of the calendar. The priests also showed the Spaniards some ornaments which they said had been worn by the chief of these strangers.

The positive declarations about white people having landed upon the shores of the Mexican Gulf have been carefully investigated. It has been usually

---

of them were habited in the Castilian costume." The same author relates that at "a short distance, there was a portal constructed of stone, on the columns of which were the figures of men likewise represented in Spanish habits, with hose, ruff round the neck, sword, cap, and short cloak". . . .

"All the circumstances," observes Juarros, "lead to a belief that there must have been some intercourse between the inhabitants of the old and new world at very remote periods."

The information given traditionally by the Indians living at Copan, is singularly in accordance with the traditions of the priests and caciques in Mexico and Yucatan with respect to the arrival of a stranger who commanded temples and pyramids to be built and then went away and never returned.

It is remarkable that, in the first interview between Montezuma and Cortes, a singular tradition was mentioned by that Emperor. Cortes in his second letter (Segunda carta-relacion) dated 30th October, 1520, relates that Montezuma spoke to him as follows :—" We know from our writings that we received from our ancestors, that I and all those who live in this land are not the natives of it. We are strangers and came into it from very distant regions. We also know that our nation was led here by a chief whose vassals all were. He afterwards went back to his native country. Afterwards he returned and found that those he had left had married the native women (mujeres naturales) and had many children, and had built villages where they lived, and when he wished them to proceed with him they did not want to go, or even receive him as their chief and therefore he went away."

considered that they were the result of a myth, or
that they were based upon vague traditions relating
to events which, if they had any foundation, must
have happened at a period exceedingly remote and
possibly referred to early migrations from Asia.
But it has to be remembered that the facts reported
by the caciques and priests invariably related to a
period when their tribes were established in Yucatan
or Mexico; and the arrival of the strangers was
always said to have taken place on the eastern sea-
board of those lands. As the Toltecs according
to the Indian records were not established there
before the sixth century the event, if it occurred,
must have happened after that date.

There are also other circumstances connected with
this legend which appear, to some extent, to remove
it from a mythical character and to place it within
the limits of legitimate inquiry and investigation.
The Indians who described the events spoke of
them in a manner which was not vague, but was
clear and decided, and as being within the personal
knowledge of their ancestors. They also always
gave a description of the monuments of the strangers
or of their chief. Thus, in Yucatan, the leader was
said to have left that region for the coast of Mexico.
At Cholula, it was the tradition that Quetzalcoatl,
with several of his companions, went away to the
sea shore near Goascoalco, in the direction of Yucatan and never returned. In the regions of the
interior of Chiapas and Guatemala, it was stated that
in several of the native manuscripts accounts were
given of a great leader or chief named Votan who
was believed to have arrived in that country with

nineteen companions or other chiefs. Votan was supposed to have landed in America near the Laguna de Terminos and to have established his first settlement near Palenque.*

The most singular circumstance relating to the worship of Quetzalcoatl is the fact that a cross should have been the chief emblem in the temple especially dedicated to him at Palenque. The fact of this symbol being worshipped by the Indians in the New World may perhaps not be deemed particularly strange, but it has to be taken into consideration that there is no record of any figure in the shape of a cross having been an object of devotion in any part of America, except in the regions that had been occupied by the Toltecs.

When the Spaniards arrived in Yucatan they reported that they saw in the court of a temple at Cozumel a cross made of lime and stone which was worshipped by the natives. There were some doubts about the precise meaning assigned to this image, possibly owing to the difficulties of understanding the Maya language, but it was afterwards ascertained that it represented the god of rain.

The cross on the altar at Palenque is of an entirely different character, and evidently forms the principal part of the emblem representing Quetzalcoatl. How did it come to pass that this exceptional figure of a cross should have been sculptured upon the tablet representing the emblems of the white

---

*The author of the Popol Vuh, does not mention the tradition about Votan.

stranger who, according to the Indian traditions, landed upon their shores, coming from the east in a sacerdotal dress, wearing sandals upon his feet and having red crosses embroidered upon his cape?*

It is this coincidence that causes attention to be directed to an endeavour to form some reasonable solution of the problem. It will be observed, upon an examination of the illustration of the tablet of the cross, that the name Quetzalcoatl is represented by the quetzal, the emblematic bird of the Quichés, and by peculiar marks surrounding the cross which are thought to be intended to denote a serpent (coatl) which, as at Uxmal, was probably the Totem of the tribe.‡ But the principal figure placed in the centre of the altar is the cross. This by its shape and position must have been intended to have had an especial significance.

---

* Las Casas in commenting upon the subject of the Cozumel cross, mentions that it was ten palms high. In the course of the extensive explorations carried out by M. Desiré Charnay, in 1880-82, a similar stone was discovered at Téotihuacan. It is considered to be the emblem of Tlaloc, the god of rain.

‡ Professor Rau in his memoir upon the Palenque tablet, states that it is his belief that the Maya language, or a kindred dialect, was spoken by the builders of Palenque.

With regard to this subject it has to be observed that when the Toltec tribes, or the tribe that built the temples, settled at Palenque they had possibly forgotten their own original language, which may have been a Pawnee or Dakota dialect.

It would naturally happen after their wives had been taken from among the aboriginal race, that the children would speak the dialects of their mothers. It has been mentioned by an early Spanish writer that the Aztecs, when they settled in Mexico, endeavoured to establish their own language, but without success.

It is related by Gomara that, upon the occasion of the discovery of Yucatan by the expedition under the command of Francisco Hernandez in 1517, the Spaniards observed in the country near Cape Catoche, crosses of brass and wood placed over graves. The unexpected finding of these crosses in an hitherto unknown land attracted the attention of geographers in Spain and, to some extent, led to theories with regard to the possible arrival in Yucatan of the Spanish ecclesiastics who had, according to an ancient legend, fled from Spain when that country was conquered by the Saracens in the eighth century, and were believed to have reached an island in the western parts of the Atlantic ocean called Antilia.

What Gomara wrote upon this subject is as follows :—

"In that place there were found crosses of brass "and wood over the dead, from whence some argue "that many Spaniards had fled to this land when the "destruction of Spain was done by the Moors in the "time of the King Don Roderick : but I do not "believe it ; since there are not any in the islands "that we have mentioned : in some one of which it "is necessary, and also compulsory to touch at, "before arriving there."

Gomara was undoubtedly correct in not believing that these crosses were placed over the graves of Spaniards who had arrived in Yucatan after the defeat and flight of King Roderick. It is not requisite to go back to events that occurred in Spain in the eighth century to account for the existence of crosses on the promontory of Cape Catoche. When Hernandez landed there in 1517, nearly a quarter of

a century had elapsed since Columbus had founded
his settlements in Cuba and Hispaniola, and during
that interval many small expeditions had been
organised by Spanish adventurers for the purpose of
exploring the coasts in the direction of Honduras
and Nicuaragua. In pursuing these voyages of discovery their vessels must have frequently passed at
no great distance from the eastern shores of Yucatan
where, on their return from the south, they would
have been baffled by contrary winds and currents.
Under such conditions it is not improbable that one
of the vessels may have been wrecked or abandoned
off Cape Catoche, and that some of the crew perished
and were buried by the survivors near the seacoast.

The Spanish legend to which Gomara refers is,
with respect to America, chiefly remarkable for its
surprising concurrence in date and other circumstances with the Toltec legend. of the arrival of
strangers wearing cassocks. It is therefore necessary
to ascertain if there are sufficient reasons for placing
any confidence in statements that appear to be
founded upon tradition, and whether the event that
was believed to have taken place could have been
possible. The tradition did not escape the attention
of Washington Irving. In his "Life of Columbus "*
he states that " It was recorded in an ancient
" legend, that at the time of the conquest of Spain
" and Portugal by the Moors, when the inhabitants
" fled in every direction to escape from slavery, seven
" bishops, followed by a great number of their people,

---

* Vol. iv., p. 333.

" took shipping, and abandoned themselves to their
" fate on the high seas.   After tossing about for some
" time, they landed upon an unknown island in the
" midst of the ocean.   Here the bishops burnt the
" ships to prevent the desertion of their followers,
" and founded seven cities." *

In the principal maps published during the
fifteenth century, before the discovery of America,
the island of Antilia was usually given a position in the

---

*According to Gibbon, the Goths under the command of
King Roderick, were defeated by the Saracens on the plains of
Xeres in the neighbourhood of Cadiz, upon July 19-26, A.D. 711.
This great battle decided the fate of Spain.   It was supposed
that Roderick was drowned in the river but it was not known
with certainty what became of him as his body was never
found.

Decline and Fall of the Roman Empire, chap. li.

The subject of the flight of the bishops, was afterwards
brought into notice by a report of the discovery of the island
where they had settled.   This fabulous report was believed, in
the fifteenth century, to be true.   An historian states that :—

" In this yeare also, 1447, it happened that there came a
Portugal ship through the Streight of Gibraltar ; and being taken
with a great tempest, was forced to runne westward more than
willingly the men would, and at last they fell vpon an island
which had seuen cities, and the people spake the Portugall
toong, and they demanded if the Moores did yet trouble Spaine,
whence they had fled for the loss which they had received by
the death of the King of Spain, Don Roderigo.

The boatswaine of the ship brought home a little of the sand,
and sold it unto a goldsmith of Lisbon, out of the which he had
a good quantitie of gold.

Don Pedro, understanding this, being then gouernor of the
realme, caused all the things thus brought home, and made
knowne, to be recorded in the house of Justice."

The Discoveries of the World, by Antonio Galvano.

middle of the western Atlantic, south of the Azores.
In the chart of the geographer Toscanelli, which
was sent to Columbus, Antilia was placed in the
direct track by sea from the Canary islands to
Cipango (Japan), the large and prosperous country
supposed at that time to be situated in the extreme
west, near the eastern limits of Asia. It is evident
that Columbus firmly believed in the existence of
Antilia, for when he left the Canaries on his outward
voyage, he shaped his course for that island and
steered due west for about sixteen hundred miles.

Upon reaching the latitude and longitude where
he expected to see land, the admiral conferred with
his captains, but as nothing had been observed it
was thought that the ships must have passed the
island.   At sunset, the captain of the Pinta hailed
the admiral and reported that land was in sight
to the south-west. The course of the ships was
accordingly altered towards that direction. On the
next day it was found that what had been seen
was cloudland. The ships resumed their course and
proceeded until the landfall was made upon the
island of Guanahani.

The belief in the existence of the legendary island
was, however, not then dispelled and it is remarkable,
as a proof of the opinions of geographers, that in the
important map of the world by Ruysch, published in
1508, in which were placed the latest discoveries in
the west; Antilia still retained its position.*

---

*Antilia appears as a large island in the Atlantic in the
rare maps of Andreas Bianco (1436) and Bartolomeo Pareto

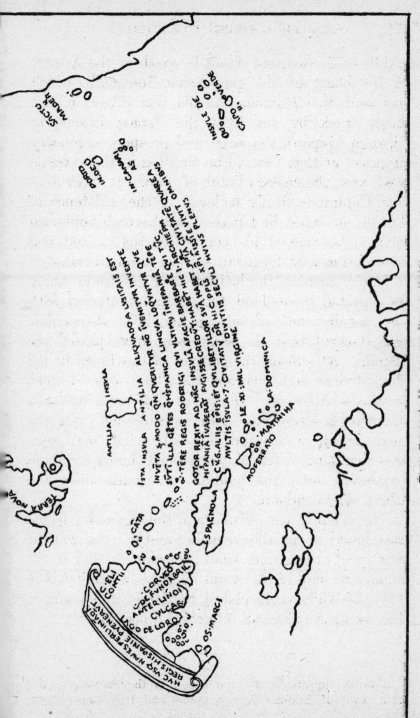

FROM RUYSCH'S MAP OF THE WORLD (1508).

(NORDENSKIÖLD'S FACSIMILE ATLAS.)

In the early part of the sixteenth century, several
expeditionary fleets were fitted out and sailed
across the seas towards the New World. Many
islands were seen, but Antilia was not found. Thus
when it became known that Yucatan had been
discovered and that a cross placed within a stone
temple was worshipped by the Indians, and that
other crosses had been seen placed over graves, it
was surmised that the bishops must have finally
reached that distant land.

Such an event may be thought to be improbable,
but as, in consequence of the trade-winds, it is not
impossible, it is expedient to consider in what
manner it might have happened. It has to be
assumed that the legend, so far as it relates to
Christian fugitives escaping from the tyranny of
Mahometan conquerors, may be considered as being
within the limits of reasonable historical inquiry.

(1454). On Martin Behaim's globe (1492) it is placed about
eighteen hundred miles west of the Canaries. In the earliest
maps published after the return of Columbus to Spain, Antilia is
placed near the newly discovered islands of the West Indies.

The legend upon the accompanying map may be rendered as
follows :—

"The island of Antilia was, at some period, discovered by the
Lusitanians, but the exact time is not known. There have been
found there in it families who speak Spanish as it was spoken in
the days of Roderick, who was the last King of Spain in the time
of the Goths, and they are supposed to have fled to this island
from the face of the Barbarians who had then invaded Spain.
They have here one Archbishop with six other Bishops, each of
whom has his own proper city, hence it is called by many the
island of the seven cities. The population are strict Christians
and abound in all this world's wealth."

Men deliberately leaving their own country to seek a place of refuge where they would be free to establish their religion, would, before embarking upon unknown seas, take with them supplies of provisions and water, and thus, by proper precautions, secure themselves from the risk of starvation. It is also probable that they were informed by the pilots or other navigators acquainted with the adjacent shores, that there were islands situated beyond the Mauritanian coasts within a distance not too great for them to undertake the voyage with a fair prospect of reaching land.

In the eighth century the Canary Islands had not been discovered by Europeans, but their position was known to the Arabs and Moors and rumours concerning them and their proximity to the coast of Morocco were doubtless familiar to the sea-faring men living near Cadiz. The pilots would, therefore, have shaped a course for the Canaries. They would have expected to reach those islands within eight or ten days. But a slight error in their course would have taken the vessels into the trade-winds and, in that case, they would have been driven across the Atlantic in the direction of Florida, whose coasts might easily have been reached in less than six weeks from the date of the departure from Spain. It is also possible that they may have been chased by some of the armed vessels which had conveyed the Saracens from Mauritania.

It is not, however, necessary to pursue this investigation to any greater length. It is sufficiently clear that if the event, as recorded by tradition, actually happened, there is no difficulty in accepting the conclusion that several of the bishops and their companions may have reached America in safety.* Thus the statements of the Indian priests, that white strangers wearing beards and dressed in cassocks had arrived from the East, would be confirmed.

Upon an examination of the laws that govern the direction of the trade-winds in the Atlantic and Pacific oceans, it is found that there is a strong easterly wind continuously blowing across the Atlantic towards Florida, Mexico and Yucatan. There is also a strong westerly wind invariably blowing across the North Pacific, over the regions between the fortieth and fiftieth parallels of latitude, from Japan towards the north-west coast of North America. In consequence of this prevailing wind several junks have

---

* In the first voyage of Columbus the vessels left the Canaries on the 6th of September and arrived off Guanahani on the night of the 11th of October, having been thirty days at sea. They had traversed a distance, according to the Admiral's journal, of 1,092 leagues or 3,276 miles. On the second voyage from the Canaries to Dominica they left on the 3rd of October and arrived on the 3rd of November. Upon the last voyage, Columbus left Ferro (one of the Canary islands) on the 26th of May and reached St. Lucia in the West Indies on the 15th of June. This was a quick passage and only occupied twenty days.

In the Vestal, a sailing frigate of 26 guns, we left the island of Gran Canaria in the year 1852, on the morning of the 27th of September, and passed between Antigua and Guadeloupe at noon on the 16th of October after a voyage of nineteen days, having sailed over a distance of 2,800 miles. During the whole of this time we were running before the wind with our studding sails set, steering West. A favourable N.E. wind prevails from Florida to Yucatan and the Mexican coast. With respect to Columbus's first voyage it should be observed that his landfall at Guanahani was four or five days' sail further west than the islands of Dominica and St. Lucia.

been driven out of their course and have reached the American seacoasts. In 1833 a junk was wrecked near Vancouver island and several of the crew landed and were received by the Indians. In the previous year a Japanese junk laden with fish arrived at the Sandwich islands. She had been driven across the seas by a violent storm which had caught her off Japan. Four of her men were alive and they were taken to Honolulu.

Taking therefore into consideration the prevalence of trade-winds blowing towards America, and the peculiar conditions of architectural and astronomical intelligence possessed by the Mexican Indians, there are certain inferences which may be accepted. It is not improbable that men belonging to European, Moorish, or Asiatic races arrived in Central America during a period between the sixth and eleventh centuries. There is not sufficient evidence to determine in what manner this may have happened; but after giving due weight to the statements of the Indian priests and caciques, and the traditions of the circumstances under which their knowledge was introduced into Mexico, together with the adoption of monastic institutions, and the systems of education, it is reasonable to conjecture that the comparative civilisation of the Toltecs and Aztecs was originally caused by the influence and instruction of strangers who came to their land in vessels which had crossed the Atlantic.

INDEX.
